In the Shadow
of Serenity

DIEU BAO

In the Shadow of Serenity

DIEU BAO

In the Shadow of Serenity

Dieu Bao
3807 NE 202 Avenue
Fairview, OR 97024

Ordering Information:
Quantity sales. Special discounts are available on quantity purchases by corporations, associations, and others. For details, contact the Author at the address above.

First Edition
Printed in the United States of America
ISBN-10: 1977903002
ISBN-13: 9781977903006

Dedication

To my mother, Kieu Thi Van, who taught me love, gave me hope, and guided me into adulthood. I owe everything that I am to you.

To all my children and grandchildren, Trung, Bichphuong, Thuannha, Hoaitram Thuanphong, Thithu, Thitho, ThiThoung, and Thithanh: Your joy of life, your wonderment, and your insatiable curiosity have renewed the child in me.

Acknowledgments

I would like to give a special thanks to Valerie Couch, who assisted in the writing of this book. You are my best friend, my confidant. Through the laughter and tears, you have always been there. I am proud to call you my little sister.

CONTENT

DEDICATION

ACKNOWLEDGMENTS

III

Prologue New Beginnings

1

ONE Turning the Dharma Wheel

3

TWO Expanding Horizons

25

THREE Testing Endurance

51

FOUR Transcending Boundaries

71

FIVE A Thorn in My Side

97

SIX Knowledge of Self-Actualization

121

SEVEN Another Spin of Fate's Wheel

143

IV

EIGHT The Devil's Advocate

165

NINE The Fourth "I Do"

185

TEN The Stranger Within: Who Am I?

209

ELEVEN Different Winds

233

TWELVE Noble Eightfold Path: Journey to the End of Suffering?

259

FOURTEEN Sự trở lại đến Việt Nam: Return to Việt Nam I

283

FOURTEEN Sự trở lại đến Việt Nam: Return to Việt Nam II

305

FIFTEEN The Demon Within

327

SIXTEEN Saṃsāra: Endless Suffering

351

SEVENTEEN Paññā: Wisdom and Insight

371

EIGHTEEN In the Shadow of Serenity

393

EPILOGUE Last Trip to Việt Nam: The
Promising Wings of Hope

419

ABOUT THE AUTHOR

435

III

Jump! Jump, Bảo, a persistent voice resonated in my head. Jump and you will find happiness and a respite from all this suffering.

"I want to die," I shouted. "I want the pain to stop. I want this nightmarish life to end. I'm going to jump—I want peace of mind. This is the only way."

I looked into the helpless, innocent faces of my children... who idolized me as Mommy. I was shaken back to reality. Jim, on the other hand, was neither supportive of my misery nor willing to validate my efforts as a wife and mother. Instead, he demonstrated only apathy for my struggles and indifference to my anguish.

"Go ahead—jump," he shouted, playing a risky game with my fragile spirit.

Shocked by his reckless, unsympathetic behavior, I realized that my children would be in his hands if I died—a reflection that awakened my reasoning, carrying me away from my own self-centered concerns.

Prologue
New Beginnings

In my last book, "Without Boundaries, My Life During the Việt Nam War". I had finally escaped the horrors of the Việt Nam War. Here I was a daughter of Việt Nam, no stranger to overwhelming fear, pain and violence standing in the San Francisco Airport, in America! I felt so much of my anxiety disappear as I looked around me. I felt something deep stir inside of my soul. It was a realization, something I had never felt before. I could finally be what I wanted to be: without boundaries.

For me, life has always been a test of faith and endurance, a repeated crossing over through a progression of events and situations governed by struggles, conflicts and a substantial dose of pain. Usually, it was a battle just to keep my head above water. And, more often than not, the certainties were meager reassurance.

I have been keeping a diary since I was sixteen and continue entries even today. This is my true story. I decided to write this as form of therapy, a way to release my inner demons...My path to escape the Shadow of Serenity and discover my drop of Nirvana here on Earth,

CHAPTER 1
Turning the Dharma Wheel

Recognizing my native dress, two Vietnamese college students approached and inquired if I was meeting an American or a Vietnamese. I told them I was meeting some American people and handed the girl Jim's address and phone number.

"Could you please phone Jim for me?" I asked. "He lives nearby and will come pick us up."

"This number and address are not located here in San Francisco," she told me, gazing at the crumbled slip of paper I'd thrust under her nose. "This man lives in Georgia—that's another state across the country. Its two thousand miles away! Do you have a dollar fifty to call him?"

"I don't have any American money," I stammered," but if you call him, I'll change some *dong* and pay you back."

"Don't worry about the money," the young woman said. "I'll call Jim for you."

3

After her conversation with my fiancé, she informed me that I had to fly to Dallas and catch a connecting flight to Nashville, where Jim's stepmother would be waiting for me.

At least I knew what I was doing. Thanking the girl for her kindness, I boarded the plane for Dallas. Landing in Texas, I proceeded to the boarding gate to catch my Nashville flight.

At eight o'clock in the morning, I arrived at Nashville International Airport, nervous, exhausted, hungry and fearful of all the unknowns in my new life. However, no one was there waiting to meet me as they had promised.

Exasperated but still doing an excellent job of keeping it together, I found a seating area and, together with my restless and by-then-irritable children, remained until Jim's stepmother made an appearance four hours later

My first impression of Jim's stepmother, Kay, was that of a distant woman who harbored an unjustified dislike for my children and me. After her unwarranted late arrival at the airport and her paper-thin alibi, she had no additional words for me. A hand motion invited me into her car. No smile, no "hello"—nothing, just an extended finger. If it weren't for her flimsy excuse, I would have believed she was speech challenged.

We sat in silence during the ninety-minute ride to her house in Columbia, Tennessee. She and Jim's brother, Jerry, who had accompanied her to the airport, further quashed any suspicions I had about Kay's ability to speak when they engaged in a quick dialogue between themselves as if I were not present. It seemed she did have a voice.

Eventually, I learned that Jim was the oldest of five children: David, twenty; Jerry, nineteen; Gary, fourteen; and sixteen-year-old sister Sandy.

As we drove along, I noticed most of the trees were barren—just huge branches, some knotted, all bare. *How odd,* I thought. *There are no leaves in America!* And what looked like smooth, pure-white sand covered the streets. I was amazed, even though this desolate panorama of skeletal trees and dusty streets saddened me. Where were the flowers—those delicate, white, yellow, orange, pink, violet, and red blooms that made me smile? It was all white and brown. Was this the face of America, so stagnant and colorless?

Of course, I would soon became familiar with the facts of nature: Some trees shed their leaves in the fall and during the winter months, an icy, white fluff referred to as "snow" showered down on people and places like rain. Certainly, it was interesting to discover how different the nature cycle was in America. In Việt Nam, trees stayed fertile year round and snow was virtually nonexistent. I soon discovered that in America, there was the bitter cold to deal with—the teeth-chattering, bone-quivering, ear-, nose-, toe- and finger-burning cold!

But, on my first day there, I did not know all of that yet, and I was surprised and disappointed by the general appearance of my new country's landscape. Movies I'd seen featuring America always had lush, colorful scenes with thick, verdant lawns, flowering plants and wide-armed trees dressed in various shades of green. Was that all just movie scenery?

When we pulled up to the property, a large tree caught my eyes. Its thick branches sprouted tiny, twig-like arms. Just beyond the tree sat a diminutive, wood-framed house, resembling a Lincoln-era log cabin. Stacks of yellow-orange leaves carpeted the roof, porch and lawn, painting a dismal, unwelcoming portrait, similar to Jim's mother and brother. Sadness penetrated my spirit, breeding a reluctance to enter the house.

A feeling of anxiety and a hesitancy to move forward left me frozen at the door.

"Go on in," Kay said unconvincingly. "What are you waiting for?"

Drawing a deep breath, I obliged. Much to my surprise, the interior did not mimic the dreary exterior. Instead, a tidy, warm atmosphere prevailed. Decorated with photos of smiling children's faces and a large, three-dimensional landscape painting, the room was inviting. A quick glance around left me convinced that the sturdy, worn furniture reflected a comfortable lifestyle. My spirits were lifted, and I slowly recovered from my initial impression of the place.

A call from Jim bearing the news that his tour of duty would be completed in eight days curled my lips into a smile. In just a week and a day, Jim would be there, and that was encouraging. Certain I would live through it, I settled in, trying to acclimatize myself to the different surroundings.

What intrigued me most was the snow phenomenon. It just fell like rain but after a while, the snowflakes accumulated into a soft, fluffy, ice-cold carpet. Best of all, when the rays of the sun beat down on the snow, it glistened like mounds of tiny diamonds. But when I leaned over to grab some I noticed I could form it into a hard ball. This was so different from the hot, slippery sand in Việt Nam that escaped through my fingers like granules drizzling through an hourglass.

Jim arrived at midnight, while I slept. Though exhausted, I awakened to the sounds of his voice and Kay's discussing my presence.

"You know, she arrived penniless," Kay said. "I had to buy everything."

"Here, Mama," he responded, slipping her eighty dollars. "Don't worry, I'll look for a job next week and contribute more."

Jim kept his word and was hired by the telephone company with wages totaling fifty dollars a week. Immediately, he handed over forty dollars to Kay and kept the remaining ten to purchase baby supplies for Thaun.

"Bảo, I gave Kay some money for groceries," he confided as we walked to the store.

8

"No problem," I said. "I guess we're a pretty big family to feed."

When we reached the store, we looked around a bit before heading to the baby-supplies section.

"Oh, honey, look!" Jim said. "We should buy that electric blanket."

"It's too expensive," I said. "How can you pay for it?"

"I'll make monthly payments."

"How much a month do you have to pay?"

"Just five dollars."

"How do you know?"

"Because I bought clothes here before I enlisted in the Army and I charged them. Plus, I worked here during my high-school years."

"Do you want to get it?" I asked.

"Sure. Let's get one each. I'll take a blue one. What color would you like, Bảo?"

"I like the pink."

After we made our selections, Jim went to the cashier to complete the paperwork.

"Can you lend me two dollars?" Jim asked as we left the store. "I have to call Kay to pick us up."

"Two dollars for a phone call?" I asked, puzzled. "I thought it cost a dime."

"It's for gas, not the phone call," he said, irritated.

"Didn't you just give her forty dollars?"

"Don't worry. Just give me two dollars."

Opening my hand bag, I retrieved two dollars and handed them to Jim. *What kind of family is this?* I wondered. Of course, I expected to contribute for my room and board; with two children, I knew my responsibility. However, I couldn't believe how much money Kay milked from Jim. There were constant requests for more and more.

I'd never paid my mom to live in her house. How would Jim and I be able to save any money for a home of our own if Kay repeatedly depleted him financially?

We discussed plans to legalize our relationship as soon as possible and just ten days after my arrival in Columbia, Tennessee, Jim and I became husband and wife in a ceremony at the West Street Church of Christ. We had one guest in attendance—Jim's brother, Gary.

Although the wedding was far from a romantic or elaborate affair, Jim was thrilled to have acquired a family of his own. We applied for a marriage license the following day, which was an accomplishment, considering my previous two experiences.

Returning home to a vacant house, my curiosity spiked, leading me to explore the lower level of the property. Taking the steps, I entered the cellar, a dark, humid room, dusty and filled with ceiling cobwebs. Pulling the light switch, my eyes fell on a large, white box with buttons. Unaware it was a washing machine, I advanced, opened the glass door and peered in.

It was empty, but the buttons and knob were interesting. Never one to quit without answers, I pushed, pulled and turned the knob just to see what, if anything, would happen.

I didn't expect the gush of water that sprouted up, filling the machine and spilling on the floor in splashes and puddles. Unable to stop the deluge, I disengaged the electrical cord.

Feeling very embarrassed and stupid about the mess I'd created, I darted up the stairs, not wanting anyone to see the calamity I had orchestrated. Of course, once it was discovered, the finger would be pointed at me.

My identity in this extended family was ambiguous, leaving me open to create one as a big sister assuming responsibility for Jim's younger siblings. I cleaned their rooms, did the laundry once I learned how to operate the machine, and invaded the kitchen and made delicious egg rolls. My efforts were not without applause. The siblings loved me to death for all my help and attention.

Although Jim's father and stepmother were separated, his father made sporadic, often-unannounced appearances. In contrast to Kay's cool, aloof demeanor, Jim's father was gracious and congenial, greeting everyone, patting me on the head and picking up my children, lavishing them with hug and kisses.

"These kids are not just yours," he'd say every time, "they're mine, too. Make sure you take good care of them."

Whether or not he meant what he said was irrelevant; he certainly had a master talent for raising my spirits, especially since Kay's strategy was to tread as if my children and I didn't exist. Eventually, I came to know her as mean, petty, bossy, manipulative, greedy woman who was always squeezing Jim for money.

In the quiet of my thoughts, I compared and contrasted Jim's family with my own. How different they were. *Could this be the American way?* I wondered. In my heart, I hoped Kay was, in essence, the exception to the rule instead of the norm.

Everyone seemed happy when Jim's father was at home, including Kay. But, when he returned to his other family, they had only angry words for him.

Kay continued to drain Jim's finances. It almost seemed as if it was her purpose in life.

"We have to get out of here!" I said to Jim one day, trying not to show my disdain for his stepmother. "I'm tired of her intrigues." Earlier that day, Kay had swatted Jim across the face, ordering him to sit down as if he were a delinquent ten-year-old. I'd also had enough of her rages.

"Be patient. We will leave," Jim said, anticipating my comment. "As soon as I get some time off, we'll look for a place and move out."

Exasperated, Jim, David, and Gary set off after supper to look for a house. Thankfully, it didn't take long for them to find a little, mobile home. Happy to be free of Kay, I gave my approval and we moved the following morning. Finally, I was free.

Jim worked hard, returning at day's end with mud-plastered clothes, which, to save money, I laundered every evening by hand in the bath tub. Since I was pregnant again, it was difficult to lean over the tub. Upset by this, Jim asked Kay if we could possibly use her washing machine, at least until the baby was born. Angry and aggressive, Kay made it clear to her stepson that the answer was "no" and that he was never again to ask her for anything.

My love and admiration for Jim deepened as he demonstrated concern for my

13

children and me. Although we barely had enough money, he continued to feed Kay's greed. I tried my best to always prepare hot, nourishing dinners for him. I also drew him a warm, relaxing bath every evening, had his slippers ready and laid out a fresh change of clothes.

Jim was gracious and appreciative, able to evaluate my efforts and give thanks when merited. However, his immature habit of stopping at Kay's after work to discuss our life together was irritating. I neither understood nor approved of this behavior and made no secret of my displeasure. It did, however, fall on deaf ears. Jim continued to confide in Kay. Eventually, she had him running errands for her, which, I might add, caused him to neglect me.

This was the kind of control that Kay exerted over Jim. Eventually, he began to absent himself from me and his obligations, without notification, to fill all his stepmother's orders.

We started to have problems when I confronted Jim about his unacceptable behavior.

"Why do you have to run errands for her every day?" I asked.

"Well, if I don't, Mama will get mad."

"Then let her get mad. What if I get mad?" I shouted, my blood pressure skyrocketing. I knew I had to get a hold of myself.

"Jim," I went on, "it is okay to help her out once in a while, but not every single day. You told me you ran away to join the Army because your stepmother and family were giving you a hard time. Now that you are free and have a family of your own, why do you keep going back there? Don't you see the game she's playing? She's just using you to upset me and cause trouble between us. This is a selfish woman who cares only for herself. Does she ever thank you for all that you do?"

I was wasting my time and energy. Jim was in denial.

The following Saturday, he left and remained out until late. Although I was seething, I had supper waiting when he returned.

"I came home to tell you I'm going to pick up Jerry from work. I'll be back in a little while," he said, giving me a quick look. "Keep supper hot."

"Jim, Jerry is eighteen. I think he's old enough to be responsible for his own transportation. Why don't you just come in and sit down for dinner?"

15

Without a word, he stomped out the door.

Grabbing some fishing poles hanging on the wall, I ran after him, hurling them wildly as he was driving away. Blind from rage, I fell short of my target, hitting instead an electrician working on the lot. Thankfully, he was not injured, but eventually, Jim had to give the landlord an explanation for my violent outburst.

Unsatisfied with his job possibilities, Jim enrolled in night school under the GI Bill. Miraculously, our relationship with Kay changed. She told Jim that I was welcome to use the washer and dryer anytime. When Jim repeated her message, I was furious.

"Really? Why didn't she offer when we didn't have a car or money?"

Actually, I didn't need an answer. I understood the sinister machinations of her calculating mind. Now that we had the means

16

to live somewhat more comfortably, she thought she could wring his pocket harder. It was always about how much she could extract from him. Nothing else had any importance.

She had neither compassion for nor an understanding of his responsibilities to me and the family. And, she cared only about herself. It mattered not that we had two children and a third on the way.

Her wheedling money from Jim knew no bounds as far as I could see. Jim received his tax refund check of $350, and Kay told him to sign the check over to her because the money was rightfully hers.

"How can it be yours?" Jim asked. "I've been looking forward to this check for a long time now. I'm going to save it for the hospital bill when Bảo has the baby."

"When your family was here, the bills were higher and now I owe a lot of money," Kay shouted.

Refusing to endorse the check, Jim left. Later, after dinner, Gary came to visit.

"Mama needs some money and so do I. I have to fix my motorcycle and pay for gas because got a job delivering papers."

Unfortunately, Jim succumbed to Gary's requests. Storming out the door, he cashed the check and handed Gary $15 for his motorcycle and $20 to give Kay.

Additionally, Jim had been paying Kay $50 a month for the time we'd spent with her. When he posed opposition, she insisted that he still owed her money for groceries. Jim and I quarreled almost daily over money. The more he gave Kay, the less he had for his family.

"I'm your wife, Jim," I reminded him during one skirmish. "Whatever money you have is also mine. I asked you not to go over to Kay's all the time. Whenever you're there, she milks you broke. I don't want you to go back there ever again."

"Bảo, she's my mother. You can't stop me from seeing Mama."

"Damn it Jim, it's always Mama—she comes first in your life. She's the only one who counts for you."

Frustration and anger cajoled me into losing my temper. Overturning the table, I shouted as food-filled plates crashed down, splattering morsels of our still-unconsumed dinner on the floor and walls. Since the dishes did not splinter into tiny pieces to satisfy my rage, I stomped on them one by one, crushing them to powder.

"Damn her, Jim," I yelled. "She's a selfish, uncaring bitch, taking every penny we have."

18

His calloused hand was cold and abrasive when it slammed against my cheek—once, twice, three times, sending me face down into the chaos of shattered glass and food bits. Blood oozed from my nose in bright-red drops, imprinting a Rorschach blot on the front of my shirt. Apparently, it neither bothered Jim nor worried him that I was pregnant. His rage was irrational.

My eye would be swollen and black for two weeks, compromising my sight. It was more than obvious my marriage was precipitating into a danger zone, and all because of Kay's incessant interference and demands for money.

After his vicious attack, Jim darted out the door, seeking refuge in his stepmother's house. Of course, listening to his lament, Kay advised him to be wary of me, insinuating that I would eventually pack up and abandon him. She instructed him not to purchase anything in co-ownership with me.

"Women today are evil and conniving," she cautioned. "She will leave you, return to her country and meet someone else."

Following Kay's advice, Jim acquired an insurance policy and named her as the beneficiary. His auto was titled to him exclusively. When I found out and confronted him, he admitted that Kay had advised him. But it didn't end there.

I asked Jim for a lightweight jacket, and he related my request to Kay.

"Jim, I have an old jacket Bảo can have for fifteen dollars," she said.

When he told me, I was furious. "I don't want her old jacket," I shouted. "Tell her to give it to anyone she wants. I don't want to hear another word about it." However, despite my protestations, I did not get a new jacket.

On October 8, 1974, I brought into the light my fourth child, my first American-born child, a darling baby girl I named Tram. She was perfectly formed, with a full head of dark hair and the tiniest toes I had ever seen. The moment I cradled her in my arms, I knew it was all worthwhile—even Kay's atrocious behavior in my regard.

The hospital billed us $333 dollars a week. I asked Jim to satisfy the bill with the money in our savings account.

"We have only one hundred twenty dollars," he said.

"How can that be possible?" I questioned. "We're supposed to have four hundred."

"Well, Mama keeps giving me trouble, wanting this and that, so I have to take money out of the bank and give it to her."

Speechless and stunned, I fantasized about killing him. Right or wrong, the scenario, if carried out, would free me from him and the horrendous fallout from his greedy, demanding and miserly stepmother. Thankfully for Jim and Kay, it was merely a fleeting fantasy.

A week later, the bank sent a notice advising us that we had overdrawn the account—the amount was forty-three cents.

"We just deposited sixty dollars," I said. "How can we owe forty-three cents?"

"Bảo, we had to pay a service charge for withdrawing all the money from the account."

"Why did you withdraw all the money?"

"Honey, I can't help it," he said, lowering his gaze to avoid mine. "Kay keeps sending me to the store all the time and never gives me any money to pay for her stuff."

A few days after this disturbing confrontation, we received a bill totaling $14 for the bouquet of flowers Jim had sent me when I was in the hospital. Enraged beyond all limits of self-control, I realized that even the Lord could not pacify my spirit. Reaching for a vase, I hurled it against the wall. Emulating the echo of a detonating grenade, it brought Jim to his feet.

"I don't need your flowers if paying for them pushes us further in debt," I yelled. "I don't appreciate this kind of gallantry."

My love and admiration for Jim began to wane like the radiant rays of the sun at dusk.

Sadly, not only was he not the man I'd thought he was, but he didn't live up to my expectations of a kind, caring and loyal husband and father who had his priorities straight.

I put my family above all, even if Jim made his stepmother the number-one person in his life. Disappointed, I asked myself why I stayed, why I accepted his emotional and physical abuse.

Perhaps my commitment to keep the family together, mixed with the fact that I was a foreigner, encouraged me to stay in the marriage. But, how much more would I be willing to take? When would it all end? When would I enjoy the serenity I so coveted?

Chapter 2
Expanding Horizons

A serious car accident on December 10, 1974, on the way home from work in a torrential downpour, left Jim with minor injuries and the car totaled. Money was at an all-time low and my husband made the decision to reenlist in the army.

When informed that he would be stationed in Key West, Florida, I was delighted. The climate was tropical, similar to my birthplace. Maybe life would get better for us in the Sunshine State.

The trip was smooth, and we arrived shortly before Christmas, on a warm, balmy day.

With Jim's decision to serve his country again, I had been exonerated from carrying a suffocating burden—Kay was miles away and I was free from the snow, the shivering cold and the sadness of barren foliage.

This move represented a new lease on life. Without the tyranny of Kay, I was hopeful that Jim would focus on his family as a responsible husband and father. Regardless, I vowed that I would never again let him treat me as a doormat. Instead, I would put myself in a position to be self-supporting and independent.

Maintaining my promise, as soon as we arrived in Key West, I found a job as a bikini seamstress for a local boutique, working right from my home. Once I had sufficient experience, I moved on, applying for and obtaining a position at the Key West Hand Print Factory. At minimum wage, $2.10 an hour, my take-home pay averaged between $70 and $90 a week.

My marriage was calmer, and Jim expressed a desire to adopt Thaun and Phuong, to facilitate their rights to the military medical care that covered his family. I agreed with Jim, and he adopted the children without any problems.

A year and a half following our transfer to Key West, Jim's youngest brother, Jerry, phoned to ask if he could stay with us for a month before reporting for duty in the Air Force. We told him that he was more than welcome and that we would be happy to accommodate him for a while.

"I'll be driving down tomorrow," he said, so I'll see you soon."

We cautioned him to drive carefully, realizing that youth doesn't always realize the mortality of the human body. However, the following day, he called apologetically.

"I'm sorry," he said. "I'll be a few days late. Mama wants me to paint the house."

Once again, Jim's intruding stepmother had intervened to redirect the course of life to suit her selfish whims, regardless of the resulting consequences and the effect they would have on others.

We waited near the door and near the phone, but Jerry never arrived. David called us several days later.

"I'm afraid I have some bad news," he said somberly. "Jerry was killed in a car crash. I'll phone you later with the funeral arrangements."

When Jim related the news to me, I froze. In my mind, I tried and condemned the culprit.

If only that dreadful woman would have left him alone, I thought, *Jerry would be here with us.* This time, Kay's meddling had ended in a terrible tragedy.

Several hours later, David called to give the details. On the rear of an envelope, I penned the date, time and addresses of Jerry's funeral service.

While packing for the trip to Columbia, tired and heavy-hearted, in the dimming glow of sunset, I saw Jerry standing before me—his young, handsome face, cut and bruised; his eyes puffed and violet; his nose flattened; his neck disfigured from the break. Caught off guard, I gasped, running into the bathroom where the light was brighter.

Was my mind playing a trick on me? Or was I just anxious and pushed to the extreme? Drawing a deep breath, I returned to my luggage. *The dead are at peace,* I reassured myself, *and once a soul passes, there is no motive for alarm. How can we fear the deceased?*

Jim chuckled and called me "paranoid" when I told him of the apparition.

"Jerry's dead, Bảo. There is no way you could have seen him. He's gone—and, hopefully, at peace."

"Well, he's certainly free from the horrible, monstrous Kay," I blurted. It may have sounded unkind, but had I not expressed myself in that manner, I would have been lying.

The following morning, at six o'clock, we left for Columbia, driving all day and night. Since no one was at home when we arrived, we went directly to the church. Of necessity, I glanced at Jerry in the casket. My heart was invaded by stampeding horses vying for the Triple Crown. I gasped. Jerry was exactly as I had seen him in my room—the wounded face, the distorted neck, the darkened, swollen eyes and crushed nose. What did it mean?

The service was sad, but thoughts of such a young life lost, and Jerry's ghost appearing before me, tormented me during the drive back to Key West. Jim, thankfully, did not seem to share my anguish.

I returned to work the following day. Our financial situation did not permit the luxury of extended time off. Money was a commodity. It afforded me independence and the power to buy the necessities for myself and the children.

Oddly, I noticed Jim's disapproval over my new empowerment. Perhaps he feared losing his command status in the family, since I was now exercising the role of breadwinner and nurturer. He complained about the better-quality shoes I was providing for the children. I just couldn't escape his consternation. Then, one day, he pushed it beyond the limits, chastising me for purchasing a purse with the money I had earned and saved after taking care of the children's needs!

What was happening? Was Jim turning into a clone of his mean, stingy stepmother? Best of all, his lamentations were unwarranted because the dollars spent were my hard-earned wages, not his.

I worked diligently, and my salary increased to almost $300 a week. The added cash flow, together with Jim's earnings, allowed us not only to satisfy our debts and pay our bills but gave us the possibility to save $2100—the down payment on a new car. A ray of sunlight was forcing its way through the heavily clouded sky. Could I dare believe in a reprieve, in the dawning of better times?

Miraculously, Jim no longer hassled me about money matters. My spending patterns were no longer a source of condemnation. Working two jobs, I put in sixteen-hour days. Waking at sunrise, I packed my lunch, prepared breakfast for Jim and the children, accompanied Phuong to school, and took Thaun and Tram to the babysitter. Afterwards, I headed for the factory. At quitting time, I picked up more patterns and materials for the bikinis and headed home to cook dinner and get the children fed, bathed and ready for bed. Then, I was free to sew the bathing suits until midnight. Of course, Jim never lifted a finger to help out. Instead, he sat like a *pasha* awaiting the service of his harem of wives.

The store was soon giving me more work than I could handle because, as Lori, the owner, shared with me, I was their best seamstress. To stave off total exhaustion, I decided to quit my job at the factory and work full time for Lori, and I remained with her until 1977, when Jim received orders for his transfer to Germany.

Another country—another life change. Where would this adventure take me? On the positive side, I would be a continent away from Kay. Taking a deep breath, I prepared for a new journey.

Before my departure and residency in Germany, I was advised to apply for American citizenship. Heading off to the post office, I obtained the handbook filled with the questions and answers I had to master in order to satisfy the exam criteria. The process also required two American citizens who knew me for a minimum of a year to stand as witnesses on my behalf. Although a five-year residency was mandatory for most immigrants to reside in the United States before applying for citizenship, because I was the wife of a military man, this condition was relaxed for me.

Upon my return from the post office, I visited my friend and next-door neighbor, Mary, who babysat for my children. I asked her if she and her military husband, Bill, would be willing to stand up as witnesses for me. They were honored and, once they agreed, I concentrated on studying for the exam.

When the day arrived, Jim, Bill and Mary accompanied me to the Southern District of Miami, Florida, to take my test. It was January 19, 1977. While I was called before the examiner, they sat in the waiting room.

The examiner asked me to raise my right hand and state my full name. Then, the questioning began:

"Have you ever deserted the military?"

"No, sir," I responded.

"Are you a member of any clubs?"

"No, sir."

"Have you ever been arrested or served jail time?"

"No, sir."

"Who is the current president of the United States?"

"Richard Nixon."

"If something should happen to the president, who will be sworn in to undertake his duties?"

"The vice president."

"Who is responsible for trade laws?"

"Congress."

"How long have you been in the United States?"

"Three years."

"Could you write that down for me?" he said, handing me a sheet of paper. I obliged.

"What will you do after you finish taking this test?"

"I'll return home," I responded.

"Could you please write that for me?" he repeated. Once again, I obliged.

Though apprehensive, I did remarkably well when answering the questions I was asked. Rising from his high-backed, black-leather chair, the examiner exited in silence, returning moments later in the company of Jim, Bill and Mary.

Bill and Mary were asked to raise their right hands; they were administered an oath and requested to sign an affidavit attesting to the length of time they had known me. Afterwards, Jim signed the necessary documents for Thaun and Phuong, making him the husband and father of three new Americans. I was thrilled and proud to be a citizen of the USA. A beautiful dream had been spun into a reality.

On the way home, in celebratory mode, we invited Bill and Mary to lunch at Kentucky Fried Chicken. I was a true American.

Leaving Key West was difficult, as I had grown attached to the city, which shared climatic similarities with Việt Nam. Many questioned why I did not let Jim go to Germany alone for his tour of duty. Perhaps it would have been easier, especially with young children.

However, in part, my priorities governed that decision. Family was my most important concern, and Jim had threatened to sever his financial obligations if I refused to accompany him. There was no way I would have been able to maintain myself and three children without his financial contributions.

Furthermore, our relationship had steadily improved, which made my choice less of a hardship. Even if our marriage was a long way from idyllic, we had managed to iron out some of the twisted tenets that had made it a battleground. Amicable and civil, we were actually enjoying a wave of compatibility.

In January 1977, we left Florida to visit Jim's birth mother, Helen. Believing it would take about six months for the government housing to be ready to accommodate us, the children and I remained behind while Jim reported for duty in Germany.

"Bảo, if I find a suitable apartment for us," he said, "I'll send for you earlier. In the meantime, I think you'll be happy here."

Helen confirmed Jim's words. She was a gracious woman of congenial personality, and we got along beautifully. We held barbeques in her backyard in the summer and just played around like two schoolchildren. Sometimes, I carried her on my back and ran around the yard, even though she outweighed me by about fifty pounds. The children loved the lighthearted, playful ambience and willingly participated in our games.

In the evenings, we dined together and often, I prepared Vietnamese dishes, giving an exotic air to Helen's ribs and chicken.

"Bảo, I've never been as happy as I've been during this time that we've spent together," Helen said one afternoon. "I'm glad you're all here so we can get to know each other better."

I couldn't have agreed more.

Helen had been only sixteen when Jim was born, and although she had probably tried her best, marriage and a child had done little to turn a sixteen-year-old girl into a woman. It takes a lot more than a mad dive into the pool of adulthood to do that. Although everyone is different, I firmly believe that experience is the catalyst in the maturing process. It just

36

doesn't happen overnight, but takes years of serious living.

Helen continued her cathartic soul bearing, telling me about the family's trials and explaining how they had struggled until the dissolution of her marriage.

"Bảo, Jim always held me responsible for the divorce, and at eleven years of age, he opted to move in with his father and Kay."

"Don't worry, I don't judge you even if Jim did," I said, trying to assure her that I was neither disparaging nor disapproving of her.

Encircling her arms around me, tears welled in her eyes.

"Jim hardly ever allowed me to have anything for myself," I blurted, taking her cue to unburden my own soul. "Instead, he was repeatedly filling his stepmother's pockets with money, satisfying her every whim, when we were barely able to make ends meet. Sadly, for my first Christmas in America, I did not have a cent to my name. Much as I wanted to get Jim a gift, I had no resources."

"Well, I'm sure he didn't expect anything from you, knowing you had no money," Helen said, coming to my defense.

"Perhaps, but I wanted to give him something and devised a plan to get some money."

"What did you do? How did you get money?"

"Over the course of several nights, I waited for him to fall asleep. Once he was snoring, I picked his pocket, dug out his wallet, carefully removed a five-dollar bill and reinserted the billfold as I had found it. Several times, I grabbed his pants, hurling them on the floor, admonishing him for leaving them on the bed."

"Why make such a fuss?" Helen asked, not following my train of thought.

"The idea was not to scold Jim for not properly hanging his pants, but to empty his pockets of any loose change or bills."

"Did it work, Bảo?" Helen asked, wide-eyed with anticipation of learning the outcome.

"Yes—believe it or not, my scheme netted twenty dollars."

"So, what did you get Jim?"

"I bought him an electric shaver. It was not a big deal, but it meant a lot to me because I was participating in the American cultural tradition of giving presents—be it for a birthday, Christmas or whatever."

"People don't give gifts in Việt Nam?" Helen asked, surprised.

"Well, yes and no. Vietnamese adults exchange gifts of food among each other, but pretty, wrapped presents are given only to children."

Since I was focused on grilling chicken, I failed to realize that Helen was laughing until I looked up to ask her to bring me a plate.

"Forgive me, Bảo," she muttered apologetically, fighting to take on a somber look. "I didn't mean to laugh at you but I couldn't help myself. The creative way in which you collected and saved money was amusingly unique."

"I never saw it in that light," I said, joining her in a fully bell laugh.

During my stay in Tennessee, I did some stitching for people, earning extra money for myself and the children. Helen worked in a restaurant, leaving me free to work at home. Our weekends were spent chatting and shopping. It was a wonderful interlude in my life.

Receiving approval for government housing in June of 1977, Jim immediately sent me plane tickets to Heilbronn, Germany; receiving them was a bittersweet moment. Bidding farewell to Helen was difficult and sad. She had befriended me, treating me with love and respect that had been unknown to me before. Consequently, I knew in my heart that I would never forget her and the extraordinary kindness she demonstrated during a trying period of my life.

The trip to Europe was calm and uneventful, offering me a few hours to shut my eyes and catch my breath. Ambitious and tenacious, as soon as I arrived in Heilbronn, I sought work in the military mess hall, much to the chagrin of Jim.

"Båo, I don't want you working in an environment of rude, crass servicemen," he said, nervously scratching his chin. Much as I knew better—he didn't like the idea of my spending eight hours a day with other men—I remained unemployed there part time, and babysat for extra money.

A year later, however, I did take a full-time job in the mess hall, working five days a week. Although the work was strenuous, I enjoyed my coworkers, and the pay was good.

One day, two colleagues phoned in sick, which meant I was expected to work a double shift.

"Don't worry," said Nancy, my coworker, reassuringly. "We'll handle it. Come here—let's take a break and have a cup of coffee."

"OK," I responded, happy to have a moment's pause.

Thomas, an amicable lieutenant who often patronized the eatery, walked into the dining room while we were on break. He flashed an ear-to-ear smile and inquired if he could join us.

"May I get you a cup of coffee?" I asked,

"Oh, that's very nice, thank you," he replied. "Only two of you tonight?"

"Just Nancy and I work tonight. The other two called in sick."

"Do y'all need me to stay and help y'all out?"

"Are you sure?" Nancy asked. We couldn't believe that a lieutenant had offered to help us!

"Oh, yeah, I'm sure!"

Spotting the GIs walking in the door, we jumped to our feet, making a mad dash for the kitchen. When dinner was finished, the diners brought their plates and utensils to the kitchen window.

Amazingly, Lieutenant Thomas followed in our tracks. Rolling up his sleeves, he grabbed a knife and scraped the dishes. Handing them to me one at a time, I rinsed and passed them to Nancy who, in turn, loaded them into the dishwasher. Since the window was narrow and Thomas was tall, his shoulders were visible, revealing his rank and insignia. An officer was in the kitchen washing plates!

41

The GIs were shocked to see a lieutenant on KP duty, and speculated among themselves about the possibility of a punishment.

"What could he have done to be forced to scrape plates?" they whispered. Their gawking resulted in a slowdown as the line lengthened, moving barely at a snail's pace. Consequently, though exhausted, we had to remain an hour longer to clear up the bottleneck traffic jam, the result of Thomas' kitchen intervention.

Pulling my weight to get the GIs served and the mess hall cleaned up, I failed to realize that Thomas was sizing me up in a nonprofessional light until my supervisor mentioned she saw his eyes literally fixed on me. I did recall that some months earlier, I had noticed Thomas staring at me but had never made an issue of it as he'd never overstepped any boundaries.

"You're pretty, Bảo," he whispered when our glances locked. Ignoring his compliment, I continued to work, hoping his recent offer of help wasn't going to breed any problems.

The following day, Thomas walked into the mess hall and slid into a chair, settling himself between Nancy and me.

"What do you think?" he began nervously, clearing his throat. "Did I do a good job last night?"

"Yes, Lieutenant," I replied, "you did a great job. Thanks—you certainly bailed us out. We needed the extra hands."

"I've got six months to serve before my tour of duty ends. Then I'll be discharged—a civilian again," Thomas said, curling his lips in a full smile.

A hullabaloo of colliding voices distracted my concentration as the GIs trickled in. Thomas lowered his head, pushing himself away from the table.

"I guess this is my cue to leave," he said, rising from his seat.

"Bye, Lieutenant, and thanks again for your help," I told him.

After his debut as dish scraper, he never again stepped foot into the kitchen, though he did not curtail his flirtatious game-playing with me.

Despite the mounting issues creating havoc in my marriage, living in Germany was an enjoyable experience. Furthermore, notwithstanding our marital mayhem, I birthed our second child and my third son, Phong, on August 5, 1978, in Stuttgart's US military hospital.

I was blessed with a quick labor and a smooth delivery, and my beautiful, new baby was of calm pedigree. Cooperative and easygoing, he responded well to the efforts of my older children who, I might add, joined forces to form a wonderful support team.

With my surrogates on duty, volunteering energy and youth, I was able to savor the beauty and cultural offerings of this country whose citizens, proud of their German heritage, took excellent care both of private property and common surroundings. Perhaps the threat of steep fines for negligence and littering in and around the cities served as strong incentives to maintain civic commitments.

Not a very expansive country, Germany was inviting to tour. Jim, the children and I visited a different city every weekend; I'm certain we left our footprints in every *schloß.* I think there are as many of these castles in Germany as there are churches in Italy. Majestic and stately, they left me in awe.

Once we felt we had absorbed Germany's cultural and monumental delights, we ventured into Switzerland for a long weekend. After a three-hour drive, we arrived at the US Army resort. The following morning, we crossed the German-Swiss *grenze* (border) in a *tretboot.* It was a new adventure, as we had never before sailed in a pedal boat. Like typical tourists, we toured, filming both the natural and manmade panoramas of the country, reassuring ourselves that we had immortalized some beautiful memories of this European interlude in our lives.

A month thereafter, we embarked on a bus trip to Austria. Traveling by *sammelleitung* was definitely more comfortable than the car. The bus allowed us the liberty to stand and stretch at will. Arriving several minutes before noon, we hurried over to the food vendors to get some lunch before the afternoon *mediteraneepause* would leave us with closed vendors and nothing to eat.

Jim ordered five small glasses of orange juice and five *würstchen meist in einem brötchen verkauft*—hot dogs and buns. When the vendor said, "*Fünfzig* dollars *bitte*—fifty dollars, please," I was stunned.

"Did I hear correctly?" I asked Jim.

"Yes, I'm afraid he said fifty dollars."

I questioned what was in the hot dogs— perhaps they put a smidgeon of Beluga caviar in to warrant such an exorbitant price.

After we feasted, we did a walking tour of the city, surprised to note that it was totally in shutdown mode. Eventually, we learned that most Europeans liked to take a *siesta* midday, for a leisurely lunch and short nap.

Life resurrected around two o'clock, putting smiles on our faces and quickening

45

our strides. Hitting the markets and cathedrals, we acquired souvenirs and additional photos.

During the return bus trip to the base, some of the passengers were discussing the post-World War II history of Austria and the diverse nations that had influenced and invaded the country. They mentioned that the population had withered, making the country home to just two and a half million people.

Listening to the painstaking recounting of the memories of those who had lived it firsthand, I felt saddened. A victim of wartime casualties, I was able to identify with the bloodshed, horrors, anguish and terrifying uncertainty of a country no longer at peace.

My mind wandered to those dreadful days when Schlessinger had announced the start of Operation Frequent Wind. His broadcast on April 29, 1975 had spoken of the helicopters that flew on a massive, emergency mission to evacuate remaining military, diplomatic and civilian personnel from Sài Gòn. The following day, South Việt Nam fell to the Communists. I had been crushed.

The pain had been searing and unwavering that day. Inconsolable, I had been riddled with fear—for the fate of my country and, more importantly, for the safety of my family. Living an ocean apart, in another world, a frustrating feeling of powerlessness had set in, shoving me into an irrepressible depression.

An enticing bait, the balcony of our second-story apartment had tempted me like a cunning snake charmer, with promises of amnesty from the gnawing worry eating at my spirit.

"It would be so easy," I'd whispered to myself, gazing down at the racing cars carrying people to their destinations. "All I have to do is jump and it will all come to an end—the throbbing hurt that never healed, the bitter hopelessness leaving me shivering in the sunlight."

Jump! Jump, Bảo, a persistent voice resonated in my head. *Jump and you will find happiness and a respite from all this suffering.*

"I want to die," I shouted. "I want the pain to stop. I want this nightmarish life to end. I'm going to jump—I want peace of mind. This is the only way."

I wrestled with the idea of escaping my heartaches. How simple it would be—the ideal solution. Feelings of worthlessness edged me further into despondency. What if I jumped? What about my children? Who would tend to their needs and make certain they matured into healthy, well-adjusted adults? Who would dry their tears when they cried, comfort their aches and hold their hands while they stumbled along the rocky path to adulthood? Questions erupted as I stood, selfishly concerned about my own problems, contemplating a cowardly way out!

Fortunately, when I looked into the helpless, innocent faces of my children who idolized me as Mommy, I was shaken back to reality. Jim, on the other hand, was neither supportive of my misery nor willing to validate my efforts as a wife and mother. Instead, he demonstrated only apathy for my struggles and indifference to my anguish.

"Go ahead—jump," he shouted, playing a risky game with my fragile spirit. Shocked by his reckless, unsympathetic behavior, I realized that my children would be in his hands if I died—a reflection that awakened my reasoning, carrying me away from my own self-centered concerns.

When the bus stopped, my memories vanished. We exited and walked to the car to continue our return trip.

For a brief, fleeting interlude, I gazed at the panorama of nature with its budding and blossomed flowers in flecked and spotted hues, so carefree. The beauty and awe were a panacea, reinvigorating, though I knew the benefits would be short-lived. Soon, I would be home, and the bickering would resume.

Sighing, I decided I would just settle down and savor the moment.

Chapter 3
Testing Endurance

Although from time to time, Jim declared his love for me, I didn't understand his contradictory behavior. Does a man demonstrate love for a woman by yelling at her, by chastising her as if she were a mischievous child? If such disrespect is a consequence of love, who needs or wants it? Why couldn't my husband converse with me in a civilized voice? It was a mystery I hoped to solve.

The truth is, Jim lived in eternal antagonism. It was as if he balanced a chip on his shoulder from morning until evening. He was angry with his sister and birth mother, mad at his boss and Army superiors; I was not the sole target of his rage. He also fought with the lower-ranking GIs who crossed his path. At least he was consistent.

Much as I shunned doting on these failings, I could not escape them because his irate moods were a repeated source of reinforcement. Consequently, my life with

Jim was neither satisfying nor fulfilling. Instead, it was a frustrating struggle and a font of anxiety.

Working to make ends meet, tending to the needs and demands of four children and managing the household chores from cleaning to cooking, I had a full day every day. Although Jim returned earlier than I in the evenings, he never once made an effort to assist me. His job seemed to be messing up and seeding discord as soon as I straightened things out. However, he was not shy about scolding me for what he called "domestic negligence."

"Jim you make such a mess—why don't you help clean it up?" I asked, exasperated by his sloppy habits.

"I work all day. I'm tired. I want to relax when I come home, not do more work."

"Well, I have a job, too. Did you forget that I work all day?"

"Then quit—leave the job."

"If I didn't work, we wouldn't be able to buy the extras and put some money away. Your paycheck covers only bills and groceries—that's it. What about clothes, entertainment, and money for emergencies? You don't make enough to support us. Don't forget we have four growing children."

"Bảo, when I was a kid, my mother forced me to clean the house and wash the dishes every day. Now that I have a wife and kids, why should I have to clean up?"

"Because your children are too little and your wife works. If you made enough money, I wouldn't mind staying home and cleaning up. But you don't, so I have to work."

Following that verbal reality check, Jim made an effort to collaborate with me in his way when it came to completing the domestic chores. His idea of vacuuming was to pass the appliance over a limited and specific area of a room where he actually walked. As a result, the house looked untidy, especially under the chairs and tables and in the corners. If I tried to correct his senseless strategy, he'd admonish me for being neither satisfied nor grateful.

"You're never pleased, Bảo, so I think it best if you take care of the house." With that said, Jim's half-hearted efforts came to an abrupt end.

Unfortunately, the neglect and laxity extended beyond household chores. Jim seemed allergic to hand washing and dental hygiene. My efforts to correct these bad habits were fruitless.

"Get off my back," he'd shout whenever I'd open my mouth. "Stop nagging me." All

53

attempts at communication were unsuccessful. He just never listened to anything I had to say, even if it was for his good.

One afternoon, Jim returned home earlier than expected to retrieve some documents he needed for work. While rummaging through our files, he accidentally came across some photos of David, Thaun's father.

"This is David, your old boyfriend," he said, shoving the photo in my face. A flushed complexion and an irate tone told me he was upset. "I saw him downtown."

"When did you see David?" I asked, trying to curtail my excitement and the pitch of my voice.

"The day we were looking for curtains. I caught him staring at you, so I gave him a dirty look. He understood my message, He turned and walked away."

"He's here!" I exclaimed. "Obviously, he was given a commission here, like you," I added reeling in my enthusiasm. "I had nothing to do with it. He's certainly not here for me."

Shrugging his shoulders in *faux* nonchalance, Jim dropped the photo on the table and left. Relieved, I pranced around the house, excited to be in the same city as David. Was he really here—or was this a mere reverie?

My mind choreographed diverse scenarios in which David and I met face to face and fell into each other's arms as if our glances had been apart for just a day. Life is ironic—I had looked for him in every city I had been in during the past six years, eyeing ever man in uniform who crossed my path. And, as if by some magical hocus pocus, now he was right here in the same city. My heart still fluttered for him. Undoubtedly, time was not an accommodating ally in clouding my feelings for Thaun's father.

As my marital problems intensified, my thoughts of David became more frequent. I no longer doted on what I had with Jim, but on what I could have had with David. However, instead of feeling joyful, I relished a bittersweet disdain for the man who, at one time, had captured my heart.

Though I had written to him throughout the years, David had never once responded with even the courtesy of a few lines. If he had, perhaps our destinies would have unraveled in a different manner.

Dismayed by his diffidence, in the hopeless corners of my mind, I chose to leave behind the closed door and walk through the open one with Jim. Consequently, I blamed David for my miserable marriage. It was always his fault. Undeniably, he was a deterrent to my happiness. These feelings continued to influence my mood because I had absolutely no reason to dispute his role in my troubled life.

Although a drizzle of rain mixed with snowflakes created a dismal panorama, when the children returned from school, I enticed them into taking a walk with me along the Neckar River. Rippling water was always therapeutic and with my emotions twisted in disarray, I knew I had to get out and get moving or I would totally lose it.

Ignoring the steady precipitation drenching our heads and shoulders, we strolled as if a clear, blue sky splashed with golden rays of sun accompanied us. Deep in thought, I hardly noticed the arrival of an auto.

"Where are you going?" Jim asked, rolling down the window.

"Just for a walk," I sighed.

"Will you wait for me while I change out of my uniform? I'd like to join you."

"OK," the children blurted in unison, thrilled to have Mommy and Daddy together. I, instead, merely nodded in agreement.

Heilbronn is a midsize, subdued town, where activity at various times of the day is at a bare minimum. Hence, many businesses and shops were already closed, leaving us the sole pedestrians on the cobblestoned streets.

The children chatted among themselves as we crossed over to begin our return to the house. Suddenly, something in a store window caught my eye. I peered more intensely, raising my hands to my forehead to shield my eyes from the light. An elderly gentleman looked at me askance in passing.

"I like this," I said, pointing to an object on display. "It's better than the one I used to have."

His mouth dropping, the stranger glared at me through condemning eyes, then rotated them up and down over each member of my family.

"You never had that!" Jim said, grinning.

"Yes, I did," I insisted.

"Bảo, do you know what that is?" Jim asked.

57

"Of course—it's a curling iron. I've used it before to wave my hair."

"It's not a curling iron," he said, breaking into a hearty laugh. "It's a vibrator—a pleasure toy for women."

To say I was embarrassed is an understatement. However, I understood why the elderly stranger had given me such a weird stare—there I was with my husband and children, gloating over a vibrator! Apparently, I was still a novice in life, even though I had married three men and birthed five children.

Jim was reassigned to Fort Sill in Lawton, Oklahoma, and on January 30, 1980, we returned to the USA, taking a detour to spend three weeks with my friends, Hoa and Michael, in Nashville. I'd been introduced to Hoa, also a native of Việt Nam, by Jim's mother, Helen, during my last trip. Throughout my stay in Germany, we had maintained contact through letters. Therefore, upon learning of our return, Hoa immediately extended an invitation. Thankfully, the visit was both relaxing and productive.

While in Nashville, we bid on a twenty-two-acre property, agreeing to the $22,000 asking price. A $4,000 down payment, with a ten-year mortgage with monthly payments of $200, closed the deal.

Once the contract was signed, we ventured on to Hazard, Kentucky, to visit Jim's father and third wife, Sheri, whom we politely referred to as "Mom" to put a smile on her face. Extroverted, amicable and upbeat, Sheri was easy to relate to. We shared the familiarity of old friends, a warm and relaxed feeling that made it seem as though I had grown up in her company.

Famished, we arrived at Sheri's house several hours past lunchtime. Accompanying her to the local country store to purchase some groceries, we argued over who would pay the tab. Since the food was acquired to accommodate my family I felt it was my responsibility to take care of the cost. Disagreeing with my method of reasoning, Sheri won the discussion, snatching the bill from my hand.

"I'm older than you, Bảo," she said, smiling, "therefore, you must listen to your elders."

"OK," I said, laughing. "I surrender—you win."

"Let me know when you would like to eat," Sheri said as soon as we entered the house. Reaching for the produce, meat and dairy products, she began loading the refrigerator.

"I'm about to die from hunger," I blurted. "Can we eat now?"

"OK, we'll have lunch," she said, laughing as she went into reverse mode, unloading the refrigerator.

"I'll cook, Sheri," I said, lifting the food from her hands. In less than twenty minutes, the house was filled with an enticing aroma, leaving everyone salivating. Suddenly, a crowd formed—I could see that my cooking was like a magnet.

"Lunch will be ready in five minutes," I announced. There was no question in my mind that I had prepared a delicious meal. The confirmation arrived when empty plates returned to the kitchen.

When we left Germany, among our possessions and souvenirs were two cuckoo clocks.

One I gave to Hoa and one I saved for Sheri, who was thrilled to receive such a fun and unique item. It was my way of expressing gratitude to these gracious ladies for their generous hospitality in accommodating my family.

Soon after bidding farewell to Jim's father and Sheri, we departed for Fort Sill, finding temporary lodging in an Army motel for a couple of weeks before settling in a house near the base. Eager to get acclimated and meet people, I went to the commissary, where I immediately encountered Que, a Vietnamese woman. Bonding at first sight, we chatted and exchanged telephone numbers. Shortly thereafter, she phoned me.

"Bảo, I have to give you a warning," she said. "You must be very careful where you choose to live."

"Why? Is this a dangerous area?" I asked, taken a bit by surprise by her words. "You must have a reason for cautioning me."

"Well, yes, I do. About five months ago, two men patrolled the neighborhood, knocking on doors. They were well dressed in dark business suits and ties. Each carried a couple of books. Hearing their knock, a woman opened the door, believing they were nice gentleman. Aggressively, they pushed

61

her aside, forced their way into her home and raped her."

"How awful! I'll be certain to discuss this with Jim," I said.

After we ended the conversation, I bedded the children down for the evening, then closed my eyes for a moment of relaxation. Dozing in and out of a light sleep, I bolted upright when the doorbell sounded. Rising to my feet, I walked over to the window and peered out.

Startled, my heart thumped, leaving me gasping for air. In front of my door were the two men my friend had warned me about earlier, dressed exactly as she had described, complete with books tucked under their arms.

I thought of the children. Terror invaded, mixed with nausea. I fought it. This was not only about me. The children were asleep in their rooms. I knew I had to get a hold of myself, stay calm and not panic. Glancing at the door, I was relieved to note it was locked. These men were dangerous criminals and intended to hurt me.

I was afraid that if I ran to the phone, they would catch sight of me through the window and perhaps force the door. Not daring to breathe, I waited and prayed. If I was really quiet, I thought, maybe they would just disappear, believing they had no prey to pounce on.

Instead, impatient to add another crime to their already-delinquent penal records, they pushed the bell several times while pounding with their fists on the door. The echo was penetrating, and rendered ear-shattering by the intensity of my own fright.

Presumably assuming the house was vacant, they waited for a couple of minutes then departed. Thankfully, the children were safe and asleep. Realizing it could have been a harrowing nightmare for all had I not been forewarned, I broke into sobs. My mind sailed through various gruesome scenarios of what could have been—the kind of experience that would have undeniably resulted in tragedy. My children could have been permanently traumatized or even killed!

Shaking like a weeping willow caught in the bands of a passing hurricane, I debated my next move. Should I phone the police or wait until Jim returned? After several minutes of deliberations, I chose a no-action option.

When I told Jim about the incident that evening, he scolded me.

"Bảo, you should have phoned the police immediately," he admonished. "These are dangerous criminals. They have to be caught and thrown in prison to protect innocent people."

I had to admit Jim was right. I should not have allowed fear to manipulate my ability to reason and influence my judgment. Criminals should be reported to the authorities and apprehended for the safety and protection of all. Actually, it was my civic duty. I reassured Jim that I would never be so hesitant again in the face of such peril.

The following week, as I was serving dinner, the phone rang. Resting the platter on the table, I walked over, lifted the receiver to my ear and responded.

"I'm at home all alone," a female voice whispered. "I need someone... I'm desperate for a friend... I need you, honey."

"Who is this?" I responded, irritated.

"I want to take you in my arms. I want to lick you all over. I want to—"

"Don't call here again," I shouted, slamming down the receiver.

Naïve in some areas of life, despite the traumatic war experiences that had cut short my childhood, I was stunned, never before hearing about a woman who desired another woman sexually.

"What's the matter, Mommy?" the children blurted, confused by the aggressive way in which I'd slammed down the phone.

"Nothing, don't worry. Someone just dialed the wrong number. Eat your dinner before it gets cold."

However, upset by the obscene proposition I had received from a stranger, I lost my appetite. Trying to eat was useless—the food would not go down regardless of the super-small, bite-size pieces I cut.

After the children went to bed, I told Jim about the disturbing phone call.

"Jim, I think we should have heeded Que's suggestion," I said. "She warned me about being careful. I don't feel safe living in this neighborhood anymore.

Believing military housing would be a safer, more cost-effective option to pursue, Jim chose to put his name on the waiting list. I, on the other hand, lost my patience. The two frightening incidents had furnished credible evidence that Que was right. Therefore, I preferred to keep searching until we found exactly what we wanted in a safe and sound neighborhood.

Actually, my idea was to save enough for a down payment on a house while the children were still young. Growing up secure equated to living in a family-owned dwelling—a blessing not granted to me as a child. Consequently, I wanted my children to have all that I'd never had. Fortunately, Jim was in full agreement.

Three months thereafter, subsequent to searching the housing market, we located a property that not only suited our needs and tastes but represented a profitable investment. Closing the deal, we moved in. Of course, all the motel living, dining out and signing a land contract in Tennessee had absorbed our savings. We were totally broke.

Not one to sit still in acquiescence, resigned to the lacks and losses in my life, I ventured forth in search of employment. Although Thaun, Tram, and Phuong attended school, two-and-a-half-year-old Phong, was still at home. Finding a suitable sitter, I went directly to the employment office to apply for a job and collect the benefits due to me.

Unable to read or write English, I panicked when the receptionist handed me an application. When I confessed my handicap, a staff member came to my rescue.

"You must go out and search for a job at least three times a week," she instructed, handing me a card. "And when you apply for a job, remember to document in writing the date you applied as well as the company name and location."

The following day, I applied at Haggar Slack Factory on Bishop Street in Lawton,

Oklahoma. Two days later, I applied at a fan manufacturing company, and on day four I contacted Goodyear.

Returning to the employment office, I turned in my card, signed in at the reception desk and waited to be summoned. Next to me, a woman was seated. She was holding her card, and a quick glance told me she had an entry on every line.

"Excuse me," I said, looking to iron out my confusion. "May I ask you a question?"

"Yes," she responded politely. "How may I assist you?"

"I thought we were instructed to apply for a job three times a week, but I notice you have a full card."

"Don't worry," she responded, "just go out and write down the name and address of any business you see advertised. Walk around and jot down the companies listed on buildings—then write it down on your card. It'll look good."

"But why? I'm really serious about finding work—I'm not interested in looking good."

"Well, then go look for a job!" she blurted, clutching her card.

Departing the employment office, I drove down the street, rehashing in my mind the conversation that had transpired between the woman and me. Maybe she'd meant well, I thought; perhaps she had been imparting some valuable advice. Maybe it was me—maybe I just didn't get it. Feeling somewhat silly, I decided to follow her instructions. After all what did I have to lose by filling up my card?

Recognizing that time was not a luxury for me, I rode around the block a couple times, looking for company names. The name Don McCurdy appeared, posted on a board attached to the side of a building. I wrote it on my card. I also wrote down Lee Borlova, a name familiar to me from the Gold Dragon Restaurant and Lounge.

Hurrying back to the employment office, I deposited my card on the desk, turned on my heels and headed for the door, mulling over in my mind the list of things on my to-do list. Pulling the doorknob, I heard my name called.

"Follow me, please, and have a seat," the administrative assistant said, pointing to a vacant chair.

She glanced at my card, held firmly in her right hand.

"Do you know who Don McCurdy is?" she asked, not raising her gaze.

"Yes, ma'am," I began. "He's a big businessman whose office is located in the white building about three blocks from here."

"Are you absolutely certain about that?"

"Oh yes—one-hundred-percent certain," I lied.

"Well, I'm afraid you're mistaken," she said, raking her side-parted hair with her long, slender fingers. "I'm sorry to contradict you, but Don McCurdy is a member of the House of Representatives, currently running for a seat in the Senate."

He was a politician! I felt a wave of heat rush over my face and chest. *Whoops—this is a serious* faux pas, I thought.

Caught off guard and desperate for an acceptable comeback, I looked down at my feet for a brief interlude, until the assistant cleared her throat—a signal that she wanted my attention. Raising my eyes, I noticed her quick smile. Luckily, my English, heavily laced with an Asian accent, was an asset. She was gracious, and she understood that I had serious language difficulties.

"Let me give you some advice. The next time you look for a job, go inside and speak with someone in charge of hiring. Also make sure you write down the person's name and phone number on your card, so we know who to contact. Do you understand?"

"Yes ma'am."

"OK, good luck," she said, handing me a new card.

"Thank you, ma'am," I said, and quickly left. Embarrassed by my foolishness, I wanted to get as far away from her as possible.

On the way back, I stopped at Home Land Grocery to pick up some chicken for dinner. I arrived home at the same time as the kids. All three of them ran toward me as I stepped out of the car.

"Mama!" Tram called loudly.

"Mama! What did you buy?" Phuong asked.

"I got some chicken for dinner," I told him.

"Mama, where did you go?" Thaun asked, dancing around me.

"I was out looking for a job."

He didn't seem exceptionally interested in my job search and abruptly dropped his line of questioning. Presumably, it was merely a sprout of curiosity over the motive behind my absence.

While the children played, I prepared dinner. When Jim returned at six, we sat at the table for the evening meal. Though exhausted, I knew I would not end my quest for a job until I was hired. Quitting was never part of who I was.

Chapter 4

Transcending Boundaries

A week later, I applied for a job at Memorial Hospital. Approaching the human resources office, I waited, anxious for someone to appear. Several minutes thereafter, a middle-aged woman of petite stature entered.

"How may I help you?" she asked, smiling broadly.

"I'm interested in applying for a job either as a kitchen aide or janitor."

Walking over to the desk, she sifted through a small pile, lifting an application.

"Fill in your name, address, phone number, date of birth and Social Security number," she instructed, handing me the document.

"Could you please help me with the rest of the information required?" I asked.

"I need the name and address of your last employer and three references. Can you supply that info?"

"I just moved here," I stammered, "but I can give you the names of two references."

I was somewhat hesitant, fearful that I would not hear from the hospital because I knew that both of these individuals did not really know me well enough to endorse my character. However, five days later, I was contacted and offered a janitorial position in the hospital, where I would cover the morning shift with a staff of six nurses and a maximum of thirty patients.

My post started at seven o'clock and concluded at three-thirty, with a half-hour midday lunch break. I worked for eight consecutive days followed by a three day pause every other week. The job description stated that I was responsible for picking up a cart and stocking it with tissue, plastic bags, soap, Windex and whatever products I needed from the supply room to satisfy my job requirements.

The staff, with the exception of the head nurse, was open, agreeable and friendly. I enjoyed interacting with them during chance encounters in patients' rooms or while having lunch. Seated together, we laughed, joked and discussed the day's issues.

Moody, predominately disgruntled and sour, the head nurse never smiled or greeted me. He behaved as if I willfully had wronged him in some mysterious way. Frustrated, it behooved me to determine what, if anything, I had done or not done to cause this aloof reaction on his part.

One day, he mentioned his tour of duty in the Việt Nam War, a confidence that explained his coolness in my regard. Nevertheless, in opening the lines of communication with me, he let down his guard. In so doing, he discovered that I was really not at fault for his traumatic battle experiences, despite my Vietnamese origins.

From that day forward, the nurse's icy demeanor melted, encouraging me to build a pleasant friendship.

Racism is and was equated with an ignorance bred from narrow-mindedness, a global dilemma that, for the most part, has been alleviated in the twenty-first century, thanks to the power of knowledge. Though in many parts of the world the journey has not been completed, generally, I like to think that people are moving in the right direction.

Transgressors have always existed and will continue with their bigoted thought processes, but they represent a small minority, unlike years ago when bias was more stridently pronounced.

Years ago, while living in Việt Nam, I'd been hurriedly heading home one day with my

73

eighteen-month-old daughter, Phuong, scared of being caught in a bombing raid or some other skirmish. Arriving at the bus stop, I noticed an American military truck pull up at the intersection. One of the soldiers riding in the rear spotted me at the bus stop. Without any provocation on my part, he leaned out and hurled the contents of a thirty-two-ounce cup of pineapple juice in my face.

Startled, I caught my bearings and tried not to panic. Concerned about Phuong, I clutched her closer just as the soldier, snickering derisively, threw the empty cup in my face. Tires screeching, the truck drove off, the soldiers' mocking laughter still audible over the din of their speedy getaway.

I was confused and unable to decide on to whom I should focus my rage. Instead of releasing my pent-up feelings, I opted to forget the incident. Realizing it was ridiculous to blame or hold a grudge against all Americans based on a solitary demonstration of ignorant behavior, I learned an important lesson about cultural relationships. Just as I could not in good conscience point a condemnatory finger at one race for the stupidity of a few, I did not hold any grudges against the Americans. However, I also felt that Americans should not repudiate the

Vietnamese for the actions of some. It just wasn't fair.

As a rule, I enjoyed meeting people and making friends, defining the process as another of life's interesting challenges. While walking down the hallway one afternoon following my lunch break, I noticed the arrival of a new patient. Curious, I entered his room to introduce myself.

"Hello, sir," I said cheerfully, "I'm Bảo."

My overenthusiastic approach was met with silence.

"OK, I'll come back tomorrow," I said, and left him in peace.

Keeping my promise, I returned the following day. Once again, my greeting was received with more silence. Determined to crack his hard exterior and vow of silence, I revisited every day for five days—all to no avail.

What now? I thought, reluctant to admit defeat. Deciding against surrendering to the glacial reception I received from the icy patient, I persisted.

I asked myself what harm would a "hello, how are you?" approach do anyway, even if my words and smile were ignored? Tenacity and patience, persistence and determination, pay big dividends.

On the sixth day, when I entered his room, he said, "Hi. Do you still put *nước mắm* on your food?"

"I'm shocked," I replied. "How did you know I'm from Việt Nam?"

"I can tell by your voice."

"Were you ever in Việt Nam?"

"Oh, yes! I was stationed in Tam Ky for a year."

"Really! I lived in Tam Ky—even had a restaurant there that was patronized by many GIs."

"I bet I ate there sometime."

Surprisingly, the icy patient seemed to have melted. His eyes glistened, his smile broadened and he called me "ma'am" as a sign of respect. Thanking him for his graciousness, I departed.

"I will see you tomorrow," I said strutting out door, proud of my accomplishment.

Such triumphs, regardless of importance, raise my spirits. Therefore, with a light, springy step, I walked into the room of another new patient. In keeping with my style, I imparted an exuberant greeting, which once again was reciprocated with an apathetic silence.

Was this becoming a pattern? I remembered that I had heard about many GIs who had been to Việt Nam, loved the country and culture and reenlisted after their tours of duty were completed just to remain there. Perhaps this new patient also was a Việt Nam veteran.

Again, I opted to leave him in peace. It was a tactic that seemed to work. Finally, he decided to acknowledge my presence.

"What will you do if Americans and Vietnamese engage in combat?" he said almost derisively.

"I will continue living my life," I responded.

"You can go now," he growled. "Just get out and leave me alone!"

"I'm on my way," I blurted, eager to head for the door. "Goodbye, sir."

Despite his sudden and unexpected aggression, I felt good about our encounter. At least I had been successful in getting a reaction from him, albeit not a very gracious one. Experience had taught me that people often misunderstand each other because they don't take the time to get to know who is standing before them. However, once knowledge overcomes unfamiliarity, it becomes easier to communicate and more difficult to misinterpret what is said.

Alienation, hostility and a stubborn attitude are, in my opinion, parents of prejudice. People are biased and intolerant because they refuse to familiarize themselves with those who look, speak, think and believe in a different manner. Nonetheless, taking the time to know the various individuals with whom we share the planet leads to tolerance, openness and acceptance as well as many interesting, significant and endearing relationships.

"Time for lunch, Bảo," my coworker, Dee, called, cutting through my thoughts.

"Thanks, Dee. I'm coming over."

Quickly rolling up my sleeves, I disinfected my hands and made my way to the cafeteria to join my colleagues. A warm feeling of camaraderie prevailed. Happy to be accepted by my peers, I tried not to focus on the handful of cranky patients who were somewhat aloof towards me. In my heart, I knew I would eventually win them over—all they had to do was invest some time and energy into getting to know me. It was that simple.

Walking down the hall one morning, I overhead a frail female voice screaming.

"They took my husband from me—they hurt me!"

I followed the voice, trying to find the room in which the wailing woman was located.

"Number one—number one, please come in," her cracking voice shouted.

Confused, I quickened my stride.

"Number two, please come in," the voice called next.

The bizarre counting continued. Except for the escalating number, the phrase was the same.

Reaching the woman's door, I knocked and strolled in just as she as she said,

"Number forty-five—number forty-five, come in, please."

"Hello, ma'am," I said, hoping to break her chant.

"Who are you? Where did you come from?" the elderly woman blurted, sitting upright in her bed. Eyes open unnaturally wide, she dared not blink. I neared her bed, intent on appeasing her restless spirit.

Having seen me, she almost immediately forgot that I was there, and her counting chant resumed. Her trancelike state seemed impossible to suspend. The counting and beckoning persisted with a pronounced, staccato rhythm until she wearily slid back on her pillow and fell into a deep sleep.

Patience was in short supply among the nurses and staff, and the elderly woman's difficult behavior kept everyone at bay. Isolated in her own world, it was impossible to establish any contact with her.

Nurse Anne and I were working in the old ladies room one day. She started screaming just as we were about to leave.

"They took my husband away from me. They hurt me," she yelled.

"Anne, those are the same words I heard her say a week ago. I don't think she is thinking clearly. She probably doesn't realize what she is saying. I wonder if she is really here with us."

"They did," the old lady said, slapping her fist on the bed. "They took him away."

"Yes," Anne said, "I know they took him away."

Although I wondered why the nurse humored her in that rather dishonest manner, I kept silent, not questioning her action.

I was unable to distract myself from thoughts of the elderly lady who appeared so alone and lost. Unqualified to diagnose the nature and gravity of her malady, I assumed she was repressing the memory of some painfully traumatic event experienced in her earlier years.

Fascinated by her strange disconnectedness, and eager to discover what was at the root of this bizarre behavior, I returned to her room, intent on checking the chart tucked in a slot on the outside of the door.

Slipping it out, I hurriedly scanned through the documents on the clipboard. I noted that her age was listed as eighty-six, and the date of her arrival was one month earlier. Most of the other info was illegible.

Her room was unadorned—no flowers, no cards, no candy—which equated to the heartbreaking reality that neither family nor

81

friends had visited. Saddened, I bought a single rose, set it in a vase and decided I would deliver it to her in the morning.

When I arrived the following day, she raised herself on her elbows, eyeing me as if she had suddenly reconnected with her surroundings and was meeting me for the first time.

"Where did you come from?" she screamed.

"I'm from Việt Nam," I said, gently lifting her hand, "and I'm here to see you. I know you must feel lonely, but I want to tell you that everyone in the hospital loves you. I love you also. Do you now that? You are very pretty, a really attractive woman."

"Thank you. You're pretty, too," she whispered. I had actually gotten through to her!

"You should get some rest," I said, leaning over to plant a kiss on her densely lined forehead. "I have to clean and straighten up your room. But look what I have for you— I brought you a rose."

"Oh, thank you," she cooed shyly.

"May I place it on your dresser?"

"Yes. That would be lovely, please do."

After I left her room, I felt a spray of energy infiltrate my body. I questioned if I had played a role in the unraveling of a miracle. Had my efforts, persistence and nurturing released this lady from her prison of silence?

Glimpsing my watch, I noticed it was quitting time. Returning my cart, I punched out at the time clock, thus ending my workday but not my thoughts of the elderly woman.

Walking back to her room for a final "good night," I discovered she was fast asleep. Tiptoeing so as not to disturb her, I left.

Sadly, my first conversation with her was also my last. My supervisor caught me at the door just as I was leaving the room.

"Bảo, starting tomorrow, you will be working on the third floor for a few days."

When I returned to my old floor ten days thereafter, I was informed, much to my chagrin, that the elderly woman had been dismissed from the hospital two days previously. Disappointed that I had missed the opportunity to bid her farewell, I felt empty and useless, as if I had lost someone very dear to me. I wondered if she had felt disturbed or abandoned during my absence.

"Bảo, I'd like to see you in my office at nine-thirty," said Randy, the department supervisor, as he handed me my paycheck. Unable to discern if his request for a meeting would result in a positive or negative outcome, I opted not to squander time dwelling on it. In reality, it made no difference. It would be what it would be whether I worried or not.

"Come in, please, Bảo," Randy said when I knocked on the door. Rising from his chair to greet me, he grinned. I wondered what was so humorous about my presence in his office.

"Bảo, you're not only excelling in your job, but you're also a good, warm-hearted person. You go above and beyond in trying to help patients when they need extra attention. Nevertheless, I'm sad to say the nurses prefer that you refrain from assisting the sick while they are on duty."

Pausing, he cleared his throat and took a few sips from the coffee mug on his desk. "You're different from most people," he continued. "I can see that you just can't walk away when you see someone in trouble. It's very nice of you, but you have to understand that I can't encourage this behavior. It is not your job to care for the patients, and if anything were to happen as a result of your intervention, you'd be in serious trouble. So, I have to ask you to please stop it. If I ever catch you again, I'll have to suspend you for three days without pay. Do you understand?"

"Yes, sir," I said, trying to swallow the knot in my throat.

However, when I returned to my janitorial post, one of the patients lit up when I came into the room.

"Where have you been?" she asked.

"I was transferred to the third floor for a while," I replied. "How are you?"

"Much better now that I know why they send you all around."

"Why?" I asked, puzzled by her strange answer.

"Oh, that's easy—they send you around so that you can take care of the whole hospital. Everyone else just poses at the door, looks around, and then leaves. They don't seem to want to get their hands dirty. I'm glad you're back."

"Thanks. I'll see you later."

Although Randy had been clear and firm in his admonitions, I continued to help patients, risking suspension and the loss of my job. It was stronger than me. It was who I was and impossible to suppress. When I heard a patient cry out for help, I knew they probably needed assistance walking to the bathroom or getting some water. Consequently, I continued to intervene without getting caught, attributing this fate not to luck but to the fact that I was merely doing what I was meant to do.

To increase my earnings, I continued to sew at home after my evening English classes at the neighborhood school. Then, one day, while shopping, I ran into Sally, a friend who informed me about a job opening for a seamstress. Sally owned a tailor shop located in the Central Mall, where I would sometimes visit. I hadn't spoken with her since I'd started working at the hospital, so she really was not updated on my professional life.

"Edwards and Son's Clothes, across the street, is looking for a tailor," Sally said.

"Really? I'm going to shop for some things for the children, but afterwards I'll stop by and inquire."

"Would you be interested in working there?"

"Maybe. It depends on what they are willing to pay."

"Why don't you come over on Saturday? We could spend some time together," Sally offered.

"Sorry, I can't. I have to work on Saturday. But would Sunday be OK?"

"Sure, Sunday is fine. Now, don't forget to give Edwards a thought. It might be something good."

"Thanks—I'll give it some serious consideration."

I heeded Sally's advice and stopped at Edwards and Son's. A well-dressed woman, of voluptuous proportions and in her late fifties, greeted me as I entered.

"Hello, I'm Mrs. Wood," she said. "How may I assist you today?"

"Hello, Mrs. Wood, I understand you're looking for a tailor."

"Yes, we are. How long have you been tailoring?"

"About fourteen years," I responded.

"Is that so? You look very young."

"Thank you!" I replied.

"How long have you been in the United States?" she asked me.

"I lived in the US three years before moving to Germany with my husband and children. We returned a year ago."

"Is your husband in the service?"

"Yes, he is."

"You're interested in working for us?"

"Yes. But, may I ask about the salary?

"We pay minimum wage," she told me.

"I'm sorry. I expected more than minimum wage. I heard you pay four dollars an hour."

"Our starting salary has never been that high. No new employee was ever paid that amount, but, if you're skilled enough to resolve the problems we have right now, we

87

will pay your asking price. When can you start?"

"I'm currently employed at Memorial Hospital. I'll need to give them two weeks' notice."

"Could you possibly work a couple of hours today? I'd like to see what you can do."

"Yes, I could. May I please use your phone? I'd like to call my family to tell them I'll be late."

"Of course. You can use the telephone in my office."

After I phoned the house to inform the children of my whereabouts and what I was doing, Mrs. Wood instructed her son, Ed, to escort me to the tailoring room on the second floor and show me the rack of clothes. Once upstairs, Ed invited me to browse through the garments.

"Bảo, you can start with these. Choose whatever item you wish. When you finish, my mother and I will take a look at what you've done."

"OK, Ed, as soon as I'm finished I'll take it downstairs."

Selecting a man's blazer, I altered the sleeves. The tag indicated that the customer requested they be shortened by an inch. About an hour later, I showed Ed and Mrs. Wood. Slipping on her glasses, she scrutinized my work, carrying the blazer over to the window for a brighter light.

Though I had a fair amount of self-confidence and was certain my work was of quality, I felt a bit tense to be the object of such scrutiny. Holding my breath, I waited for her judgment.

Removing her tortoise-shell glasses, she approached with determined steps. In the fast-arriving dusk, her shadow kept pace on the camel-colored carpet.

"Beautiful job, Bảo," she said, her voice changing from courteous to enthusiastic. "I would like to offer you the job. Will you come work for us?"

"Mrs. Wood, I'll give you an answer as soon as I speak with the hospital," I said, finding her sudden burst of enthusiasm intriguing.

On Monday morning, I presented my letter of resignation, effective in two weeks. Summoned by my supervisor, I presented myself immediately.

"Bảo, I'm disturbed by your decision to resign from the hospital. Who will I rely on when difficult situations arise? Furthermore, you're the only person who could teach me something," he added jokingly.

"You're too smart," I quipped. "There's nothing you could ever learn from me."

At lunchtime, I broke the news to my colleagues that I was resigning. They also tried to reverse my decision.

"Maybe you'll change your mind," said one of my coworkers, said patting me on the shoulder. "You're so good at what you do, Bảo, and everyone just loves you."

On my last day, Dee met me in the hall during my morning shift.

"Would you like to join us for lunch today?" she asked, smiling.

"Why are you asking? Don't we have lunch together every day?"

"Yes, but today we're lunching in the break room. Mrs. Kim is retiring and we're giving her a farewell party."

"Why didn't you tell me about the party earlier?"

"I'm sorry. I meant to tell you several days ago but I forgot."

"I don't have anything to give her," I said, somewhat miffed. "It's embarrassing."

"It's OK, Bảo. Why don't you make some egg rolls?"

"Make egg rolls now? There's no time! I can't whip them up in ten or fifteen minutes."

This is absurd, I thought. How could she even suggest I make egg rolls if I was still working?

"Don't worry, Bảo, I'll finish your shift—just go and prepare the rolls."

"But you're a nurse, Dee. Nurses don't do janitorial work."

"Just say 'yes.' I'll cover for you."

"All right," I sighed. "Luckily, I have some egg rolls in my freezer. I'll fry them and be back in an hour."

Quietly, I darted out the back door and headed home. I couldn't understand why Dee had not told me earlier. I could have avoided all the rush and anxiety over the possibility that she could get caught and fired. Plus, I would have had a nice gift for Mrs. Kim.

Arriving home, I thawed the egg rolls and popped them in some sizzling oil. An hour and twenty minutes later, they were fried and packed to go. The aroma penetrated the house—an appetite-arousing scent, and it made me salivate.

Returning to the hospital, I looked for Dee to let her know that I was available to take over my shift. Although she was nowhere to be seen, I noticed that she had carried out my tasks perfectly.

Musing about the spontaneity of this moment, I realized that a certain excitement resonated in my thoughts. In an odd way, digressing from routine carried a titillating fascination.

A curious glance at my wristwatch told me it was eleven forty-five. Walking down the hall, I noticed that my colleagues were scurrying towards the break room, carrying bags and boxes, whispering among themselves as if they had a hot piece of gossip to share. Trailing behind, I held on to my aromatic egg rolls. Something was in the air—but what? Why all the hustling about?

I shrugged my shoulders, casting off the questions, and walked into the break room. The chatter was animated, and I was surprised to note that the room was filled to capacity.

As I entered, the volume of conversing voices gradually ebbed until silence prevailed.

Unpacking my egg rolls, I set them out for everyone to help themselves. Immediately, the room was filled with an appetizing aroma. Everybody gathered around, plates in hand, eager to savor my treats. After we ate, one of the staff members presented me with a going-away present. Caught off guard, I was momentarily speechless.

"Thanks," I said, confused. If Mrs. Kim was the guest of honor, I thought, why did I receive a gift? And why were there boxes stacked on a side table?

"This is your party, Bảo," said Dee, seeing my befuddled facial expression as I glanced around the room, clutching my

92

decorously wrapped package. "Today is your last day here, right?"

"Yes, but you told me we were celebrating Mrs. Kim's" retirement," I said, beaming.

"Well, it's your party now," she said, laughing. "We're celebrating our Bảo!"

"But why didn't you just tell me?" I asked.

"Bảo, I'm sorry. I hope you're not upset with me. I couldn't help myself. It was a strategy, albeit it selfish, to convince you to make a batch of egg rolls. Since this is our last lunch together, I wanted to enjoy them one more time."

Dee's confession triggered a deep, hearty laugh, which, judging from the foot-stomping, leg-slapping roar penetrating the environment, was highly contagious.

"Open your present," Dee prodded, grinning. "There are many more."

Obliging, with shaky fingers, I clumsily untied the pretty, pink bow, letting it slip from my grasp. It settled on my lap. Slipping my thumb under the side of the wrapping, I tugged until the paper split at the side. Then, I pulled out the box.

Lifting the lid, my eyes focused on a shiny brass and cherry-wood plaque shaped like the map of Oklahoma. On the front, the words "BEST WISHES ALWAYS, ANNEX STAFF 7-3" were engraved in large, bold letters.

Overcome, I was once again left speechless. I never expected such an endearing tribute. No one had ever given me any recognition for anything I had done with the exception of my German coworkers, who had presented me with a beautiful, crystal candy basket before I'd left Europe. Touched by the attention and kindness, I mustered my emotions.

"Thanks," I said. "I'm grateful for your benevolence, and very touched by your thoughtfulness."

I now had the confirmation that the hospital staff had taken a liking to me—especially the head nurse. It was exhilarating to witness his acceptance of the truth that not all Vietnamese people were bad.

It was a lesson for all—one that confirmed knowledge as the major force in the war against prejudice and ridiculous, preconceived notions based exclusively on ignorance. It was a confirmation that ignorance leads to the erroneous and foolish stereotyping of people who don't always fit into one convenient mold.

Chapter 5
A Thorn in My Side

Around mid-March, I joined the mother-son team at Edwards and Son's Clothes, working from nine to five-thirty for almost eight years. Simultaneously, I attended English-as-a-second-language classes three nights a week after work before returning home to my family. I enjoyed the school, which had a fun end-of-term party and bingo game. We were encouraged to don our native clothing and sing the traditional songs of our birthplaces. It was a period I remember with much fondness.

Just as life is not always a course through smooth seas, I recall that that period in my life was not always sweet. Then again, if life were an unobstructed path, we would not have nourishment for growth. Many times, adversity is the teacher of important life lessons and that which strengthens our frailties. Therefore, looking back, I regard my adversities as the stepping-stones to whom and where I am today. I seek not to forget, but to recall and be grateful for the power to survive and overcome.

One evening, when I arrived at school, four young, Asian American men were standing outside conversing.

"*Oom, oom,*" the taller of the two said, eyeing me with deliberate intent.

"I don't understand," I said, puzzled. "What does *oom oom* mean?"

"It means 'kiss me,'" his friend quipped, grinning.

"Oh, no. If you kiss me, you'll make your father jealous," I said coyly.

"What—what did you say?" the tall fellow blurted, visibly nervous.

"Can't you see I'm old enough to be your mother?" I asked him, laughing.

Caught off guard, they lowered their heads and walked away. Although I guess I should have been flattered by the attention of two young men, it left me a bit disturbed. Perhaps it was the element of teasing I just couldn't digest.

Several months later, I was the unwilling recipient of a nasty telephone call from an unidentified man. I slammed down the receiver to cut short his ugly verbiage but, determined to rile my spirits, he rang me repeatedly, every morning for two months. Although I did not respond to the phone calls, I realized I could not ignore the phone's ringing since I had a husband and children who were out of the house the better part of the day.

What if something had happened to one of them and my attention was immediately needed?

The telephone harassment continued, exasperating my nerves. I knew it was time to take action. Consequently, when the phone rang one morning, I calmly lifted the receiver.

"Hello. Who's calling?" I asked politely.

"Your friend," a strange voice replied.

"Which friend? I have many. What's your name?"

"If you answer my question, I will tell you who I am."

"Well... What is the question?"

"Do you like my..." he sneered, making a vulgar reference to the male reproductive organ.

"That's awful. You're no friend of mine," I shouted disgustedly. "Friends don't speak to friends in such a crass manner! Now, I want you to listen carefully,"

I said, believing I could perhaps get through to this ruffian. "The only reason

I'm spending time with you today is because I want to help you. You have absolutely no sane reason to speak to me, or anyone else for that matter, in such an improper, condescending way. I don't understand it and there is no call for it. I would like to assume you're a good, decent man who will eventually find a nice, suitable woman and settle down. I'm certainly not afraid of you, just turned off by your vulgarity and lack of manners. But I caution you—please, do not ever phone me again."

I could hear his newly labored breathing during my brief pause.

"Goodbye!" Waiting a respectable amount of time for his response, I eventually hung up. He neither uttered a word nor phoned again. Apparently I'd done something right.

I jumped into my car and headed for work. *En route,* I wondered if I would ever hear from my obscene caller again—or if, in effect, my words had stirred him enough to motivate him to give up his criminal behavior. Several months passed and he did not attempt to phone me. My approach had functioned.

One afternoon, a man knocked on my door, claiming to be a church member on a mission to solicit people to attend services. Confused by the ideas, principles and workings of American houses of worship, I realized that I had neither a very deep perception nor sufficient knowledge to form my own opinions. However, what I did know lead me to question some concepts of faith. It was a least a beginning—a stimulus.

"Tell me, sir," I said to him, "why do people kill and hurt others, and why does God allow this to happen?"

"God gave man the gift of free will and although he allows man to make his own decisions, he does take action. Plus, he certainly gets upset with mankind. There are a lot of sinners in the world," he replied, "a lot of sinners."

I gave his answer several moments of consideration and opted to give him the benefit of the doubt. Perhaps he was right.

"I will try my best to come to the services," I said.

"Ma'am would you be interested in purchasing a booklet? It's just a dollar," he said, holding it out to me.

"Sure. If you'll be patient a moment, I'll get the dollar."

I exchanged my dollar for his pamphlet, and wishing me a good day, he departed.

Later, during a moment of relaxation, I busied myself by comparing and contrasting the differences and similarities associated with people's spiritual beliefs. On one hand, they seemed compatible with the credence in a divine super power. All encouraged love, family, faith, charity, repentance and good works while representing mankind as a breed of sinners, striving for the rectification of transgressions and the attainment of goodness. Yet, on the other hand, it was amazing to note how many diverse denominational churches in which Americans worshiped.

There was nothing in these religions that caused any disagreement or conflict in either my heart or mind. Although I did admit that my religious culture was merely in the dawning stages, I was able to further pursue it through the options available for spiritual experimenting and investigating.

For a period of two months, I was committed to attending church regularly. However, despite the unwavering dedication, I discovered that I did not have the same feeling as when I worshiped in the Vietnamese temple where, together with my family, I went to pray and meditate several times a month.

We always arrived bearing flowers, fruit, ginseng and money, though it was not obligatory. The tithing commitment was not imposed in the Vietnamese temple as in many churches in America.

I enjoyed attending services and meeting different worshipers. One Sunday, I invited our Sunday school teacher, Amy, to share a midday meal of fried rice and egg rolls.

"Bảo, may I speak with you openly?" she asked somewhat timidly after we finished lunch.

"Of course, Amy," I responded, curious to see where this provocative preamble would lead.

"Has anyone ever slighted you for being Vietnamese?" she asked.

"What exactly do you mean by 'slighted'?" I responded.

"I mean, has anyone ever been mean to you or your children or made derogatory comments? What I'm asking is, have you been the victim of any prejudice?"

"Yes," I replied. "A woman with whom I worked in Germany told me her brother was killed in the Việt Nam War, and consequently, she neither liked nor trusted Vietnamese people."

"How did you react to her behavior?"

"I told her the truth—that I, as well as the majority of Vietnamese people, was not culpable for her brother's death and that most of us also lost loved ones in the conflict. I mentioned that the tragedies of war hit my own family and therefore, it was unfair of her or anyone else to focus anger on a race of people who suffered the same atrocities. Just because it happened in Việt Nam, one cannot implicate all Vietnamese."

"How did she react? Did she get it?" Amy asked, leaning forward in her chair.

104

"I think so. She said she understood and actually apologized, assuring me she would never again indulge in that negative way of thinking."

"Did you see each other again?"

"Yes. Actually, we be became friends."

"Well, I have a problem with immigrants taking our jobs while we pay the price with high employment," Amy blurted, catching me off guard. "Americans need jobs also and if foreigners take them, what happens?"

"The Vietnamese came to the United States in search of freedom," I said, irritated. "It was not about acquiring wealth or stealing jobs. It was about having the opportunity to live and raise their children in a free country not plagued by the atrocities of war. It was about dignity and leaving behind violence, bombings, starvation and a crippling, dehumanizing Communist regime. Simply stated, it was all about attaining and enjoying a better life."

Sadly, Amy's comment reflected a manner of thinking that was rather widespread—a view of immigrants and immigration that both angered and distressed me. I told Amy that I'd come to the US legally, as do the majority of foreigners. I reassured her that I worked hard, paid taxes, voted, contribute to society as a law-abiding citizen and I was proud to be part of a country that had developed, grown and matured into a super power thanks to the blood, sweat and tears of generations of immigrants.

Amy listened as I explained the issue from my perspective, which was, apparently, new to her. She sat quietly as I continued to tell her that I knew from where I came and I was fully aware of where I had arrived.

"Amy, you have no idea what life in Việt Nam is like. You don't know what we've been through. How can you imply that the Vietnamese people come here to take away American jobs?"

"I understand now," she replied. "I never thought of immigration in that light before. But you know, there are a lot of people, young and not so young, who do not comprehend this issue."

"This is why it is important to be knowledgeable—to ask the right questions and get the correct answers. Ignorance breeds only prejudice, intolerance and faulty thinking," I said. "It is the basis of many serious but avoidable problems both here in the USA and abroad."

Amy listened, surprised by the erroneous consequences born of her misinformed opinions. I had set her on a path leading to the rethinking of her views and attitude—but what of the millions of people still locked in faulty thinking? Would time eliminate this mistaken concept?

We said "goodbye" and went our separate ways. However, a feeling of insecurity left me apprehensive, and I doubted if I should attend church, fearful I would come into contact with many individuals unaware of my plight and guided instead by biased thoughts and feelings. They might even have resented my presence among them. Would they believe I was intruding on their country and repudiate me for seeking a better life in a free world?

Certainly, I did not desire to be where I wasn't wanted—not if I could help it. Following our conversation, Amy phoned me repeatedly, asking me to come to church with her. Unfortunately, I allowed my qualms and insecurities to mold my decision. Consequently, I responded to her invitations with little, white lies, claiming I was busy or socially committed. Promising to return soon, I never maintained my word, and was reluctant to elaborate on my feelings.

Meanwhile, Jim decided to supplement his income by taking a second job repairing sewing machines. After nine years, our marriage had settled at a comfortable plateau, and I was experiencing a harmonious, pleasurable period, which encouraged me to believe that my dream had finally come true. Had I found the happiness I'd always coveted?

Jim seemed calmer despite his extra work hours. One evening, after supper, we sat in the living room a few moments to catch the last news broadcast of the day before retiring.

"Bảo," he said, gaining my attention, "my boss, Henry, bought his wife a twelve-hundred-dollar diamond ring for Christmas."

"Sally is a lucky woman."

"When I die," Jim continued, "you can cash in the insurance policy and buy yourself a diamond."

Though all I'd ever wanted and needed was a kind loving man by my side, not a glittering diamond on my finger, Jim's words touched me. He had actually thought of me for a change. That evening, I went to sleep content, counting my blessings.

Nonetheless, Jim's docile nature was quick to spurt and sudden to fade, pushing him back into his old, selfish self. I noticed that this metamorphosis occurred in synch with his job resignation, encouraging me to deduce that Henry's kind regard for his wife had been a positive influence on Jim, who had mimicked the gallantry at home.

However, once Henry was no longer in my husband's life, Jim switched like Jekyll and Hyde back to his standard personality, treating me as Kay had instructed. Recognizing that the old Jim was back, I decided to exert my independence and take control of my life. No one was allowed to dictate how I should structure my days.

My dependence—or, rather, reliance— on cosmetics was the first issue I tackled. Jim repeatedly chided me for plastering my face with makeup, claiming I was beautiful enough *au naturel* and didn't need the extra splashes of color. One of the first things I decided to do was buy some make-up while shopping with Jim.

Sensing my newly reinforced independence strategy, he quietly retrieved his checkbook.

"What's today's date?" he asked, uncapping his pen.

"Never mind, Jim," I blurted, "I have some cash—I'll take care of it."

Little did I know that my newfound independence would soon be tested in a manner beyond anything I might ever have imagined.

While at work, I received an emergency call.

"Bảo, your son, Thaun, is on the phone," Mrs. Wood shouted from downstairs.

"Thanks, I'll be right there," I said, running down the steps.

I was not prepared for my son's screaming voice.

"Mom, can you come home right now?" Thaun stammered breathlessly. "We need you."

"Calm down," I said, "I'll be right there."

"Is everything okay, Bảo?" Mrs. Wood asked, sensing my anxiety.

"No, ma'am, I'm afraid not. I have a family emergency and will have to go home."

"Do you need a ride?"

"No, thank you, Mrs. Wood, but I appreciate your offer."

Arriving home, I discovered that Phuong and Jim had bickered over lunchmeat—a disagreement that had turned ugly, eventually escalating into physical violence. I summoned Phuong.

"Mom, I'm leaving," she said through gasping sobs.

"What happened, Phuong?" I asked, upset by the scene I had walked in on.

"Jim has been behaving inappropriately with me and Tram," she blurted.

"Inappropriately?" I questioned. "What do you mean? Is he sexually molesting you?"

"Yes, Mom. It's awful and we don't like it."

"How long had this been happening?"

"Since we lived in Germany," Phuong sobbed.

I had no reason to either discredit or mistrust the judgment of my daughter. That being the case, I was devastated. My

111

daughters were being sexually exploited by my husband right under my roof and I was oblivious to it all.

In that moment, my entire world collapsed. It was my responsibility as a parent to protect my children, yet the very person I trusted to be my ally in keeping them safe as they matured into healthy adults was actually the culprit. Had Jim violated their innocence? Had he stolen their childhoods? These were serious accusations. I had to know the truth.

As a habit, Jim would tinker with the car when he was upset or angry. Heading for the garage, I was intent on confronting him.

"Jim, I want the truth and I want it now!" I said. "Do you understand?"

"I didn't do anything," he replied.

"What kind of monster are you? I'm working long hours to provide a comfortable life for our family and you're at home, harming our daughters. This is inexcusable conduct. This is criminal.

You told me your father was abusive— he had hurt your mother and your siblings. You also swore that when you grew up and had a family of your own, you would never do anything to hurt them. And I always believed you! Why did you do this to us? Jim, they are vulnerable children and you hurt them."

I ran to my bedroom, buried my head in the pillow and cried for hours. Jim came in later and apologized.

"Please, don't cry, Bảo," he whispered, sitting down beside me on the bed. "I'm hurt, too."

Breaking into tears, he seemed repentant, but the damage was done and would never be rectified. Once children are abused and molested, the pain lingers, resulting in emotional and physical turmoil that scars for life. This was serious; worse, I felt as though I had let my family down. The children were my responsibility. I was supposed to guide, nurture and protect them from any ills.

Now, I had to discover the extent of the damage Jim had inflicted on my girls.

Approaching Tram, I mentioned Phuong's allegations against Jim. She confirmed my fears, swearing that Phuong's accusations were true. Both girls had been molested by their father.

I was despondent, and forced to meet my guilt head on—a guilt based on self-accusations of neglect. How could this have happened? Were there signs I'd missed?

Had the girls asked for help and, in focusing on providing financially for the welfare of my children, had I defaulted on their personal and emotional wellbeing? Could I still overturn the effects, or was it too late?

My mind would not stop churning. All I could think about was that Jim had been mistreating Phuong and Tram since our stay in Germany in 1977—and now it was 1983, six years later! How could I have been so stupid, so blind and trusting? My spirit was broken. My family was my life.

Unable to work, I phoned Mrs. Wood to request a brief leave of absence. Realizing I was embedded in a family crisis, she agreed.

"Take all the time you need, Bảo. Your job will be here when you're ready."

I thanked her for her understanding and support.

Three days later, I engaged the services of a divorce attorney. My marriage was irreparably broken. There was no reason to postpone the inevitable.

When the papers were served, Jim made it known that he did not want a divorce. Although he tried his best to convince me to drop the proceedings, my mind was made up. A meeting with my attorney set the record straight. Finally, Jim understood that I had no interest in a reconciliation attempt. My decision was final.

In the evenings, Jim slept in our bedroom while I moved in with the girls. However, one night, as I was drifting off to sleep, Jim tiptoed in, lifted me in his arms and carried me to our marital bed.

"Honey, you have slept in there long enough. Sleep with me tonight," he whispered. Jumping off the bed, I ran into the living room, plopping myself on the couch.

Jim trailed behind me.

"Bảo, I'm sorry—I'm so very sorry. I love you. I don't want to lose you. You're everything I ever wanted. You're my life. Can't you give us another chance? I've been transferred to Germany again and I'd like to stay together. As my wife, you're entitled to many benefits. You will be able to use the hospital and go to the commissary. Otherwise, if we divorce, you will lose all the benefits. You know I worry about you when I'm not around. Will you think about it, Bảo?"

He was making a desperate attempt to repair our marriage.

"My tour in Germany runs two years," he continued. "Please think about it. Two years is a long time. It will give you the opportunity to reflect on us. When I return, if you still want a divorce, then we'll follow that path."

Tears welled in my eyes. For a moment, my mind wandered back in time to our first meeting in Việt Nam, many years earlier.

I envisioned him carrying Phuong on his back as she giggled and screeched in joy, loving every minute of his attentions. Her glowing eyes and bright smile had told me that Jim would probably make a wonderful father. How could I have been so wrong?

I recalled some of the conversations we'd shared in which Jim told me about America, Americans and life in this great country he so loved. He told me of his humble beginnings in a small town, which, surprisingly, had a high divorce rate, including his own parents. A victim of a broken family, he'd grown up believing that American women were unfaithful, self-centered and neglectful of their children.

"Why do so many American couple's divorce?" I had asked him.

"Something makes the women unhappy and unsatisfied. Maybe they expect too much from their husbands. They fight, believe the grass is greener elsewhere and engage in 'safe' extramarital affairs thanks to contraceptives. Husbands become disillusioned, feel neglected and find other women to love and appreciate them. The cycle ends in divorce."

Jim's explanation had been confusing. He'd made it seem as if after just one fight or conflict, a couple would throw in the towel, take lovers and divorce. I had retaliated, telling him about the plight of Vietnamese women, who I felt were conditioned to tolerate and accept abuse as a part of life.

Vietnamese men sometimes mistreated their wives, using physical violence, tormenting and belittling them. When women could no longer bear the denigrating abuse, some abandoned their husbands, even if it meant facing very difficult lives alone with their children. If a woman was lucky, she might be successful in finding a wealthy man willing to marry her—a rather rare scenario.

Most paid steep prices for their independence, ending up working in the mess halls or clubs frequented by GIs. Women's rights were nonexistent and child support laws were not in the books like in the USA.

At will, men were free of their wives as well as all familial obligations, including financial. Consequently, women were forced to find employment as barmaids to support their children and put food on the table. It certainly was not a trailblazing time for women.

Jim's orders arrived and, six weeks thereafter, he departed for Germany. Much as I realized that my marriage was over, he had successfully talked me into postponing any divorce action. Some of his security points did make sense, and I had to think of my children. They were my priority.

Sometimes, I wondered what made Jim tick. I questioned his poor judgment with Phuong and Tram and wondered why he demonstrated so little respect for his family.

I wanted to give him the benefit of the doubt while holding firm to the hope that perhaps he would repent and rectify his wrongs. It was wishful thinking on my part, but I gave it an honest chance.

While he was in Germany, the children and I enrolled in a karate class. However, after a month of attendance, they expressed distaste for the art and asked if they could quit. Although I didn't exactly win black belts, I persisted, intent on acquiring some self-protection skills. Unsure of the direction in which my life was going, I knew I had to prepare myself for an eventual role as a single mom.

My marriage was on a fragile path. After the discovery of Jim's deplorable misdeeds against my daughters, I wondered if I would ever be able to forgive him and trust him again. One thing was certain: He had lost my respect, perhaps forever.

Chapter 6
Knowledge of Self-Actualization

Having earned a brief furlough, Jim returned from Germany. Hoping for the best after months of separation, I was happy to see him, fooling myself into thinking that our problems had disappeared. Sadly, the time away did little to settle his jealousy, the confirmation of which arrived soon enough. While searching for a shirt, he found the bag of men's T-shirts I had stored in the closet.

"Bảo, what are these?" he shouted, throwing the bag of shirts at my feet. "These belong to your boyfriend, don't they?" he continued, enraged.

"No, Jim, you're totally wrong. I don't have a boyfriend. Even if I wanted one, I don't have the time. I work and I take care of the children."

Mistrusting of my defense and refusing my protestations, he interrogated the kids, attempting to seed in their minds false allegations of my betrayal. Although they assured him that I did not have a boyfriend, he chose to disbelieve their words. Instead, in a fit of anger, he collected the bag of T-shirts and summoned the kids into the living room.

"Look" he ordered, pulling a shirt from the bag. "This is a man's T-shirt and not my size. Come here. Read the size—it says 'small.' I wear large. These shirts belong to another man. If you don't tell me the truth, I will whip your butt's sore. Do you understand?"

"That bag of T-shirts belongs to Mama," Phuong stammered. "She bought it."

"They are men's shirts, Phuong," Jim went on. "Who did she buy them for?"

"I don't know. She didn't say."

"It's a large bag. Where are the rest of the T-shirts?"

"They're in my drawer," Phuong said.

"Now, why are the shirts in your drawer?"

"Because I wore them."

"Go get them and bring them to me. I want to see them."

Scared and upset by Jim's outlandish rage, Phuong did as she was told.

Retrieving the shirts from her dresser, she handed them to her father.

"All right, you can go now," he said, clutching the shirts.

Still unconvinced of my loyalty to our marriage vows, Jim decided to interrogate the neighbors about my activities, hoping to receive the information he wanted in order to convict me of adultery.

When I returned from work the following day, he was waiting unwilling to renounce his conviction that he was right about the T-shirts.

"Do you see this?" he asked, again holding a T-shirt to my face.

"Yes. It's a T-shirt. I told you once before why I have the shirts."

"No, Bảo, this is not just a T-shirt—this is your boyfriend's shirt," he insisted. "Where is he? I want to drag him out like a sack of garbage."

"Jim, you're mistaken," I said, trying to maintain my cool. "I told you over and over, there is no boyfriend. I bought that T-shirt for Trung. I was keeping it until I finished the rest of my shopping and then I was going to mail it to him in Việt Nam."

"I don't believe you. It is your boyfriend's T-shirt."

"You are a son of a bitch!" I exploded. "You have no right to accuse me of any infidelity or wrongdoing. Look what you did to my daughters. I would never have expected such awful behavior from you. Yet, you don't find fault with yourself. You show no remorse for the pain you inflicted on those innocent children. But, you have the gall to point an accusatory finger at me for having a boyfriend."

Angry and offended, I sat down to gather my wits.

"Jim, I told you once before—after what you did to me and the girls, our marriage is irreparably shattered. Therefore, I was and am free to behave as I see fit, which means I can seek the companionship of another man if I feel so inclined. You no longer have any claims on me. However, I decided against another relationship not because of my loyalty to you, but for the well-being and tranquility of my family. I'm a woman of honor and integrity, and I believe in protecting the welfare of my children. As for the valid opinions of our neighbors, let me tell you a little story about them."

I was empowered and ready to put all the cards on the table. There would be no holding back or protecting soiled reputations.

"I was having breakfast in the kitchen one morning at about seven o'clock when I noticed Scott, our neighbor, walking in our backyard. To get a better view of what he was up to, I stood and moved over to the window. I saw him jump over the fence and head for his house. I thought he was fetching a ball that had rolled onto our property."

"So, what's wrong with that?" Jim asked sarcastically. "He didn't commit a crime."

"Let me finish the story. I didn't know at the time that the police were after him."

"The police were after Scott? Why?" Jim asked, incredulous.

"Denny, our neighbor, came over a couple of minutes later. He wanted to know if I'd seen anyone in his backyard. I told him about Scott but said I didn't know anything about his yard, and asked him why he was inquiring.

He told me he had spotted a man running away from his tool shop.

Then, when I left for work, I noticed two police cars stopped in front of his house. Denny was speaking with one of the officers, but I could not hear the conversation. As I was pulling out of the driveway, Tonie, Scott's mother, sped down the road, stopping short behind my car, blocking me.

Throwing open her car door, she ran up to me, "'Don't you dare step on my toes!' she yelled threateningly.

"I looked at her and asked why she was speaking to me in such a menacing manner. She continued her strange behavior, forcing me to summon the police from across the street.

One of the officers ran over, and I reported Tonie's threat. Apparently, her son, Scott, was implicated in some criminal deed at Denny's shop. I left and went to work. An hour later, the officer stopped by to tell me had spoken with Tonie."

Listening to my recounting, Jim was reflective. Although during his tour of duty in Germany he did not have the slightest inkling of what was happening in my life, he had full knowledge of my commitment to sending packages of clothing and other items to Trung. Since my brother had adopted him, Jim and I had been unable to obtain a visa for him to come to the United States. Nevertheless, we kept in contact through letters and, several times a year, I sent gifts of clothing, toys and school supplies in addition to money.

Certainly, it was a distressing hardship for me to leave behind one of my children, even if my intention was good. But, much as I tried to rationalize my decision, the painful feeling of sadness never waned. I continued to think of Trung every day, worrying he may have been wounded or killed during the gruesome war years.

But, never losing hope, I clung to the idea that one day, Trung would be able to immigrate to the USA, and I would have my family united. Eventually, Jim and I presented an application to bring my mother and her family to the USA. Of course, this initiative included my brother's family and, therefore, Trung.

Unfortunately, at the last moment, Nghe had second thoughts about emigrating; consequently, everyone remained in Việt Nam. It was a disappointment, but I had to accept and respect my brother's decision.

Ten days after Jim's return, I started to feel ill. Although I could not define the nature of my malady, I knew it was disturbing enough to seek medical attention. Jim accompanied me to the Fort Sill Army hospital, where Jim explained my health issue to the doctor.

"Do you know if there's something bothering your wife or why she may be feeling ill?" the physician asked him.

"Well, I've been home almost two weeks now and she's always tired. She's restless, doesn't sleep well and does not have much of an appetite."

"I'll prescribe sleeping pills to help her get some rest. If they don't help, I want to see her again in one week."

I took the pills as directed, but after three weeks, I didn't see any improvement. Meanwhile, Jim's furlough was over and he had to report back to Germany. He left with the status of our marriage still undefined.

After Jim's plane departed, Tram and I walked back to the car. Automatically, I opened the front door and slipped into the passenger seat. Tram stood outside, laughing. At first, I didn't understand why she was laughing, but then I realized I was supposed to be the driver, not the passenger. It was proof of my weary state of mind.

Tram remained outside when we arrived home, kicking a big, red ball that had been abandoned on the front lawn. I entered the house, sat down on the couch, lowered my head and wept profusely. I was not quite sure what triggered the deluge, but I knew it certainly was not Jim's departure.

My mind rolled through various scenarios from our decade of life spent together. Everything had been so alien and strange when I'd first set foot on American soil. It had been a cold, November day in 1973. I remembered how amazed I'd been to discover automatic washing machines and snow. It had been like thumbing through a book of fairy tales.

Then, the unknowns resurfaced. There were so many unanswered questions. Among them: Why hadn't Jim's parents attended our wedding? In Việt Nam, nuptials were a big, family event. Didn't families participate on their adult children's lives? Judging rashly, I had mistakenly thought that perhaps Americans just differed in their cultural traditions.

My mind pursued its wandering through the maze of our early years, when Jim and I would gather the children for drives in the country, sometimes stopping to visit Aunt Betty and then on to Uncle Charlie's. Aunt Betty, petite but stocky with strong, nimble hands and a brow beaded with crystal droplets of sweat, loved to prepare a sumptuous meal, home cooked from appetizer to dessert.

And at Uncle Charlie's, we always received a warm, hearty welcome.

"Bảo, my nephew is a lucky guy," he'd say, smiling flirtatiously. "I wish I had a wife like you. It would certainly make life easier."

Apparently, his first wife, Sara, had preferred to curl up with a good book. She was an energy-challenged woman who regarded the farming lifestyle as filled with indolent platitudes. Nothing and no one could convince her otherwise.

Though Uncle Charlie had made several attempts to acquire 200 acres from his mother, Sara adamantly had vetoed it. Her refusal to accommodate his wishes left him with a bitter taste and broken spirit. Yet, after meeting me, he realized that I was a different woman—one he believed would not have shunned a bit of soil stuck under my nails. Certainly not shy, Uncle Charlie made it quite clear that Jim had his blessing.

Life with Jim was not always a dramatic tear-fest. Instead, there were some endearing moments for which I will always be thankful. I remember when Phuong had been disobedient, meriting a scolding that I diligently administered. Running to Jim, sobbing like she was vying for an Oscar, she told him I was a mean-spirited mother whom she no longer loved.

"Your mother is a loving, devoted woman," he told her, putting his arms around her in a gesture of solidarity. "Phuong, she wants to buy a house for all of you so that you can grow up on family-owned property instead of living in military housing. And, when you wanted to study the clarinet, you mother took the three hundred dollars she was saving for a new mixer and bought it for you. I don't think you appreciate your mother enough. You should be more grateful. Plus, I might add, she was right to scold you. You misbehaved, and it is her duty as a parent to discipline you."

There was no shortage of surprises in my life. Oddly, one day, I received a compliment from Kay during one of her few rational moments.

"Jim," she said, "I have come to the conclusion that Vietnamese women make wonderful wives. I guess I should apologize for all the aggravation I caused you and Bảo. She is truly amazing."

Realizing that the clock was ticking, I halted my stream-of-consciousness spin down memory lane, planting my feet back in the present moment. It was amazing to note how powerful time was in altering the course of events. Living day by day, unaware of what my tomorrow would resemble, I tried not to dwell on my problems. I was wise enough to realize that focusing on the negative would never culminate in a positive end.

Concentrating on my karate class, I prepared myself and headed over just as everyone was running though the warm-up exercises. When Master Jang arrived, the class stood at full attention and saluted him. For some inexplicable reason, I suddenly lost control of my nerves. Tears rolled down my cheeks like water from an overfilled goblet. I tried to interrupt the flow, but when my hand movements were not adequate to remove the evidence of my outburst, I walked out, feeling too distressed and embarrassed to participate in the class.

Ten days thereafter, I received a letter from Jim in which he informed me that he would no longer oppose my request for a divorce. I read it three times, marveling over the fact that feelings of sadness or gloom were nonexistent. Instead, I felt elated and relieved, as if a massive weight had been hoisted from my shoulders.

With the calming release came the realization that finally, I had achieved that for which I had been wishing and praying. Amid the changing destiny, I could smell the invigorating freshness of a newly acquired freedom. At this point, my priority was to disengage my children and myself from Jim's abusive behavior; I was certain that we would not only survive but find ourselves empowered to move forward toward the happiness we not only desired but deserved.

Once the emotional tsunami had abated, I sought healing and recuperation. Turning my fears to productive energy, I voted in favor of a new lifestyle. In an attempt to regroup and get my bearings as a single mom, I dropped my English and karate classes and focused on my work. Willingly or otherwise, I arrived at the shop every morning.

"Oh, I'm terribly sorry to hear about your divorce," Mrs. Wood said after receiving the news.

"There is no need to feel sorry. This is the best thing that could happen," I replied. "My marriage was too broken to be repaired."

"Well, Bảo, if you're comfortable with that decision, then I'm happy for you."

"Although it is what I want, I'm still feeling a lot of pain, even if I can't understand why. In a way, I am now able to relate to my mother's feeling when my dad was killed. I often wondered how she dealt with all the gut-wrenching anguish. Eventually, I learned that somehow, strength arrives in the darkest moments, just when things seem beyond hopeless."

"Death is a different situation," Mrs. Wood offered. "It is not comparable to a divorce. Your father did not want to leave your mother."

Musing over her words, I realized she was right. My parents' circumstantial split did not involve free will. Conversely, in my current situation, I had chosen to eliminate Jim from my life.

Now, I would have the opportunity to rear my children according to my own philosophies and theories, without having to compromise my beliefs and ideologies to accommodate Jim's way of thinking.

Often, as biracial parents, we had discussed our cultural differences, expressing childrearing strategies that we truly believed were best for the children. We were not always in agreement, though, and I was stunned when Jim mentioned that at eighteen years of age, children are expected to leave the family home and fend for themselves.

In my opinion this outlandish, cultural mindset was totally absurd. I couldn't understand how teenagers could survive, let alone flourish, with empty pockets and no experience on which to depend. Presumably, it was the "sink or swim" mentality. A child was hurled into the water of independent life and either he learned to swim in that moment and survived—or he drowned.

In Việt Nam, kids remained in the family home, and were fed and clothed as in childhood, while they accumulated work experience and sufficient funds to permit a more venerable entry into adulthood.

It galled me to think of parents pushing their children out the door with neither financial backing nor concern for their lack of coping skills. Therefore, I was not timid in communicating to Jim my distaste for this traditional rite of passage.

"I don't agree with your mentality," I told him. "In fact, I find it rather outrageous."

"Why? I don't understand your reasoning. Once the kids are done with school, it's time to get out and get working," he said, convinced that his way of thinking was right.

"Well, I'm not of the same opinion. I intend to put aside money until the time is right for a dignified exit."

"What do you mean by a 'dignified exit,' Bảo?" he asked, chuckling.

"I mean we can buy them a car and put some money in their pockets until they have steady jobs that will guarantee their independence—not years of struggle and hardship while living on the margins of society."

"That's the Vietnamese way, not the American way," Jim said, sounding irritated. "Our children are Americans—or have you forgotten?"

"That is not true," I retorted. "When I was still living in Việt Nam, we often watched American movies. Many times, the plots involved parents who helped their children get good starts in life."

"Maybe some do, but they are the exception to the rule."

"Well, if some do, then perhaps we can join ranks with them, can't we?"

"Hardship builds character, Bảo. It turns boys and girls in to men and women of value. When I was a child, I had only two sets of clothing," Jim continued. "One pair of pants had a big hole in the knee. If I was too embarrassed to wear torn pants, I was obliged to patch them by hand. And if I ever dreamt of new clothes, I knew I had to earn the money to buy them."

"As a child, how could you earn money?" I asked, eager to hear the rest of his tale.

"When I was eleven, I got jobs mowing lawns in the neighborhood. With the money I earned, I bought new clothes."

"Jim, I feel sorry for you, but I had only two outfits also. At the start of the new year, I received two sets of new clothes, a pair of new shoes and a new hat. My family did not have much money. Before my father was killed, we were comfortable. He was a wealthy man who focused on the well-being of his family. It was his priority to make our lives as pleasant as possible.

According to my mother, he was continually searching for ways to provide more luxuries.

"Unfortunately, he died before his dreams could be realized. As a result, we had to struggle just to make ends meet. Our house was soon demolished by bombs, leaving my family in total poverty. I don't want our children to be forced to endure such suffering and deprivation.

Thankfully, these are different times. Why should they have to experience the devastation of misery when we can afford otherwise? The American dream is not exclusively about our success and achievements. It spans generations. It is about being in a position to offer our children the means and opportunities to have head starts—to avoid all the anguish we had to plough through.

"My dreams involve a forward direction for my family, not a shifting into reverse. Why should our children be forced to travel over the obstructed paths we had to follow? We fought to clear the way for them."

Jim looked at me, sighed and excused himself from my company without another word. I interpreted his silence as a troop withdrawal—a kind of surrender that handed me the victory.

Before work the following morning, I sought an appointment with a divorce attorney. Graciously greeted by a smiling secretary, I waited while she checked Mr. Knight's schedule and gave me an appointment for the subsequent Monday. Decision made, I was taking control of my life.

I met with Mr. Knight, informed him of my intention to file for a divorce and gave him the necessary information to draw up the papers.

When the documents were ready, I was summoned to the attorney's office for my signature. Mr. Knight reassured me that Jim would be served immediately.

"Once you and your husband sign the papers, we will set a court date," he said.

My emotions had settled. I was more than sure that this nightmare would be over soon.

However, when Jim received the papers, he expressed a reluctance to put his signature on the dotted line.

"Bảo, I can't sign these papers," he blurted. "I need more time to think this through. This is a big step and I won't do it until I'm absolutely certain."

"OK, Jim," I said, somewhat annoyed. "You can take some time to consider, if that's what you need."

A month later, I reintroduced the divorce topic.

"Don't worry, I already signed and mailed the papers," Jim said rather stoically.

"Weren't you going to inform me about this?"

"I hear you have a boyfriend. Is that true?" he asked, changing the subject. "Bảo, if you don't remarry, I'll send you four hundred dollars a month until our son's eighteenth birthday."

"No deal," I replied.

"I still love you, Bảo."

"I'm sorry, Jim. I don't love you anymore. This is goodbye."

Chapter 7

Another Spin of Fate's Wheel

Once the divorce papers were signed and delivered, I returned to my daily routine, working and tending to my children, with a lighter heart, clearer mind and calmer spirit, knowing that in a short time, I would be a free woman. With the source of my conflict removed, everyone would be protected from the traumatic consequences of Jim's evil deeds. Spousal abuse based on obsessive jealousy is an awful torment to bear, hurtful and denigrating, but when the malady turns into child molestation, it becomes a grave criminal act.

My busy schedule kept me occupied and unaware of the passage of time. Thoughts of Jim were now pushed into the back of mind. Days flew by in a sequence of ups and downs. Convinced this was due to my sudden and rather radical life change, I talked myself into believing it would all iron out one day soon. Then, one morning, the phone rang, and I was pleased to hear the agreeable voice of Mr. Knight's secretary.

"Hello, Bảo. Jim has signed an acknowledgment of the receipt of service. The court has entered judgment. Your petition for divorce has been granted. At your convenience, you may come by and pick up the papers."

"Thank you, ma'am. You bring me good news."

I was released from my marital contract—what a liberating feeling. Though I was enjoying the moment, I never contemplated any celebratory rituals until I ran into my friend, Que, the following Saturday.

"Hi, Bảo. How are things with you?" she asked.

"Well, my divorce from Jim is final."

"Really? That's great news. We should go out and celebrate your new freedom. It's time to get back out there! "

"Any ideas about where we should go?" I asked, excited by her enticing proposal. She was right—it was time I started enjoying life.

"Leave it to me. Just get ready and I'll drop by after supper on Saturday, around nine o'clock. Will that be OK?"

"Sure! I'll be ready."

On Saturday, I fed the children, phoned the sitter, dressed myself and waited for Que. Prompt as always, she arrived at the top of the hour.

"All set for some fun?" Que asked, greeting me with a hug.

"Yes. It's been such a long time since I had a fun evening. Let's go."

We arrived at the Sandpiper Club around nine-thirty. The place was abuzz with voices and the clinking of glasses hitting the tabletops, and I immediately shifted into fast gear.

Que had hit it right on the head—it was time to get out and meet some new friends.

Less than ten minutes later, I was approached by a tall, slender gentleman with dark, chestnut hair and a pair of intriguing, flirtatious eyes.

"Hi, may I invite you to dance?" he asked, extending his right hand.

A certain anxiousness surfaced within me. My breathing quickened, and I prayed he didn't notice.

"Oh, no," I replied. "I'm not much for dancing."

"That's OK. Actually, I'm not much of a dancer myself," he said, smiling. "But we could talk."

Reserved and soft spoken, the gentleman, who answered to the name Danny, caught my fancy. Judging from his open, flirtatious approach, I suspected he was single and eager for female companionship.

Our conversation was light and friendly, though no intimate details were volunteered. He did mention he was thirty-two, which made him four years younger than I. Danny's gracious manner made it clear that he hailed from different stock than my previous male suitors. He glanced at me pensively, and I decided I liked him.

Several hours later, concerned about my babysitter's having to burn the midnight oil, I announced it was time to go.

"I'd like to see you again—would that be possible?" Danny asked, jumping to his feet.

"Here's my phone number," I replied, tearing the napkin in half. I scribbled the series of numbers and handed it to him. I guessed there was definitely good chemistry that evening.

"Thanks, Bảo, I'll give you a call in a few days and we can get together again."

"I'd like that, Danny."

As promised, Danny phoned and we began dating—even though I discovered that he had added three years to his actual age. He was really twenty-nine, which made me seven years his senior!

After a month of lunches, dinners, walks and talks, Danny expected a bit more than platonic dating. However, I made it clear that I did not appreciate any pressure to transfer a budding friendship into a passionate, sexual relationship.

Although it was no secret that I had feelings for Danny, I felt as though he didn't truly understand why I was unwilling to take our relationship to the next step. Past experiences had left me deeply scarred but wiser and decidedly more cautious. Despite the emotional confusion my decision generated, he agreed to my terms, demonstrating once again his gentlemanly status.

I realized that my behavior was not exactly the norm in post-sexual-revolution America and probably caused him some anxiety. However, I was not willing to compromise my strategy or principles.

A bit of depravation usually makes the prize more appetizing, appreciated and treasured, anyway.

Eventually, Danny confided that he would often wonder why I was with him. I didn't want sex, and I never asked him for money or favors.

One evening, he invited me for a drink after work. His gaze was moist—it was apparent he was hopelessly smitten. Leaning forward, his breath was warm as it tickled the tip of my nose. Taking my hand, he cleared his throat.

"Do you have any feelings for me, Bảo?" he whispered.

"Yes, Danny," I replied. "Sometimes, I even think I love you."

"What did you say?" he asked, his eyes dancing.

"You heard me, Danny. I think I'm in love with you."

"Then why won't you let me make love to you?"

"Because I don't think sex is the most significant part of a relationship. Instead, I feel it is more important to discover who we are and what makes us tick. I want to know our strengths and weaknesses and build an intimate, emotional bond.

Before we consummate out relationship, we must know each other in depth—our thoughts, feelings, interests, passions, successes and failures, likes and dislikes. Do we have much in common? Can we be best friends? Are we compatible?

Have we achieved unconditional emotional and psychological intimacy?

148

"Danny, these are the imperative elements of a successful, happy relationship. If we can provide affirmative answers to these questions, then I believe we are ready for physical intimacy."

"Wow, Bảo, I've never heard a woman speak like that before. Apparently, you have put much thought into the relationship phenomenon. You are very different from the other women I know."

"I think I am, too."

"I've never met a woman like you before, but I have to admit, you make a lot of sense. I love you and I'm serious about our relationship. Bảo, I'll wait, no matter how long it takes. I can't believe I found you. I'm just thrilled."

My love and respect for Danny deepened from that day onward. Certain I had finally met a man who sincerely cared for me, I continued to see him with greater frequency. Sometimes, we went to the club for a drink and light supper; on occasion, we went to a movie; and from time to time, we met at the mall for a quick lunch. It pleased me that Danny was an action-oriented man, a doer who showed initiative and creativity. A tennis player, he also liked to shoot hoops on the basketball court and seemed to genuinely enjoy getting to know my children.

Even though we were no Fred and Ginger, one night, we decided to step out of our comfort zones and go to a dance.

Surprisingly, it was not as traumatic as we'd imagined. In fact, we actually enjoyed the foot-tapping, disco rhythms.

After the dance, we agreed to a romantic night in a motel. Danny was wonderful, tender, attentive and sweet, making our first encounter a beautiful and memorable experience. Consequently, I received the confirmation that not scurrying into sex was beneficial to the relationship.

I returned home beneath penetrating sunshine, my path illuminated by this radiant gift of nature. Totally in love, my thoughts centered exclusively on Danny. I understood that he was the man I had been waiting for most of my life, despite my interim marriages and erroneous past judgments. That he loved and cherished me was a certainty. Our night of love had been evidence of this—a reputable testament.

Then, my feet suddenly crashed down on the ground, I awakened from my reverie. Danny phoned neither on that evening nor during the five days thereafter. At that moment I wondered if I could have possibly committed another error in judgment. Was I mistaken about Danny? Was he just looking for a good time? Was he like the others?

As the days passed, my pain and disappointment escalated. Whenever the phone rang, I ran to it breathlessly, hoping I would hear Danny's voice—all to no avail. It seemed as if everyone I didn't want to talk too phoned.

Finally, frustrated by his sudden, inexplicable interruption of our relationship, I summoned my courage and phoned him.

"Danny, this is Bảo," I said, trying not to stammer.

"Hi, Bảo, how are you?" he asked as if nothing had happened between us.

"Actually, I'm not that good. I thought you'd call after the other evening at the motel. Why the silence?"

"I'm sorry, Bảo. Remember Sim, my old girlfriend? Well, she suddenly came back to town. I told you I was looking for her when we met."

Did he say 'Sim'? I wondered, feeling a twinge in the pit of my stomach. I didn't quite understand what all this meant, but Danny's words were painful, hitting me hard. I knew that Sim, with whom he had shared his life for over a year, had left him without notification when he'd been deployed overseas. She'd just disappeared in a cloud of dust. Upset and

151

desperate, he'd searched for her upon his return but had been incapable of determining her whereabouts.

When Danny and I had met, he'd been able to forget her and move on—at least until now. I knew from experience that I was not destined for a fictionalized life in which I was penned to ride off into the sunset and live happily ever after. But, I did not expect this heartache from Danny. I had proceeded with caution. How could I have been so wrong again?

At the conclusion of our brief conversation, I slipped the receiver onto the cradle, knowing our relationship was over though I did not commit to this decision vocally. I did, however, regret not waiting a bit longer to consummate our union. On the other hand, how could I possibly have guessed that Sim would return to Danny's life on the day after our romantic night of love?

That evening, I wept until I was tearless—until, uninvited, the light of dawn peered through my blinds and signaled the start of another day.

Although the next few weeks were difficult, I tended to my familial obligations and my professional commitments, grinding my teeth in an attempt to squash all thoughts of Danny. I fantasized about meeting a nice gentleman who would pull me out of my sadness. Was I being unreasonable? Was I living in a mist of false illusions?

Perhaps still clinging to a slither of hope, I felt it best to see Danny one last time before I reentered the dating world. With my mind focused on a final, face-to-face encounter with Danny, I awakened early the following morning to allow some extra time for a quick visit.

Unsure if I was searching for closure or a new beginning, I went to Danny's house, drew in a deep breath and knocked with the strength of a determined woman seeking to recapture a treasure that had slipped between her fingers. Bruising my knuckles, I ignored the stinging pain as Danny enveloped me in his arms.

"Bảo," he shouted, visibly elated to see me. "I'm on my way to work. Can I come over to see you later? I'd like to talk to you."

"Danny, I didn't come to speak to you. I came to say 'goodbye.' You have Sim now."

"She is not serious. She plays games with me."

"But she's still in your life, Danny. That leaves me out," I said, annoyed.

"I'd still like to see you later. I'd like to just talk."

"OK, I get home around six. You can stop over if you wish."

"I'll see you later."

Leaving Danny's house, I wondered what, if any, effect my visit had on this situation. At the traffic light, I bore right and accelerated up the hill. Clumps of thick bushes delineated the boundaries of private property. Should I have interpreted this as a message? A delicate wind gently rustled the leaves on young and not-so-young oak trees. The world was certainly alive and flourishing—but was I?

My thoughts meandered toward Danny and our relationship. Recalling past events, I realized he had treated me better than most. Undeniably, his love was as real as mine. As memories once blurred in time cleared, I evaluated what I'd had years earlier and what I had then with Danny.

Even though he had reversed the course of our relationship, he had not been successful in truncating my feelings. I loved this man. Of this I was certain.

Promptly at ten past six, Danny's knock resounded. Seconds later, before I had a chance to open the door, he was standing in the living room.

"Thanks for giving me a chance to talk to you," he said, nervously lighting a cigarette.

Exhaling a dense, circular cloud of smoke, he continued, "You know, as I told you, Sim is not serious. She comes and goes in my life like the seasons. Besides, she's married."

"Sim is married! Where's her husband in all this? Doesn't he have anything to say about his wife's behavior?"

"She left him, and from what I understand, he has quit trying to get her back," Danny volunteered coyly.

"Maybe she's not worth pursuing. Are you up for taking a walk?" I asked, feeling a bit suffocated. "We can get a breath of air and continue our chat."

Danny was game. He jumped to his feet, walked over to my chair and extended his hand. Grabbing my keys and handbag from the table, I let him escort me out the door.

The wind felt cool on my flushed cheeks. Dusk was settling and the panorama resembled an artist's palette with muted colors spilling onto each other from frequent dabbing with a brush. We took several leisurely steps in silence. The moment was tense. Halting my stride, I turned, fixing my gaze firmly on Danny's dark eyes.

"Do you have any idea how hard it was for me to clear you from my heart and mind, especially after the beautiful night in the motel?" I asked him. "Can you imagine how

155

painful it was to hear about Sim—to realize there is another woman vying for your love?"

"I'm so very sorry, Bảo," he said, squeezing my hand. "I love you so much. Can you ever forgive me? I know I hurt you. But I didn't mean it. Sometimes, things happen, things over which we have no control. I didn't plan this. It just happened."

"Well, Danny, at least you could have called to explain."

"You're right, and I'm so sorry. But if you'll give me another chance, I promise that it will never happen again. I'll never hurt you, Bảo."

Though physically and emotionally wounded, though I'd been fed injurious lies by unfaithful, abusive men, I decided to forgive Danny's transgression and give him another chance. The power of love transcends all reason.

"Bảo, can I take you to dinner tomorrow evening?" he asked me.

"That would be nice."

He came calling for me, and we spent a lovely evening chatting and gazing into each other's eyes. Danny and I dated regularly after that, enjoying each other's company while trying to iron out some of our differences.

"I'd like to move in with you and the kids," Danny said several months later." I love you and I want us to build a life together."

I nodded enthusiastically. Leaning across the table, he planted a kiss on my lips. Warm and moist, his demonstration of affection sent a chill down my spine.

Danny's move into my life brought joy, conflict and challenges. Although his love was welcome, we had many issues to work out.

From day one, we shared my car, a kindness on my part that eventually turned into a hardship.

"I think you should get your own car," I said one afternoon when I needed the vehicle unexpectedly. "I'm busy with work, the kids have appointments, and it's too complicated and frustrating to share."

"I'd like to, but I don't think that's possible," he responded. "I doubt I can get financing. I have poor credit. The only way I can get a car is if you cosign the loan. Are you willing to do that?"

"Yes, I'll cosign, if that's what it takes."

Several days later, we set up the loan and Danny took possession of his vehicle. *One dilemma resolved,* I thought to myself, unaware of what lay ahead. *This should*

definitely make life less complicated. I was
independent and likewise so was Danny.

When the payment book arrived, I
noticed the coupons were issued in his name
only. A bit of investigating resulted in the
discovery that Danny had arranged for my
name to be removed from the coupon book.
However, still listed on the loan, I was held
liable for any defaulted payments.

Looking back, I think Danny was still
undecided about Sim and perhaps unwilling to
risk losing his car if she returned and he chose
her over me. Realizing I was possibly a
second choice was neither comforting nor
reassuring.

Furious and offended, I waited for him to
return so I could kick him out. I was seething,
but the hours were an ally, allowing my rage
to subside and a sense of reason to take
control. I had to plan my confrontation with

Danny, taking into consideration the fact that my children would be within earshot. I didn't want them listening in on my diatribe.

When Danny arrived that evening, I revealed my discovery, demanding an explanation, fearing his response and knowing it might change the course of our fate.

Eventually, Danny unraveled the mystery of my cancelled name, explaining that his motive was to protect my credit in the event of nonpayment. Though skeptical, I just let the issue drop. With my girls maturing, I had too many other, more pressing matters to pursue.

Eleven-year-old Tram needed a new pair of shoes. Accompanying her to the TG & Y store, I purchased them. A few days later, I noticed her running around barefoot.

"Tram, where are your new shoes?" I asked.

"I don't like them, Mom, they're not what I wanted. I don't want to wear them."

"What did you do with them?"

"I left them on the school playground."

"Young lady, we're going right now to the playground and you'd better find those shoes and put them on immediately."

She obeyed, though visibly irritated by the nature of our outing.

Luckily, we found Tram's shoes where she had left them. At least she had been honest.

"You'd better wear the new shoes from now on. I don't want to see you barefoot again."

"I want Nike shoes," she said, bawling. "Everyone wears them except me. I'm the only kid in school with weird shoes."

"If you study and do well in school, I'll buy you a pair of Nikes for your birthday. In the meantime, you'll wear these. They are perfectly acceptable. Do we understand each other?"

"Yes, Mom," she whispered between sobs.

"Then why are you crying?"

"Phuong will hit me when she finds out I'm wearing these stupid shoes."

"Why would Phuong hit you if you wear these shoes?"

"She said those shoes are creepy and I look dimwitted."

"That's not true. These shoes look as good as the Nikes. The only difference is they're another brand. Don't worry—I'll talk to Phuong. I'll make sure she doesn't hit you again."

When I confronted Phuong, she neither denied Tram's accusations nor provided a defense against them. Instead, her stoic demeanor left me wondering if my words were being processed. Little did I know that this was merely the rustling before the tempest and the beginning of some rather rebellious behavior. We were dealing with puberty and the mutinous circumstances of teenage rebellion. The die was cast.

IV

Chapter 8

The Devil's Advocate

Dressing for work one morning, I was bothered by a raw feeling in the back of my throat. Believing I was coming down with a cold, I opted to select heavier clothes. When I went to my closet, I noticed a strong smell that resembled bleach. Surveying the area for spills, I couldn't find any reason for the odor.

Puzzled, I reached for my favorite sweater. Tugging on the arm to disengage it from the hanger, I was surprised to see it was frayed and tattered, therefore no longer wearable. Something was not quite right. The sweater had been perfect when I had put it away.

That evening, I questioned the girls about my sweater.

"Something disturbing happened today," I said at the dinner table. "I planned to wear my best sweater but discovered it was practically threadbare, which is strange because it was fine when I put it away. Does anyone have any idea what happened to it?"

165

"Mom, I accidentally spilled bleach on your sweater," Phuong stammered. "Maybe the chemicals in the bleach ruined it."

Though I found her explanation somewhat incredible, I didn't feel like instigating a major family conflict. Brushing off the incident, I changed the subject.

Several weeks later, in a rush to get to work on time after awakening twenty minutes later than usual, I grabbed my bottle of hairspray and pushed down on the nozzle. In a split second, my shiny, black, perfectly coiffed head of hair turned sparkling white.

Horrified, a look at the container confirmed that it was not my hairspray but glass cleaner with ammonia! Furious, I suspected that Phuong had coerced Tram to switch my hairspray with the glass cleaner.

The disturbing, strange events did not end there. Each day brought new challenges and battles. One evening, exhausted, I flopped onto my waterbed. An icy chill ran down my spine; jumping off, I discovered it was ice cold. A closer scrutiny revealed that although the heating mechanism was functioning, the bed was cold.

Initially I was unable to understand what was occurring until, days later, playing private eye, I caught Phuong red-handed—she was tampering with the controls. Apparently, she had been switching the bed's heater off every morning and turning it back on right before I returned from work. Presumably, the intention was to rattle my nerves.

It didn't end there, despite my recriminations. The line of attack changed when my buttons started disappearing. Whenever I shortened the sleeves on a customer's jacket, I would remove the buttons, alter the sleeves, and then reattach the buttons. Upon completing my work one evening, I noticed that the buttons were missing.

"Has anyone seen the buttons I removed yesterday?" I asked the children once.

"No, Mom," they shouted in unison.

"I need them for the customer's jacket. Could you please help me look for them?"

"Here they are," Phuong said, opening her hand to reveal four buttons.

This pattern of behavior occurred repeatedly. However, when she went beyond teasing and actually hid the buttons, I was obliged to purchase new ones, squandering time and money.

One day, while searching for a misplaced shirt, I pulled open Phuong's drawer and *voila*—there, nestled in the corner under her T-shirts, was the stolen treasure: piles of my lost buttons. Not expecting such bad-

167

intentioned behavior from my daughter, her calculated sabotage of my work saddened and distressed me. Although the mystery was resolved, I felt neither joy nor serenity.

Similar outbursts and mischievous plots continued with unexpected frequency.

Undoubtedly, Phuong was in conflict with me and this was her way of expressing anger, resentment and disapproval.

As time passed, her pranks became more prominent and wicked. She tinkered with my cosmetics, blending pepper into my foundation. My skin became irritated, red-splotched and sensitive. Eating was painful, likewise smiling. Exasperated, I began to lose my patience. I knew neither what line of discipline to follow nor if I would ever succeed in halting my daughter's seemingly vindictive reign of terror.

Foolishly believing it would all end as it began, I discovered the error in my thinking when Tram became troublesome.

"I'm going to cut my hair," she announced upon returning from a five-day field trip with her class.

"Why would you want to do that?" I said, startled. "Your hair is gorgeous—almost to your waist."

"I don't want long hair anymore."

Tram's hair was thick but silky to the touch. Caught in the midday sun, it produced a glittering gloss. When she walked, it danced back and forth, caressing her back and shoulders. Hers was the most luxurious mane in the family. I never dreamt she would express a desire to cut it.

"Absolutely not," I said, determined to get the message across. "Your hair is too beautiful to be cropped."

Once again, I suspected Phuong's conniving influence. She was well aware that this issue would upset me.

Tram met my firm, unwavering "no" with a cold shoulder and expressionless face whenever I was in her presence. The lines of communication were not only blocked but were practically nonexistent.

By nature a sweet and loving young girl, she suddenly grew into a rebel. I represented the enemy and to avoid confrontation, she returned home late, had dinner and retried soon after. Her antics were totally out of character.

Weeks later, I was summoned by the school principal who expressed concern over Tram's slipping grades. Her teacher was worried because she was disruptive in class, didn't listen or follow instructions, and failed

169

on numerous occasions to complete required homework assignments.

Returning from the principal's office, I notified my boss that I was taking the rest of the day off to deal with a family matter. Mrs. Wood, as always, was agreeable to my request. Heading home, I awaited Tram, orchestrating in my mind the dialogue I would use hopefully to reach her.

Finally, she showed up. Pushing open the door, she seemed surprised to see me already home.

"You're early," she muttered, refusing eye contact.

"No, Tram, I'm not home early. I was here most of the day."

Sensing something was dangling in the air, Phuong went to her room and the other children scurried outside to play.

Tram sat in the living room, nervously shaking her legs. Her worried glance was evidence that she understood what was about to happen. It was more than appropriate that I demand and get an explanation.

"Tram, I had a meeting with your principal today and I'd like to know why you aren't listening to your teacher or turning in your homework."

"I wanted to get my hair cut, but you wouldn't let me," she said, starting to cry.

170

"Is that why you've been ignoring me and misbehaving in school? Your grades are slipping and you're not paying attention in class. Didn't we already discuss this issue about your hair?"

"Yes, Mom."

"Tram, we already discussed this issue. You know how I feel about your hair. I told you in plain English that I will not give you permission to cut it. You are not old enough to make that decision and until I think you are, you will wear your hair as I say. Now, is that clear? I don't want to have to repeat this every day. Do you understand?"

"Yes, Mom."

"Furthermore, I want you to pay attention in school. Listen to your teacher and get your homework done. What do you have to say for yourself?"

"I'll study and do my homework," she muttered, standing up and walking towards her room.

Convinced I had put an end to Tram's rebellious crusade, I breathed a sigh of relief. Denial is just a quick and convenient panacea—too bad it is of fleeting duration.

A contrarian, she continued her defiant attempts to always move against the grain. Sullen, insubordinate and stubborn, she was unruly in class and consequently, her grades continued to plunge.

Pushed to the limit, I caved in, too exasperated to fight any longer. Grabbing a pair of scissors, I called Tram.

"How short do you want your hair?" I asked, flashing my shiny scissors.

"Just up to here," she said, pointing to a spot on her neck about three inches beneath her ear.

"OK, come over here and I'll cut it."

Grinning broadly, she skipped over, her face revealing the glow of triumph. As I snipped, she giggled, struggling to heed my instruction to keep still.

I was amazed to note how much more sophisticated she grew before my eyes. There was no doubt that Tram was beautiful regardless of the length of her hair. More importantly, my daughter was happy—joyful because she'd won her battle and in high spirits because she felt grown up with her new coif.

A month later, on her twelfth birthday, I handed her a rectangular box wrapped in shiny, blue paper and fastened with a silver bow.

"What did you get me, Mom?" she asked excitedly.

"You'll see. Pull the ribbon and lift the cover."

Opening the box, Tram let out a scream of delight.

"My Nike shoes!" she shouted, dancing around the room.

I had kept my promise. And for a brief time thereafter, Tram seemed pacified with her new shoes and hairdo. I'd often catch her staring at herself in the mirror, all smiles. She was agreeable; she no longer contested my requests or neglected her studies. Was the reign of adolescent terror truly terminated?

Not exactly. I soon discovered that the truce was short lived. A new behavior pattern was budding on the horizon.

Every evening, after the family had retired, Tram would dress up and sneak out. For a while, she actually got away with it. Then, one morning, while walking down the hallway towards the kitchen, I accidentally stepped on a window screen left outside the girls' room.

Pushing the door open, I gazed at the window—it was missing a screen. Afraid an intruder had broken into the house the night before, I awakened Tram and Phuong.

"Did you girls hear any noise during the night?"

"No, Mom," Phuong replied. "Why?"

"I found the window screen in the hallway. I think I'll check to see if anything is missing. Maybe a burglar prowled around."

Turning over, they went back to sleep. It seemed a bit odd that they were not the least bit concerned. Perhaps kids were lackadaisical that way—too young to know or stew over the real dangers of life.

I inspected the house, giving every nook and cranny, drawer and closet the once over, but nothing appeared to be out of place or missing. Dismissing the incident as insignificant, I made breakfast, reinserted the screen, dressed and went to work.

A few days later, I stepped on the misplaced screen again when I walked down the hallway. Worried, I ran to the phone and dialed the police. Once could have been a coincidence; twice was intentional. Something was not right and I had to get to the bottom of it before a tragedy occurred.

Red, rotating beacon lights alerted me that the patrol car had pulled up in the driveway. A double knock got me to my feet.

"What is the problem, ma'am?" asked a tall, husky officer, tipping his hat.

"Someone removed the window screen, officer. I think a thief may have wandered in during the night. It already happened twice."

"Where was your husband last night?" he asked.

"My fiancé was here with me all evening."

"What does he do?"

"He's in the Army."

"And he was home last night?"

"Yes, sir, he was."

"What time does he leave for work?"

"Five-thirty—about an hour before I get up."

"Then surely he would've noticed the screen before you," he said dryly, wrinkling his brow in puzzlement.

"Huh! I don't know. I'll ask him tonight," I said, somewhat confused by his line of questioning.

"Ma'am, everything looks OK here. I don't think any crime has been committed, but just to be sure, we'll watch the house closely to see if there is any strange activity."

"Thanks, officer, I appreciate it."

When Danny came home, I asked him if he knew anything about the misplaced window screen.

"No, Bảo, I didn't see any screen in the hallway."

"Danny how could you have missed it? It was right there," I said, pointing to where I had found it.

175

"Well, it wasn't there when I passed," he growled, visibly irritated.

"You don't have to get so angry."

Realizing he was too jumpy to pursue a reasonable discussion, I let the topic drop. However, I decided to take matters in my own hands and uncover the mystery of the hallway screen.

After everyone had retired for the evening, I paid careful attention to any strange sounds and movements. After a while, a noise, coming from Tram and Phuong's room, awoke me abruptly. I ran to the window just in time to catch Tram crossing the front lawn.

Scurrying to the door, I stepped outside.

"Hey! Where do you think you're going?"

"I don't know," she replied.

"What do you mean you don't know? You're out of bed and wandering around outdoors. I won't tolerate lies, so don't even try. Get back inside right now, young lady. I know what's going on. It was you—you removed the screen and threw it in the hallway. How long did you think you would get away with this? How long have you been doing this?"

"Since my birthday," she admitted.

"Your birthday was two months ago! You've been sneaking out at night for two months? I bet you were upset because I didn't catch you. What's the sense of defying me if I don't know about it, right? That's why you used the screen as evidence of your misbehavior."

Recognizing that I was furious, Tram knew she was in serious trouble. Cowering, she lowered her gaze.

"You can be certain I'll be paying strict attention from now on, and you'd better not cross me again. Is that clear?"

An exaggerated nod was her only response.

"I'm tired," I told her, "and we both need to get some sleep. Go to bed. We will discuss this tomorrow and I will decide your punishment."

Walking back to my room, I understood why Danny had not seen the screen. Tram had waited until he'd left before setting it in the hallway for me to find.

In the morning, I informed Danny that Tram had crawled out the window the night before.

"Bảo, I'll make an appointment with a family counselor," he told me.

"What is a family counselor?"

"A trained therapist—a doctor specialized in problems involving kids and parents."

"Why do we have to talk to a doctor? Tram isn't sick."

"First of all, a therapist is a different kind of doctor—one who deals with psychological and emotional problems. And secondly, she is not well. Her defiant behavior means something is wrong within, and if we want to help her, we need to know what it is. It's getting late. I've got to go. I'll see you tonight. We'll talk some more about this."

After dinner that evening, Danny announced that he'd made a doctor appointment for one o'clock the following Thursday, which meant that I would have to ask Mrs. Wood for time off and take Tram out of school early.

Having absolutely no experience in the world of counseling or therapy, at the appointment, I sat quietly, waiting for Danny to take the lead. The therapist posed several pertinent questions geared towards encouraging us to discuss our family issues openly. After the session, I felt terribly embarrassed to have shared our private matters with a stranger. This was a first for me and I was uncomfortable with the humiliating tell-all fest. Such things were not common practice in Việt Nam. We did not speak of family troubles in a public forum.

178

Although the open-door policy was not part of my heritage, I tried a cooperative approach and participated all for the end result of attaining positive results. A few days after our first and last counseling session, I received a call from the school announcing that Tram had been truant. Quickly thereafter, the police notified me that they had picked up my daughter and settled her with a foster family.

"Mrs. Wood, I have a family emergency," I said. "I have to leave immediately."

"Did something happen to your husband or one of your children?"

"No, but I have a pressing situation that requires my immediate attention."

"Then you'd better go. Don't worry—you can finish tomorrow."

"Thanks," I blurted, running out the door.

Immediately, I phoned Danny.

"Tram has been picked up by the police for truancy," I shouted as soon as he said hello. "They put her in foster care."

"Bảo, I can't leave now. I'm busy. Tram will be safe in the foster home. She can't get into trouble. We'll take care of it as soon as I get home."

179

I paced up and down for two hours, waiting for Danny to return. The seconds ticked, the minutes ticked, followed in sequence by the hours. I was a nervous wreck. What had Tram done now? Why was I unable to get through to her? Was I not a good mother?

Was her insubordinate behavior a manifestation of a deep-seated problem, or was this merely the offshoot of an impulsive rebellion, perhaps carried to the extreme?

When the echo of car wheels crunching the gravel reached my ears, I darted out the door and into Danny's car.

"Let's go directly to the foster house—here's the address," I stammered, reading from a matchbook cover on which I had hurriedly scribbled the contact information. "I think the counselor will be there."

We pulled up to a modest, one-story home sitting on a somewhat-neglected piece of property. Clumps of weeds had invaded, bending the heads of red-and-white blooms no longer in their prime. The house had a pronounced lived-in appearance, an inexplicable appeal that lessened my fear and anxiety.

Once inside, I was met by the counselor, whose open-arm gesture and smile invited us to join him and Tram around his heavily notched dining table.

"I think we all need to clear the air," he said, nervously pinching the tip of his nose with a broad thumb and index finger. Silence prevailed.

"Who wants to start?" he asked, shifting his glance from face to face.

"I don't like my parents, so I did drugs and drank alcohol," Tram cried, rupturing the stillness.

I fought a scream that swelled in my throat, forcing it back into my stomach.

"What kind of drugs are you taking and where did you get them?" the counselor asked, seizing the opportunity to pursue.

"I got the drugs from my parents."

"That's absurd—it's a lie," I blurted. "Danny and I don't have any drugs in the house, and we would never be so foolhardy and evil as to give anything dangerous to our children."

I had been waiting for Tram to speak, eager to finally discover what was at the root of these reckless and defiant antics, but never had expected her to fabricate tales implicating her parents in abusive wrongdoing.

"I've heard enough," I said. "Tram, if you're not going to tell the truth, we might as well just get up and leave."

181

"No, ma'am, I think it best if Tram remains here for a while. I'd like to get her drug tested at the hospital to identify what substance she has been ingesting."

Danny and I agreed that the counselor was right in his approach. We had to know the truth. In the car, we discussed the day's events.

"I don't think Tram is doing drugs," I said. "I know her better than anyone else and I'm certain this is a plea for attention."

"Bảo, I know you want to think well of your daughter, but let's just wait for the test results," Danny responded.

"Well, from now on, you're going to have to deal with her if you believe she has a problem. Not me. I've not only lost time and money from work, but I'm also hurt and ashamed."

"Bảo, the counselor said that Tram told him Jim had given her a beer every day for a long time."

"I know he wasn't a good father, but don't forget, she told the counselor lies about us. How can we believe that she's not lying about Jim?"

"Well, let's just take it one day at a time."

Difficult as it was, we both agreed to wait out the nasty tempest. In the meantime,

182

Tram's test results came back negative and she was permitted to return home.

Drawing a long, deep breath, I tried not to heed the signs of my body becoming weary of it all. Exhausted, I pushed myself beyond limits. I understood that adolescence was not exactly a happy, joyful period, but Tram seemed to be a nine on a scale of ten for chaos and problems. The trail was lined with stumbling blocks, a contrivance that changed my little girl from a loving daughter into an irreconcilable antagonist. Worst of all, in her eyes, I was the enemy.

Chapter 9
The Fourth "I Do"

The journey continued. Several weeks thereafter, while at work, I received an emergency call from the police.

"Ma'am, this is Officer Carl. We arrested your daughter, Tram, for shoplifting at the Kmart."

"Oh, my God! Where is she?" I screeched.

"Don't worry, she's OK. She's in custody at the station. We're waiting for you to get here."

Near hysteria, I phoned Danny. In a voice crackling with fear and desperation, I related my conversation with the police officer.

"Be calm, Bảo. I'm getting off in a half hour. I'll go down to the station."

When Danny arrived, the police officer informed him that Tram had been interrogated, and that they would release her. She'd told the officers that her friend, Katy, was the culprit who had shoplifted the candy and when the police had been called, Katy had hurled the evidence at Tram and run away.

The police were sympathetic to the young girl. They believed her recount and let her go home with Danny. Although the situation was resolved, my problems were not put out to pasture.

Later that night, Danny chastised Thaun for playing his radio too loudly. It was easy to see that his nerves were frayed. Therefore, I was not surprised when he focused his anger and frustration on me for release.

"Bảo, you don't discipline Thaun. Instead, you give him too much freedom. It's not good. Kids don't know how to deal with permissiveness. He's allowed to do whatever he pleases with no supervision. This is why we are having all these upsetting incidents."

Danny's words sent a red flag soaring in my mind. Recognizing that Tram's outrageous behavior was putting us dangerously on the razor's edge, I understood Danny's anxiety and predilection for emotional flair ups. His temper often instigated more conflicts with Thaun and Phuong. Sometimes, he paid too much attention to Phuong's rendition of situations, failing to realize that she was focused on searing my nerves. How could I get him to see the truth? What could I possibly do to stop this reign of rebellion?

I realized that I had the leading role in this drama and that I had to find a solution that would allow us to deal with the turmoil in a manner that would not spark any additional blazes.

Initially, when Danny and I had begun dating, Phuong had resented his presence in my life. Though forewarned, I had been searching for a man who would love and protect us as well as be a good, fun-loving father. Phuong had been stubborn and hesitant to accept his role in the family.

"I don't care about having a father," she'd repeated endlessly. Her inconsiderate, rebellious behavior had been consistent with her feeling. Therefore, when Danny had appeared, Phuong immediately had pitted herself against him, assailing him neither with physical nor verbal protestations. Instead, armed with the power of her intention, she fought his intervention in the family by convincing her siblings to conspire with her against me. If my life was miserable, there was no way his could be happy.

Thaun was loyal to me. He saw through Phuong's conniving tactics and wanted no part of her warfare. Consequently, sister turned against brother. Although it upset me to give in to negative thoughts about my own daughter, her menacing intrigues led me to entertain the idea that something in her was not quite right. This seemed a bit too extreme for just teenage rebellion.

Eventually, I learned that Phuong conducted daily meetings with her siblings during which she would coach and practice with them how to tell Danny lies about how mean and cruel I was. When he asked them, "Is that really true about your mom?" they would respond in unison: "Oh, yes."

The thought of my children using someone with whom they were still unfamiliar to hurt me caused unbearable pain even though I didn't know the exact content of their lies.

But I found out one day when I couldn't find some lingerie.

"Did anyone see my nightgown?" I asked the kids.

"You're always accusing the children of naughty pranks," Danny shouted, running into the room. "You're jealous because they are doing well in school and you take it out on them. No wonder Jim couldn't live with you!"

Danny's words pressed a dangerous button. I was livid.

"How dare you speak to me in that manner," I shouted. You don't know me well enough. You have absolutely no idea who I am, and you have no right to pass judgment on any part of my life. Did I ever blame you for your failed relationships?"

"Bảo, you're being unreasonable. I think—"

"What exactly do you know about me?" I interrupted. "You stink like garbage! My children do well in school because I brought them up to be responsible. I told them that if they want to be successful, they must study hard and earn good grades. That is my dream for each child, and I do my best to make certain they will grow up and have all that I was denied. Plus, I work hard so they can have all the opportunities possible. This is who I am!"

Danny's aggressive accusations pulled the trigger, setting off a blast of gunfire in my mind. Enraged and beside myself, I could have strangled him right then and there for the malicious way in which he admonished me.

Shocked by my indignation, he seemed to have misplaced his tongue. This was certainly a first. Lowering his gaze in a sign of withdrawal, he walked away.

How I wished Danny could be more emotionally involved with my family. Believing he was pulling apart instead of uniting us, I felt he was not a positive influence.

Befriending my children in lieu of parenting them, his role, both emotionally and financially, was more in tune with a guest than family member. Never bothering to slip a hand into his pocket, Danny did not contribute to the household maintenance.

On rare occasions on which I asked for assistance, my requests received refusals. "I don't have a dime, Bảo," he'd say, exhibiting neither embarrassment nor guilt despite the fact that he was telling me a fib. I knew he had given money to his old girlfriend. Consequently, I decided our relationship was not functioning. Although I experienced difficulties communicating my feelings, I realized that I no longer had a choice. A decision had to be made.

After Danny finished arguing with Thaun, he stormed out, slamming the door in his wake. Several slivers of wood rained down on the floor. The message was clear: Danny was furious.

Walking away, I thought it best to just let him simmer down. Sitting on the front porch with my head nestled in the palms of my hands,

I waited for him to come back, struggling with the confusing thoughts and feelings tangoing in my mind. What would I say to Danny when he did return? Sometimes, I thought it best to delay setting in motion any tactics until the moment swept me into a decision.

I didn't have long to either wrestle with my options or ponder a strategy. Fifteen minutes later, a placid Danny returned like a regretful dog with his tail between his legs. Awkwardly, he sat beside me as if nothing unruffling had ever occurred between us. However, no longer willing to play the victim game, I knew it was up to me to reset the curse of my life. Hurt and offended far too often, I was now armed for combat. This time, I had gathered my strength and felt ready to confront him.

"Danny, we need to talk," I said dryly, fixing my gaze on the side of his face. I could see the muscles in his jaw contract.

"It sounds important, Bảo," he responded glancing at me sideways.

"Yes, it's very important, Danny. I have tolerated enough abuse and disrespect from you. Apparently, our relationship is not working. We are in two different places. I'm not happy and the children are nervous and rebellious. I think you should leave. You're young and you should find someone your age, without children. I know you're not yet ready to have a family of your own and I think it's time you follow that path. I realize it is very

191

challenging for you to have to deal with my four kids."

"But Bảo—"

"Danny, I love you, but I cannot raise my children with you. There are too many conflicts and problems. I want to find a man who will love me and my kids—someone who is willing to be a father to them, someone who will care for and treat them as if they were his. If this is not possible, then I will be a single mom. My children need consistency in their lives. They have to learn the difference between right and wrong in order to mature into men and women of sound principles and integrity. Do you understand?"

"Yes, Bảo. We can do it together."

"No, Danny, we cannot. Look at what is happening. We bicker all the time. This is a dysfunctional environment. Will you please leave?"

"Is that what you really want?"

"That is what I want."

"It's kind of late now and I have no place to go. Could I sleep on the couch just for tonight?"

"OK, but just for tonight. Tomorrow, I would like you to go. Is that clear?"

Rising to his feet, he nodded in agreement.

192

Although Danny was not at home when I returned from work the following evening, I noticed that his belongs had not been removed. Later, after dinner, he visited.

"I have to talk to you," he said nervously. "Can we take a walk?"

As we walked without a destination, Danny reached for my hand.

"What is on your mind?" I asked.

Pausing his stride, he pulled me into a tight embrace.

"Darling Bảo, I love you," he whispered in my ear. "I don't want to leave you. This is all my fault. I should never have let things disintegrate to this level, but I hope it's not too late. I've been thinking about you all day. I can't get you out of my mind. I thought about what you said yesterday, and I've made up my mind. I want you—I want to be with you. I'll do whatever it takes to make you happy. I'll try to be a good father to the kids—the best I can be. Will you give us another chance?"

"I haven't had much luck choosing a good man," I said. "We've been living together for seven months and during that time, I've supported you financially and emotionally. I asked you to help with the bills but you refused. Why should I believe you now?"

193

"I don't expect you to believe me, and I don't blame you for being angry. All I'm asking is for you to give me one more chance. Can you find it in your heart to forgive me and let me prove my love for you?"

Although my mind had one answer, my heart was quick to contradict. When our eyes locked, I melted.

"Alright, Danny, let's go home."

It was a fantastic evening. Enveloped in his long arms, I surrendered.

Five days thereafter, Danny received his paycheck from the Army. Immediately, he cut me a check in the amount of $1300. On the memo line, he wrote, "For love."

Arriving late the next day without warning, he was met by my confrontation.

"You're late, Danny," I said to him.

"Yes, I know, Bảo. I dropped by Sim's apartment to clear the air. I told her that I didn't love her anymore, our relationship was over and she was free to find herself another man."

"Why did you have to tell her in person? You could have spoken on the phone."

"She called, but I couldn't talk on the telephone. I wanted to say 'goodbye' face to face."

"She certainly didn't call you to declare her love but to remind you it was payday."

"That's enough, Bảo."

"It's the truth—face it. I've been around servicemen for a long time, and I've learned a lot."

Of course, Danny didn't like hearing my views, especially since he recognized my words as accurate. Therefore, refusing to counter my comment, he headed for the bedroom, gently taking me by the hand. Exhausted, I followed without resistance.

Restless and anxious, I spent a sleepless night stewing over Danny sharing his paycheck with Sim while living with me. In my mid were the echoes of his protestations— "I'd like to help you out, but I don't have the money!"

I might have been able to forgive him, but would he ever be worthy of my trust?

During the next few months, however, Danny tried his best to slip into the role of the man of the family—a role he played quite commendably. His efforts and admirable performance won him my trust. Certain that he and Sim were history, when he took my hands, locked his gaze with mine and whispered, "Bảo, I love you, will you marry me?" I answered, "Yes, Danny."

He was jubilant, but instead of uncorking a bottle of iced champagne, he pulled me towards him and gave me a kiss. Then, dropping his arms, he turned and headed for the phone to give the good news to his mother. Upon hearing of her son's imminent nuptials, she insisted the ceremony be held in Washington instead of Oklahoma to facilitate family attendance.

Agreeing, we programmed our trip to Washington for the end of May, coordinating our plans with the scheduling of school's summer closure to permit the children to participate.

On May 30, 1986, at six o'clock in the evening, Danny, the children and I embarked on a cross-country journey to Washington. Arriving in New Mexico around two in the morning, we exited the highway and rested for a couple of hours. We continued our trip, reaching Salt Lake City for lunch just before noon.

Our hunger and thirst satisfied, we drove to the Holiday Inn in Twin Falls, Idaho, pulling into the entry just as the sun dipped behind the horizon, veiling the city in a light shadow.

In the morning, after a restful night and a gratifying breakfast, we climbed into the car for the final lap of our journey. Danny announced that we would be in Longview, Washington, before nightfall. As we drove along the Columbia River, I was mesmerized by the beauty of the city's natural wonders. It was the longest river I had ever seen, but after five hours of driving along it's never-ending banks, my eyelids started to droop. Breaking my stupor, Danny's voice announced that his parents lived on the opposite side of the river.

"Over there?" I asked, pointing my finger towards the river. "How will we cross over? By boat?" I joked.

"No," he laughed. "There is a bridge— the 205 bridge. We will cross it in about a half hour. Just relax and enjoy the scenery. We should arrive at my parents' house in several hours, probably around five o'clock."

We arrived in late afternoon on June 1. Jewel, Danny's mother, who had been leaning against the door in anticipation, bolted to the car like a child running to get a promised treat. An expression of elation covered her face as she encircled me in her arms.

"This is the lady I've been waiting to meet. Welcome, Bảo!"

I was relieved and happy that she approved her son's choice.

The following day, Danny, Jewel and I drove around, visiting different churches.

Stopping at the Oak Point Community Church, located just outside Longview, I was immediately captivated. A small, white church with a slender steeple, the beautiful house of worship, surrounded by lush, wide branch trees, stood distant from the road, overlooking the mighty Columbia, as the natives called their river.

"I like this church," I said, walking through the front door. "There is an aura of serenity here."

"We'll talk to Minister Rod about marrying us," Danny said, thrilled by my enthusiasm. "He knows my parents very well."

After Danny and Jewel introduced me to the minister, he agreed to perform the ceremony on our preferred date—Saturday, June 7.

Our wedding was small, intimate and romantic. We pronounced our vows and promised our love in front of family and a handful of friends, totaling forty guests.

Both Danny and I wore *áo dài,* traditional wedding garments. I covered my shoulders with a red *áo choàng,* a formal coat, and wore a gold *khan dong* entwined in my long hair.

Danny's *áo dài* was a shimmering, royal blue; mine was red and gold. All forty guests, including Minister Rod, were invited to the reception at my new in-laws' house.

Following the nuptials, we remained in Longview for about three weeks, sightseeing and taking trips to the Oregon coast and Seattle, where we toured the Pike Street Market and Chinatown. Before returning to Oklahoma, Danny and I visited with his family. It was an opportune moment to bond with my newly acquired in-laws.

When we arrived home as Mr. and Mrs., Danny was surprised to discover that he was being deployed to Korea for one year. The honeymoon was over. Taking advantage of their stepdad's absence and my vulnerability, the children returned the rebellious pranks.

Correspondences authored by Tram's teachers arrived with clock-like regularity, communicating the same message over and over: Tram was truant. Eventually, the principal threatened expulsion if she failed to amend her delinquent behavior. In addition, she was required to attend reparation classes to recuperate the skipped lessons.

After the sunny brightness of my weeks in Washington, I slipped back into the darkness of my unresolved dilemmas. Recognizing I had serious problems, I was frustrated with my inability to find a solution.

Forced to admit my incompetence, I knew I could no longer allow the situation to precipitate further. But how could I gain influence over my daughter? How could I impress upon her the importance of accountability and responsibility and the consequences of not seriously pursuing an education?

Absent from the family home for one week, I was clueless about my daughter's whereabouts. If I didn't even know where she was, how could I possibly have any control over the situation? Something was terribly wrong. Admitting I was failing as a parent, I knew it was up to me to change the course of Tram's reckless, insolent life. In so doing, perhaps I could save her from her own condemning behavior.

"Mom, I know where Tram is," Thaun said, relieving me of my disturbing thoughts.

"You do? Why didn't you speak up sooner? Let's go get her and bring her home."

Thaun led the way, gently swinging his arms as he walked down the road. Several minutes later, he paused, turned and pointed to a white-shingled house.

"Tram is staying there," he said. "Shall we knock?"

I nodded as he tapped his knuckles on the oak door three times.

"That's enough, Thaun," I said. "Give them time to get to the door."

We watched as the door sprung open. A diminutive woman stood in the entry. From the network of fine lines encircling her eyes and mouth and running across her brow, I estimated her age to be about sixty. I stepped forward, leaving Thaun several steps behind.

"Hello, I'm Bảo, and this is my son, Thaun. I'm looking for my daughter, Tram. Is she here with you?"

Suddenly, Tram appeared at the door. Every muscle in her face was contracting—I knew she was angry.

"I want to stay here!" she cried. "I'm not going home with you."

"Stop it, Tram. Don't be difficult. I want you to come home and stay where you belong. We are going to have a nice, long chat. It is way overdue."

"Bảo," the woman interrupted, realizing there were serious issues between mother and daughter. "I was thinking about coming over to talk with you. Since Tram has been here, she's been a great help to us."

"She's helping you? What do you mean? What's she doing?"

"She's helping my two daughters with their homework and reading. We really love having Tram here."

"Is that why you're keeping my daughter in your home? Are you aware of the laws governing minors? You cannot harbor an underage child in your home without reporting it to the police. Tram has a home and a family."

Enraged, I grabbed my daughter by the hand, opened my purse and showed her the letters I had received from her teachers and principal, reporting her truancy.

"Tram, this is serious. You have to stop this nonsensical game playing. Children, according to the law, must be in school. You have to return and you have to make up the lost lessons. Is that clear?"

In silence she went inside to collect her meager belongings. I waited, uncomfortable as blood surge through my body. During the walk home, Thaun and Tram spoke softly between themselves. In all my life I had never shied away from confrontation. However, I opted to avoid any discussion just then, certain it would trigger a war. Furthermore, I had made my point clear.

Once inside the house, I headed for the kitchen to see what Phuong was preparing.

"What are you cooking?" I asked, trying to regain my interior composure.

"I baked some chicken and steamed the rice."

At least one of my girls seems to be on the right path, I thought to myself. Maybe I wasn't all that bad at parenting

We united at the table and shared Phuong's dinner, speaking about the day's events, careful not to ruffle Tram with recriminations. Although she was not further admonished, I felt she knew my feeling on the matter, and she had to acknowledge the gravity of her actions.

But I was wrong, and misjudged her level of maturity. Two days later, Tram skipped school again. Trying not to obsess over her reprehensible antics, I went to work. At this point, it was foolhardy of me to squander time and energy worrying over what I was apparently incapable of controlling.

That afternoon, shortly after lunch, I received a phone call at work from the rather inebriated woman who had harbored my daughter in her home without my permission.

"Bảo, Tram came over here with a handful of different-colored pills and is threatening to swallow them," she stammered. "I just want you to know that she's OK and went to a friend's house to pick up her make-up."

It was like rubbing salt in a wound. My daughter preferred the home of another to mine—but why? Images of my life with Tram fluttered before my eyes. Where did I go wrong? Why was she rejecting me and the values I was trying to instill in her? Didn't she understand that she was recklessly careening along a dangerous path of destruction, compromising her future?

Left alone with my thoughts, I waited another hour for Tram to return. At seven o'clock, it was practically dark out. I snatched my purse and hurried over to the woman's house, looking for my daughter. When I received a blank stare and a curt, " Listen, I don't know where she is" from the lady, who smelled as if she had prolonged happy hour way beyond dinnertime, I became increasingly worried.

Left with the sole option of returning home to await Tram's return, I sat in the living room and switched on the TV, hoping it would pacify my nerves, now tangled in knots. Another disappointment—I kept seeing commercials starring obedient, loving children.

This time, TV was not a successful escape. Instead of an anxiety-relieving, distracting mechanism, it served only to enhance the awareness of my problems with Tram.

Upset, I packed my gym bag and went to the health club. Perhaps if I took a nice, leisurely swim, I thought, I would feel better. When I got there, I noticed a young girl, about seven, playing in the pool unaccompanied.

"Hi. Are you here with your parents?" I asked her.

"Yes, ma'am. My mom's in the steam room," she responded, smiling

It was refreshing to hear a child speak respectfully to an adult and to see her happy facial expression. Thoughts of my own children flooded my mind. How disrespectful they had grown. I found myself disliking courteous children, both those projected on the TV and those I encountered in life. Feeling guilty, I acknowledged it was not dislike but envy and frustration.

In lieu of focusing on my children's failings and trying to submerge and deny my feelings, I realized I should try to change what I was unable and unwilling to accept or resign myself to accept the unacceptable. There was no other option.

The following day, I discussed with Mrs. Wood my parenting problems and the wonderful child I had met at the pool.

"Bảo, I would seriously consider seeing a therapist," she said. "You cannot resolve this yourself."

"A therapist? Do you think I need to see a doctor about my daughter?" I asked, embarrassed.

"It is certainly not my intention to upset you. I'm your friend and I want to help you. You know I have your best interest at heart when I offer my advice. I know this is not part of your culture, but here in the USA, people seek therapists and counselors when psychological or emotional problems arise, just like we seek doctors when we are physically sick. Bảo, you have three teenagers and a seven-year-old boy, a husband and a full-time job—that's a heavy load for anyone to handle. I think you need professional intervention."

I thanked Mrs. Wood for her advice, realizing she was right. My life was, in a sense, out of control. I had lost my power over my children, and I wanted help. I needed help.

Chapter 10

The Stranger Within: Who Am I?

The situation with Tram had ignited, leaving me treading on dangerous territory. Every word I said led me further into the mine fields plotted by my teenage daughter. If I wasn't careful, explosions and reprisals were daily events.

Realizing I could no longer manage the situation without further precipitating the circumstances, I made an appointment to see Dr. Wilson, the therapist Mrs. Wood had recommended. At that point, how harmful could it have been to consult a professional? I was not getting anywhere, and the consequences of Tram's truancy and shoplifting were potential risks.

Dr. Wilson agreed to schedule me for half-hour sessions once a week. During our meetings, he inquired about my family issues, leaving me at liberty to discuss whatever I felt was causing me worry.

Poised, reflective and attentive, he listened in silence, absorbing the content of my discussion. Our sessions ran with unerring precision. About eight months later, I was finished talking; telling all was energy consuming. My words just ran dry. However, Dr. Wilson suggested I keep our weekly appointments. Trusting his judgment as a professional, I agreed.

But, instead of my cathartic verbalizing, we sat opposite each other, memorizing each other's facial features. Something was not quite right with this scenario. Where was the assistance I needed and requested?

Spoken stillness, I soon discovered, was neither gratifying nor a help in the resolution of my dilemma with Tram. After several visits of uncomfortable quietude, I stopped waiting and hoping for costly advice that never actually materialized. Therefore, several months afterward, I ended my professional relationship with Dr. Wilson. Although my purse was lighter, my woes with Tram were considerably heavier. All I had to show for my efforts was an unproductive loss of time. Neither a suggestion was imparted nor advice. He just listened. Hence, it was not surprising that nothing changed at home except the frequency of my problems with Tram.

When Danny returned from Korea, I informed him that I thought it best to sell the house and transfer our belongings to the military housing development at Fort Sill. I was desperately clinging to the idea that a neighbored change would isolate Tram from her old school and less-than-enlightening companions. Maybe this was the solution!

Thankfully, Danny was in full agreement.

"I will register us," he said, handing me a copy of the waiting list. "This way, we will be given serious consideration."

"When do you think we'll get a house?" I asked.

"It usually takes about three months unless someone cancels—then, we could get one sooner."

Fortunately, there was a vacancy about six weeks later. Seizing the opportunity, we moved in immediately. I regarded the sudden, favorable circumstance as a good omen. Certain the tides would turn, I breathed a sigh of relief.

Expecting miracles, I was disappointed when my problems with Tram did not dissolve into thin air. Blaming the old neighborhood and bad companions for her delinquency, I had set myself up for the standard denial-induced delusion.

211

Like a magnet, my daughter always attracted to the rowdy, defiant and problematic kids who seemed to influence her more than Danny or I. Despite my efforts, scolding, punishments and long discussions in which I tried reasoning strategies, she continued to cut classes, take drugs and remain out all evening with neither parental permission nor notification. I was at my wits' end.

At the conclusion of the academic year, Jim asked if Phong could spend the summer with him in North Carolina. I agreed, giving him a deadline date for my son's return.

A month later, I phoned to remind Jim it was time for Phong to return home to prepare for the start of the school year in several weeks.

Jim, however, failed to honor our agreement and refused to send him back.

Furious, I sought legal counsel from my attorney.

"Bảo, if Jim does not return the boy as agreed, in accordance with your deadline, he will face kidnapping charges. Does he understand this?"

"I will be certain to tell him."

The following day, when Jim phoned, I related the attorney's words.

"Meet me at the old house on Bell Street and you can pick up Phong," he said.

"OK, Jim, I'll be there tomorrow morning around nine-thirty."

I felt as if I had made some progress without resorting to costly legal maneuvers. Breakfast finished and the dishes washed and dried, Thaun and I drove to our old house to pick up Phong. As soon as he spotted the car, he ran from the house, pulled open the door and slid in. Immediately I sped way, neither desiring nor willing to have a confrontation with Jim.

Phong's words and behavior took on a different flavor after that, which let me know that he had succumbed to Jim's influence. Formerly an obedient young boy who studied and completed his chores with geniality, he now neglected his homework assignments.

This was not my son! I no longer knew the boy who always had given me such

213

pleasure and satisfaction. Who was this stranger, this cantankerous, rebellious youngster?

Did Jim really have the power to turn a well-adjusted, young boy into a dysfunctional child in just a few weeks?

When I received a communication from school, I realized the gravity of the situation. Absenting myself from work with a family-emergency alibi, I agreed to a meeting with the principal. After the initial introduction and hurried update on the matter, Phong was summoned to the office.

My son was intelligent, and he understood not only that he was in serious trouble but that an explanation would be solicited. Though his restless demeanor betrayed a certain nervousness, he tried to camouflage his fear and insecurity behind a reluctance to cooperate.

In response to the principal's interrogations regarding his scholastic negligence and truancy, Phong offered either a curt, evasive, "I don't know" or silence bred of boldness, a strategy that deleted any credibility from his words. Congeniality, humility and sincerity had vanished into thin air.

Shaking his head of thinning, salt-and-pepper curls, the principal gave me a look of

214

compassion. We both recognized that I had a dilemma on my hands—one with the potential to ruin the life of a young boy if not properly and quickly resolved.

At home, I tried my best to emphasize the importance of education to all my children, using as an example the hardships of my own life and professional journey.

Although the children listened, it was no guarantee that they absorbed and understood my message.

After dinner one night, Thaun helped me clear the table of plates and linens.

"Mom, Jim calls a lot while you are at work," he blurted.

"Really? What does he have to say?" I inquired, both surprised and curious.

"He told me and Phong to beat you and Daddy."

"Do you realize what you just said? That's a pretty serious accusation, Thaun. Are you sure?"

"Yes, Mom," he replied. "Jim said it more than once. He said that Phong studied karate in North Carolina and could and should use it to hurt you. Then he told me to grab my baseball bat and beat you."

Resentment and anger overcame any fear that could have materialized into sudden death.

Dismissing Thaun with a reminder to finish his homework, I phoned Jim.

"I heard some very disturbing things from Nha this evening. Jim, you are an evil, malicious man. How dare you talk to the children in that manner. How dare you instigate the kids to perform violent acts. Why did you tell them to beat me and Danny? You're nothing but a lowlife criminal. Jim, that's abuse. You cannot speak to children in such a sadistic, vicious way. It's a corruption of minors."

"Wait a minute, Bảo. Calm down," Jim urged.

"No! You wait a minute. How can I be calm after what you did?" I shouted. "Now, you listen to me. I'm not through talking. I enrolled the kids in karate class for self-defense and protection. I wanted them to be

216

prepared if ever they were attacked or the victims of aggressive behavior by a bully. They were never instructed to use violence with anyone, especially family members. This is outrageous. You are filling my boys' minds with malicious ideas. I will not tolerate such hateful delinquency. This is sick! Now I understand why Tram became such a troubled teen. It's your spiteful influence. And now, Phong is acting up. This is your fault. You are ruining my children, turning them into dysfunctional individuals. You're trying to create havoc and discord in my family. I will not have it, Jim. You're a sinister, callous man. Well, it ends right here and now. Is that clear?"

Without pausing for his response, denial, excuses, rebuttal or apology, I slammed the phone down.

If a thought could be translated into a deed instantaneously, Jim's neck would have been wrung. I was beyond exasperation. I was a mother fighting to protect her children.

Still seething, I undressed, climbed into bed and spent the following seven hours wide eyed, counting every beat of my racing heart. Even Danny's deep, rhythmic breaths of restful sleep could neither ease my anxiety nor calm my nerves. I was too wound up to unwind.

217

About a year later, shortly before Danny's discharge from the Army, I made the decision to move the family to Oregon, certain it would be the most opportune strategy to rid my life of Jim and save my children from the harmful effects of his toxic influence.

In time, I had developed a loathing for Oklahoma and its surroundings. Fantasizing about a mysterious and sudden exit, I knew I would never reserve a special place in my memory for the Oklahoma segment of my life. It would be just a closed door.

Thankfully, in October 1989, we packed up and headed for Oregon. Taking a leave of absence, Danny accompanied the family, transporting our belongings and my sewing machine in his truck while Thaun, Phong, Tram and I made the trip by car.

Days before our departure, Phuong had dropped a bomb, expressing her intentions to remain in Oklahoma for a while longer.

Though my first reaction was a curt "no," Danny convinced me to soften my view.

"Bảo, Phuong is sixteen and old enough to tend to herself. She's not a child anymore. Besides, there is no need for concern. I'm still here and I'll keep an eye on her. She will be just fine and the time alone, away from the family, might actually do her some good. Maybe she'll come to her senses."

"OK, I'll let her remain for a while, as long as you promise to keep an eye on her."

"She will be just fine."

The trip from Oklahoma to Washington was a grueling, two-day car ride. Tired and restless, we stopped periodically for food, nature-call breaks and to stretch our legs. When we arrived in Longview, Danny phoned his parents from a rest stop pay phone to confirm their invitation for us to stay with them for several days until we located a place of our own.

My in-laws were gracious in providing comfortable accommodations. His worries appeased, Danny departed two days thereafter for Fort Sill, to complete his remaining five-month tour of duty.

"Bảo, let me know when you're ready to go house hunting," Danny's mom, Jewel, said. "We can start early in the morning and drive to Portland to look at different places until you see something you like."

"That would be wonderful. I'm ready. Let's go tomorrow."

We awakened early the following morning, consumed a satisfying breakfast and left on our quest to find suitable lodgings for Danny, the children and me.

Knowledgeable regarding our needs and preferences, we visited many diverse properties. Five days later, I walked into a house, immediately realizing it was suitable for my family. Enthusiastic and relieved, I notified the owner of my decision, completed the paperwork and signed the lease. I had a home in Portland, Oregon.

"That wasn't too bad, Jewel," I said, dropping the new keys into my handbag. "I feel relieved—as if a weight has been lifted from my shoulders. Now, I'd like to enroll the kids in school."

The following day, I drove to the school and spoke with the principal. He was eager to meet me and discuss increasing the school's enrollment. I found him warm and gracious within professional boundaries.

With my kids enrolled, I emitted a sigh of content. We had a home and my children had a school. Everything was rolling along smoothly. Something inside me warmed my heart. I felt proud of my accomplishments. In less than a week, I had settled the family in a new city.

That evening, before dinner, I summoned the children to deliver the good news. Excited, they chatted among themselves until I announced it was bedtime. Without resistance, they went to their rooms, excited to greet the morning's sunrise and all that the new day would bring.

On the first day of class, Tram linked up with a group of kids she felt were on her wavelength. Good or bad, I was thankful that she had enough interest to actually take the initiative to approach some other students. Maybe things would be different there. I could always hope.

But, perhaps that was just wishful thinking on my part. Much as I tried to keep a positive attitude, it would soon be interrupted by the truth. A new city, a new life—but the same Tram.

The change of location did little to modify the behavior of my dysfunctional child. She was who she was, regardless of the different surroundings. I feared what was to come.

Before long, Tram failed to return home one day, crushing my last sliver of hope she had matured, repented and altered her ways.

When I was later summoned by the principal, I realized I had returned to square one. Tram was truant again, and I was filled with shame and disappointment. As my eyes took on a look of despair, I realized the severity of the situation. I had lost all control over my daughter. Worse, I had no idea where she was or if she was safe or in harm's way.

Worried sick about my teenage child wandering alone in an unfamiliar city, I was exasperated. Ten days later, she phoned as if nothing had happened.

"Listen, Tram," I shouted, my relief flipping into anger, "I won't put up with your nonsense anymore. Either come home right now, or don't call me again. Do you understand?"

Before she could respond, I slammed down the receiver, thankful she was alive and safe, at least for the moment. Blotting with a quivering hand the stream of tears drizzling down the sides of my cheeks, I was forced to admit that I no longer knew this young girl to whom I had given birth. My daughter had become a stranger.

After dinner, Jewel phoned with the news that Tram was at her house.

"Bảo, don't worry, Tram is alright. But I have some disturbing news—she doesn't want to return home."

"Well, where does she plan to go? She can't live on her own and she certainly can't stay with you," I stammered.

"She has made her decision and seems unmovable —she refuses to go home. Will you sign a document granting her permission to live with my son, James, and his family?"

"James! She wants to move in with her uncle?" I screamed, shocked.

He had never called me to discuss taking her in. I had never been solicited for any information. When and how had this come about? James knew nothing about Tram— neither who she had been nor who she was that day, and what she was capable of doing. I was enraged.

"Jewel, it seems as if everyone is taking her side over mine! What makes her credible and me a liar? They don't know me and surely they don't know Tram. This is absurd. It smells of conspiracy," I yelled into the phone. "Forget it. I will not sign any paper."

"Calm down, Bảo," she said, moderating her tone, perhaps in an attempt to soften my anger. "Well, would you give your written permission for me to transfer her to a school in Longview?" she continued, trying to negotiate an amenable solution. Feeling a certain loyalty to Jewel, in whom Tram had

223

confided, my mother-in-law felt almost obliged to parley an agreeable deal.

"OK, Jewel," I sighed. "I'll give written consent."

Once again, realizing the severity of the situation at hand, and my apparent loss of control over Tram, I thought it best to compromise my wishes for my daughter's benefit.

"I'll get the paper and take it over to you. Would that be alright?" she asked.

"That will be fine."

"When can I come by? What's the best time to catch you at home?"

"Anytime in the evenings."

An hour later, Jewel arrived with the paper. Though I scribbled my name, I confess to having signed it reluctantly. But what other option did I have? Tram resisted all parenting efforts on my part. I had to admit that raising her had turned from a joyful experience into grueling work.

Lifting the pen I bit my lip, hoping the pain would distract me from recognizing what was actually happening. My thoughts raced within their boundaries to another time, years ago, when Tram was just a sweet, innocent baby. Was I to blame for this emotional vacancy in my regard that had found a home in her heart? Was I admitting failure as a

224

mother by giving my consent? Was relinquishing my authority truly the best strategy for Tram?

"If you have any doubts about signing, I can come back another time," Jewel interrupted, noting my hesitancy.

What she took for uncertainty was in realty just poking at my doubts and summoning my memories for comfort. I was seeking a release through escape.

Picking up the paper, I gave it a quick read and signed it.

"What about Tram's clothes?" Jewel asked. "Can I help you pack?"

I headed for my daughter's room and gathered her belongings. Jewel followed at my heels. Reaching for her books, shoes and make-up, I placed them in a sack and handed them to my mother-in-law. Taking the bag from my outstretched hand, she turned to leave.

"Don't worry. Everything will be alright," she told me. "I'll call to let you know how Tram is doing. I am sure that one day, she will be thankful—not now, but in the future, when she understands how hard you tried to make her happy."

With a few words and a slam of the door, she was gone, and likewise all traces of my daughter. Children grow, mature and leave home to make their own destinies. Parents step aside, excited to await the bloom of accomplishments living in their dreams from birth, eager to stand tall and proud.

But this was a different turning point. This was a premature exit, promising neither joy nor lofty expectations. At most, it was a temporary remedy, the outcome of which I could only hope would be positive.

A month later, I received a call from my ex-husband, Jim.

"Listen, Bảo, Tram wants to live with me," he announced. "I also think it would be a good idea if Phong comes along."

"If Phong tells me he wants to live with you, I will not contest his decision. He's free to go. But I will ask him."

"I would no longer be responsible for child support if Tram lived with me."

"Are you sending checks to the family she is staying with?"

"No, I haven't."

"What about Phuong and Thaun? They're still living with me, but you never send a penny for them."

"Phuong and Thaun aren't mine. I have no obligation to maintain them. Besides, I don't have any money, anyway."

"How can you take care of Phong and Tram if you don't have any money? It's expensive to raise children today."

"Well, it's a lot less costly if we live together," he replied.

"OK, send the plane tickets. As soon as I receive them, Tram will be on her way to North Carolina."

"What about Phong?"

"I'll let him decide if he wants to live with you and I'll honor his decision."

When I hung up the receiver, I summoned Phong.

"Tram is going to live with Jim in North Carolina," I said. "Would you like to go also?"

His response was silence. Fixing his gaze on the tips of his toes, he shrugged his shoulders almost with nonchalance. I turned, removing my presence from the room, and Phong trailed behind.

227

"OK, Mom, I'll go with Tram," he said.

As soon as the tickets arrived, Phong and Tram took off to live with their father. Feeling as if a weight had been lifted off my chest, I focused on Danny and my remaining family, unaware that my worries were far from over.

I didn't hear anything about Tram for a while, and accepted the initial silence as good news; I felt relieved not to have to deal with her rebellious escapades.

However, a year later, during a conversation with Phong, I discovered that Tram had opted to abandon Jim and live with friends in North Carolina. She had rejected Jim also. Though a part of me could have felt vindicated, there was no comfort in Phong's news.

"Mom, I miss you. I'd like to visit for the summer. Could you send me a plane ticket?"

I allowed my son to cajole me into satisfying his request. I phoned the airlines and sent him the ticket

Phong arrived chatty, with lots of stories to tell about his life with Jim. It was a joy to see him and to note how much he had grown. Settling in to his own room, he remained for the duration of his summer vacation before returning to North Carolina.

Two months thereafter, he phoned, announcing he had decided to come back

228

home. I secretly enjoyed my victory, and the return of my prodigal son . Drawing a deep breath to get my bearings, I bought the plane ticket and prepared to take on the necessary parental tasks.

First on my to-do list was enrolling Phong in school. Therefore, the following morning, I made certain he was assured a seat in the neighborhood middle school.

Though it was scarcely without glitches, Phong seemed to readjust rather smoothly to his return. Since he was now older, he was agreeable to accepting responsibility and showed a desire to work in the restaurant after school and on weekends. He was ambitious; he finished middle school and went forward with his education until he turned sixteen.

As a young man with a mind of his own, his relationship with Danny became conflicted. He resented his stepdad's intervention in his life and opted to move out. He found a roommate, a male friend from the Philippines, and continued to work in the restaurant.

Away from home and parental supervision, Phong discovered a newfound freedom. Exercising his independent decision-making right, he dropped out of school. Shortly thereafter, perhaps due to a series of professional rejections, he realized the importance and value of education in the job market and obtained his GED while employed as an apartment manager.

Determined and goal oriented, he noticed his achievements were coming in dribbles and drizzles. Opportunities dwindled, forcing him to sit quietly and take inventory of his life and aspirations. Mourning his lack of qualifications, he flipped the verdict around and acquired an electrician's license in 2004. Today, Phong travels from coast to coast as a troubleshooter.

Once Tram and Phong had departed the fold, I reflected on the vicissitudes of my life. It certainly had been a carousel of adversity, shattered dreams and painful pressures, spun by an often-turbulent current of ill winds. Yet, much as I questioned my survival skills, I never crawled into waves of self-pity inflated by thoughts of being doomed to a luckless destiny.

Instead, I channeled my energy into marveling about my own strength and resistance, which had kept me from a psychiatric hospital experience or dying from the overburdening stress. However, the turmoil did wreck havoc, injuring my personality and eventually my physical well-being. I became a stranger to myself, often questioning who I was. I gazed at my reflection in the mirror, scarcely recognizing the image gazing back at me.

My attention and concentration were compromised. Forgetful and easily distracted, I became unduly anxious and frustrated.

Often, an annoying malaise would force me to halt my tasks, take a break from work and seek comfort and refuge from nature.

On weekends, I drove alone through the Columbia Gorge. I stood before its sprouting waterfalls, hoping to cleanse my spirit from the toxicity of my life. When the wind shifted in my direction, I shut my eyes, welcoming the cool tingle of spray on my forehead and cheeks. It was as if I were depending on the trees, grass, waterfalls and animals to soothe my pain and heal my wounds. But would it work? And if yes, for how long?

Chapter 11
Different Winds

I faced each day thankful for the opportunity to witness the sunrise, struggling to keep my focus positive despite the curve balls thrown in my direction. Two of my children were still living at home; therefore, I was still involved in parenting.

Enterprising and responsible, Phuong, a sophomore at Mt. Hood Community College, financed her education by working at Oak Tree, a men's retail clothing store in Clackamas Town Center. Thaun, a tenth-grade student at Reynolds High, assumed a paper route to earn some extra pocket money.

Danny, employed as a carpet cleaner for Stanley Steamer, counted $600 in his monthly pay envelope. Certainly, we were living from paycheck to paycheck, not exactly in the lap of luxury. Leasing a space in the College Square Shopping Center, adjacent to our apartment in Gresham, I continued my tailoring business, spending all my hard-earned wages on provisions for the family.

233

Although every family member contributed in one way or another, our earnings were scarce and often did not stretch to cover all the bills unless we dipped into our savings.

After a little over a year of hair-tugging hardship, my tailoring business boasted a full roster of clients. Money was beginning to come in!

When Danny obtained full-time employment in the Army National Guard, his pay scale escalated to $2,300 a month. Life had definitely taken a turn for the better. Our backbreaking work schedules finally were netting fruit. Perhaps it was payback time.

Although far from reveling in extravagance, we were able to satisfy our monthly bills. My dream of a good night's sleep was more than wishful thinking or a fleeting whimsy. I could count on twisting and turning, wide eyed, to the rhythm of Danny's breathing with less frequency. It was a tiny ray of sunshine in a sky overpopulated with dense clouds. Sometimes, we must be grateful for small favors.

When the lease on my shop came due, I opted not to renew, transferring my business to my home. I took on tailoring jobs from the J. Riggins men's clothing shops in Clackamas Mall and Lloyd Center. Soon, I was inundated with customers. Clothing lay in many tiers on my sofa and armchairs. I was overwhelmed, not necessarily from the workload but from the added responsibility to my customers. I worked late into the evenings, with the moon often casting shadows along the contours of my hands as I stitched, painstakingly avoiding any slip-ups, errors or sloppy results.

Nominating Thaun as my apprentice, I taught him the art of hemming trousers. Once I felt comfortable with his work, I entrusted him with the task.

Additionally, he began retrieving and delivering the altered clothing—a great time-saver in my busy day.

Life went along smoothly, without too many glitches, for about two years—until August 1993, when, during a delivery, Thaun was informed by the manager of the J. Riggins Lloyd Center Mall store that my alteration services would no longer be needed.

"Mom, there is no more work for you," he said, returning empty handed. "A new alteration shop opened in the mall and they prefer to send their customers directly there instead of wasting time fitting and pinning in the shop, while other customers are impatient to make their purchases."

His dismal facial expression, unfocused gaze and furrowed brow revealed a discouraged, frantic spirit.

"I have to look for another job," he said. "The paper route is not enough. It pays hardly anything." Eager neither for my reply nor a suggestion, Thaun absented himself from my company. His thoughts and feelings were more than obvious. He certainly had my compassion.

Lifting the telephone receiver with an unsteady hand, I phoned Melissa, the manager at J. Riggins in the Clackamas Mall. As soon as I heard her familiar "hello," I told her about Thaun's experience earlier.

"Bảo, I doubt the manager failed to check the credentials and reputation of the new alterations shop before he decided to send his customers over."

"Does J. Riggins have a specific policy for the alterations part of the business?" I asked, searching for a loophole.

"Not to my knowledge. But I'll phone the manager at corporate to get more info and I'll get back to you."

"Thanks. Let me know. That may help me understand what's going on."

I breathed a sigh of discontent, skeptical about the results of her telephone call. Maybe I had to face the reality that a much-needed part of my business was gone.

The whistling kettle announced that the water was ready for tea, interrupting my thoughts. When the phone rang, I glanced at it, immobile. If I responded, my ability to hope would be quashed by certainty.

"Mom, aren't you getting the phone?" Thaun shouted, irritated, between the fifth and sixth ring.

Grabbing the receiver, I heard Melissa's voice. "Bảo, there is neither a contract nor anything in writing regarding your services. I really doubt you have any leeway for legal recourse."

Reevaluating my situation, I realized there was no need for panic, since I had in my possession an agreement with the Clackamas Mall store. My affiliation was secure—or so I thought! A few days later, I delivered the clothes to J. Riggins. Walking over to greet Melissa, I was somewhat stunned by her somber expression.

"Bảo," she whispered, "I gave thirty days' notice. I'm resigning."

"It won't be the same without you," I said, sad to learn of her intentions.

About a month later, after Melissa had departed, I arrived with a delivery and introduced myself to the new manager.

Peering at me through tortoise-shell spectacles, he nodded his acknowledgment of my greeting.

"Come back in ten minutes," he mumbled, "it's very busy here today." Customers excused him from making small talk.

Agreeing, I strolled around the mall and returned fifteen minutes later.

"Listen, Bảo," he said, clearing his throat, "your services are no longer needed."

"Does this mean you're firing me? I don't understand this decision."

"Yes, I'm letting you go… I'm sorry."

"May I ask why I'm being terminated? Is my work no longer acceptable?"

"No, Bảo, this has nothing to do with your work. This is a business decision."

"Let me try to understand this strategy. You fire people who do good work for no valid reason and call it a business decision. Honestly, I don't get it. How can this *decision* be profitable for your business?"

Lowering his gaze to escape mine, he shuffled his feet, jingled his keys and expected me to accept his explanation. The whole pathetic scenario took on a traitorous nature, betrayed by the shameful look splashed across his face.

Realizing I was just squandering time, I left. Wastefulness was unproductive. Instead, I decided to just let it go and move on. Usually, when one door closes, another one opens. It was up to me to walk through and continue my journey.

Returning home, I settled myself with a cup of freshly brewed tea and the daily newspaper, allowing the sweet, exotic scent of jasmine to soothe my injured spirit. Quickly browsing through the local and foreign events, I gazed over at the ads, noticing the announcement of the sale of a teriyaki fast-food restaurant.

I turned the idea of reentering the restaurant business over in my mind several times, recalling my experiences with the food industry in Việt Nam during the late '60s. I had been successful despite the war and political turbulence. Why couldn't I do it again?

Toying with the idea to buy the restaurant was a creative fantasy that came to fruition two years thereafter with the inauguration of Chat's Teriyaki.

Innovative and enterprising, I expanded and tweaked the menu selections, incorporating fried rice, egg rolls and stir-fried vegetables, all while honoring the original bill of fare: teriyaki beef, chicken sticks, steamed rice, carrot sticks with ranch dressing, and Japanese-garden, homemade dressing.

Thaun and I organized the restaurant, hiring John Peter, Ryan and Phuong to join the staff. John and I worked the morning shift from ten until two, Monday through Friday and often on weekends.

Running two businesses in addition to satisfying my familial obligations, I soon found myself juggling a grueling schedule. As soon as I arrived home, I would check the telephone answering machine for messages from customers in need of alterations. Trying to bulldoze my frustrations, anxiety and exhaustion into a distant closet, I hoped that once out of mind, they would somehow evaporate from my life.

I had too much to do and too many responsibilities to allow stress to slacken my pace. Implementing a functional time-management plan, I dedicated mornings to the restaurant, afternoons to tailoring and evenings to night-school English classes. Though it was hectic, it worked—but would it change my life?

In April 1995, the lease on the restaurant came due. Not anticipating any drawbacks, we contacted the landlord. Several days later, he informed us in writing of his intention to renege on the renewal option. I protested, but he let me know that he planned to utilize the space for his own business. Once again, I found a huge obstacle in my path—one that would cost hard-earned money.

Refusing to wallow under the weight of a defeatist attitude, we searched for another location—a quest that did not result in a positive outcome.

Either the rents were too exorbitant or the locations were unbefitting a successful business. Eventually, our sole option was to sell the restaurant—a decision that lost us $50,000.

In an attempt to heal our latest wounds and try to safeguard what remained of our sanity, we flew off to Hawaii's Big Island for a brief escape from it all, checking into the Royal Waikoloan beachfront hotel. The setting, the food and the relaxing, laid-back

241

atmosphere were just what we needed to unwind our twisted, mangled nerves.

Dining on the island's specialties of steamed Kalua pig, fresh-caught mahimahi and Polynesian sour chicken, we also had the opportunity to conclude our meals with the rich fullness of one of Hawaii's aromatic coffees. After satiating our appetites, we quenched our thirst for the state's exotic culture by visiting lava fields, coffee farms, secluded beaches on the Kona Coast, and the Hawaii Volcanoes National Park.

Three days later, we flew to Maui and visited the East Maui Volcano in Haleakala ("house of the sun") National Park, Maui's highest peak. Its awesome history boasts a lengthy list of eruptions.

When it was time to go home, we departed the island in silence, contemplating the wonders of nature and the divine force who had designed and orchestrated it all.

Although the flight back was long and tedious, we felt well rested and rejuvenated from our trip. Renewed, we jumped back into the daily grind defined as our fate.

For a few months, life continued in its usual pattern. I did alterations at home and continued my evening English classes. Although it was not an extraordinary time, I had attained a small measure of inner serenity that I dared neither dote on nor question, fearful it would evaporate into thin air as a substance-challenged figment of my imagination. Once in a while, it is best not to focus on blessings.

Then, unexpectedly, on March 19, 1996, while I was preparing dinner, the phone rang.

"Should I get it, Mom?" Thaun yelled. Before I could respond, the receiver had touched my ear.

"Hello, ma'am, this is Charles Rue from Central Casting. Am I speaking with Bảo?"

"Yes, this is Bảo, how may I help you?" I asked, my interest peaking.

"Would you consider working in a film?" his husky voice asked.

Caught off guard, it took me several seconds to get my bearings. A film? What was he talking about? Why would I be asked to work in a film? I was not an actress.

Suddenly, the precision of my memory kicked in. Just about a year earlier, I had applied to an "actors wanted, with or without experience" insert in the classifieds, never believing Central Casting would ever deem me suitable for serious consideration.

"Oh, yes, Mr. Rue! I'd like to. What do I have to do? When do I start?"

"Well, the process entails coming into the studio with your resume and filming a screen test so we can determine the best role for you. The camera is connected to a computer that automatically forwards the photos to different companies casting for commercials. Your responsibility for the cost of this procedure is two hundred and forty-nine dollars. If you think this is a good fit for you, we can set up an appointment."

"Thank you, sir," I said politely. "May I think about it and get back to you?"

"Sure, Bảo, give me a call when you decide."

Two days later, walking through the door of my home, I noticed a blinking, red light flashing on the answering machine. Hitting the "play" button, I heard the leaden voice of Charles Rue: "Bảo, give me a call when you get a chance, I'd like to talk to you."

I was curious. With a quivering finger, I dialed his number. He picked up on the first ring.

"Bảo, I have a job for you," he said, excited. "How soon can you get to the studio?"

With one quick phone call, I had become an actress.

That evening, in bed, I thrashed about, thumping my pillow in an unsuccessful bid to catch some shut eye. I focused on imagined images of starring in an Oscar-winning film. However, the moment the sun rose, introducing a new day, the curtain was lowered on my theatrical scenario.

However, reality was not as kaleidoscopic. In lieu of a major motion picture, I was starring in a commercial. The set was a church, the scene a wedding. Seventy-five women were dressed in bridal gowns and seventy-five men in tuxes. I had no idea what role I would play or if I would have any dialogue to memorize. Nevertheless mesmerized by the camera, lights and colorful make-up artists, I was soon swept into the cinematic whirlwind.

"Bảo," Charles called, approaching. "I have another job for you. The pay is between forty and one hundred dollars for a full day's shoot. We start March 26—are you in?"

"Sure, count me in," I said. The money was pretty good and it had all the earmarks of a fun experience.

It was March 25. Having made it through an encore sleepless night of pillow wrestling, I jumped out of bed, ran to the phone and dialed the job hotline number to get directions for the shoot. Immediately after selecting the information option, I was connected with an operator who instructed all interested parties to meet the cast and crew in Portland Meadows' parking lot no later than 7:30 a.m. the following day.

"Will we proceed with our cars?" I asked.

"No, ma'am, a bus will take everyone to the filming location. Please bring white shoes and a white bra, as you will dress as a bride— all in white."

Ransacking my drawers I realized I did not own the piece of lingerie requested. Heading out to Kmart, I immediately remedied the situation. Packing a small bag, I retired early, though far too anxious and excited to relax, I did not close my eyes.

The following morning, in the darkness preceding the initial glow of daybreak, I swung my legs from under the covers and stepped out of bed. Proceeding with my plan to head for the Portland Meadows parking lot, I showered and dressed myself. Not pausing for breakfast, I hurried to my destination, arriving precisely at seven o'clock, believing I would be one of the first passengers.

Instead, I was surprised to see that one bus was already filled to capacity. Noting my distressed expression, the driver slammed his fist against the window to draw my attention.

Pointing to another bus, he shouted, "That one is empty."

I boarded the second bus destined for the Academy Chapel in Vancouver, Washington. Stroking my hair, I tried to imagine how the day would unravel. Suddenly, the sun, like a fiery, red ball, cut through the darkness. I marveled at how it sprouted out of the wild, spreading a magnificent radiance across the sky.

"What a beautiful sunrise," I whispered. "What a beautiful gift of nature." Costing nothing, it was worth a fortune.

We got on the road and eventually, the bus came to a halt in front of a picturesque, stone chapel set on a tract of well-manicured land. The flourish of trees and shrubs created a romantic ambiance.

Once inside, we were given applications to read and fill in. Praying the emotion of the moment would not result in a hand tremor and illegible handwriting, I signed my name. Returning the forms, I was given a wedding gown.

"Try this on, Bảo," the costumer told me. "We need to see if it needs any alterations."

While the other women waited for a vacant fitting room, the men slipped into their tuxedos behind a bulky, green curtain. Once dressed, we waited for further instructions,

247

standing idly, engaging in cocktail-party-type banter until around three o'clock when thankfully, turkey sandwiches, fruit and cookies were served.

While we satisfied our famished stomachs, the supervisor pranced around, fastening black-plastic trash bags around our necks to protect the dresses. The interlude relaxed our nerves, actually drawing chuckles and laughs from the rather somber group, all trussed in uncomfortable bridal wear.

Eventually, we met the "minister"—an event signaling the start of the endless "I dos" pronounced in unison while we listened for the echoing clacks of the clapper that told the crew to cut, to stop filming.

The filming finished at eight o'clock that evening. Thrilled to be at liberty to peel off the cumbersome wedding gown I had been wearing since early morning, I quickly let loose, kicking off the four-inch steeple-spiked heels that had decorated my toes with huge, painful blisters. It's amazing how women will butcher their bodies for an attractive, appealing look.

En route back to Portland, I couldn't help reviewing the day's events. Certainly, it was an eye-opening experience to learn how much time and effort were at the nucleus of a two-minute commercial.

Like a rude gust of unannounced wind, the surprise came a couple of weeks later, when I received a check in the amount of $70 for my commercial participation!

Although I enjoyed the excitement and vibrancy of the camera and lights, the money I earned for twelve hours of difficult work seemed a rather inadequate compensation. However, I consented to the filming of two more commercials—"Difference," in which I starred as the protagonist, and a second that had me cast in the role of a business manager. A free lunch and drinks were offered as part of the benefits package. Furthermore, it was fascinating to discover the ABCs of commercials, how they were choreographed and filmed.

A practical person, I realized my finances were locked in stagnant limbo. Inflation was crawling, and if I didn't search for income-growing options, my hopes for a better life would lose validity.

Browsing the classifieds had, in the past, netted decent opportunities; therefore, there was little if any reason to believe my time would be wasted. I settled down with a pencil poised between my thumb and index finger and a cup of tea, expecting a positive outcome.

A quick read left me curious about an ad for an opening at Sleazy Sleepwear for Horses in Gresham, a small town east of Portland. I chuckled over the company name, imagining a horse dressed in sexy lingerie. Fantasizing aside, I phoned to express my intention to pursue employment.

My initial contact with the human resources director went well, and my inquiries regarding the nature of the job description were met with a clear-cut description of the company's offerings.

I was briefed on the product line and told that Sleazy Sleepwear manufactured all kinds of accessories for horses—stretch hoods, shoulder guards, fly and stable sheets/blankets, as well as various items for house pets.

"Ma'am, would you like to come in and fill out an employment application?" the human resources director asked.

"Yes. Would eleven o'clock today be OK?"

"That's fine."

When I arrived, I was interviewed by both Valerie and Gary, the manager and boss, respectively.

"What kind of experience have you had?" Valerie asked.

"I've been doing alterations and tailoring work for over twenty-five years."

"Have you ever worked with commercial sewing machines?"

"Yes, I have always used them," I replied.

Valerie picked up a piece of scrap fabric and walked over to the cover-stitch machine.

"Let me show you how this works," she said, inserting the material under the needle and locking it in place before setting the machine in motion.

"Are these commercial machines very costly?" I asked, keeping my eyes fixed on her hands.

"They run about six thousand dollars."

"What else do you manufacture besides horse apparel and accessories?' I questioned.

"We also make clothing for people— vests, coats, hats and swimwear."

"I assume I would have to purchase my own machine."

"Yes."

"Would I be able to work here on your machine for a couple of weeks? I'd like to see if I can earn a sufficient amount to cover the expense of buying my own. Then I will sign a contract with you."

"That would work," she said, smiling.

"How many hours a week would you consider working?" Gary interjected.

"I'd like to work from eight in the morning until two in the afternoon, two days a week. Would that be OK?"

"What do you think, Valerie?" Gary asked, nervously tugging on his lower lip.

"That's fine with me," she said. We shook hands, sealing our agreement.

Thus, I began working two days a week at Sleazy Sleepwear for Horses. Within four weeks, I calculated my income capacity, surmising I could drum up sufficient business to help offset the cost of a new sewing machine. Researching the new and pre-owned retail markets, I did comparison studies to see where I could get the best price without sacrificing quality.

Eventually, my persistence and diligence paid off. I made a deal with the Northwest Industrialist Company to trade my old Singer Serger and Consew Serger machines for a new Consew Serger and a used Pfaff, which allowed me to sew both straight and zigzag stitches. My financial responsibility was $1,800.

My next move was to head over to Dave's Sew Tag home business, where I purchased a Pegasus cover-stitching machine for $6,000. I was fully equipped; now, I needed to work not only to cover but to earn on my investment.

The plan was to retrieve the fabrics from Sleazy Sleepwear and sew the garments at home. It worked quite well. Then, one day, I received a phone call from Gary.

"Bảo, Valerie and I would like to ask if you would be willing to work part time at the factory. Two of our employees are leaving and we could certainly use your help."

Although I preferred to work at home, where I was able to answer calls from customers to promote additional business, I realized I could not refute their solicitation for my assistance. Therefore, I accepted, even if somewhat reluctantly. They had been more than gracious to me and I felt my intervention during their difficult moment was expected. Despite the upgraded, hectic schedule, I successfully completed my tailoring jobs at home while serving my customers with bravura and precision.

Additionally, as if I was not busy enough, I considered starting another business. Responding to a dry-cleaning "for sale" ad, I took time off to preview the shop. However, reflecting on the time and energy commitment part of the success equation, I nixed the idea.

It was probably the right moment to begin enjoying life. Pushing fifty, I realized I was no longer in the springtime of my life, and autumn was fast approaching. Nonetheless, when I glanced towards the horizon, I noticed there was still a discernible glow. It was far from over.

Perhaps it was time to shift into a lower gear. I wanted to pursue my English studies and improve my reading and writing skills to fill the void left by not having the opportunity for a good education. This failing left me forced to fight harder and longer to win my battles.

Unwilling to dip into the counterproductive world of self-pity, I pulled myself up from the abyss. I focused on my accomplishments—finding employment in a foreign country as an immigrant, and running my restaurants and tailoring businesses. Tenacious, determined, persistent and ambitious despite my academic and language handicaps, I recognized that I more than

254

merited a break. But, would professional and familial circumstances permit such a luxury?

Chapter 12
Departure and Arrival: A New Journey

In December 1997, looking for a more celebratory way to usher in the new year, Danny and I packed a couple of bags and headed for The Dalles, Oregon. Festivities were organized at the Best Western Motel situated on the bank of the Columbia River. All we had to do was arrive.

The weather was far from cooperative for the drive. A deluging rain obscured our view as we drove through the gorge, creating a visibility factor bordering on precarious. Danny turned on the radio just in time to hear a meteorologist announce that the main road was shut down due to dangerous rockslides.

Taking a detour, we arrived safely, though with marked delay. Within minutes of pulling into the driveway, we were inside the motel, relieved to have survived the ordeal unscathed.

The concierge was polite, though scarce of words. After signing the register, Danny and I were handed a key and given directions

259

to our room. Danny carried the bags and we proceeded to our quarters for the evening.

Eyes alive with the excitement of adventure, I was amazed to note the huge bay window opening onto the rippling river. In the background, snow-topped mountains glistened under the noonday sun awakened from a lengthy sleep, during which dark clouds had emptied their bowels relentlessly. The rain-lacquered lawn was tidy and cropped short probably a day earlier.

Famished from the drive and emotional expenditure of energy, we showered quickly and went for lunch. Upon our return, we noticed a big, multicolored bouquet of flowers and a perfectly chilled bottle of champagne set on the desk in our room. The holiday spirit was alive and flourishing.

Danny made dinner reservations for seven o'clock at the restaurant next door to the motel, asking the *maître d'* for a window seat. We arrived on time, eager to enjoy the holiday evening. After a romantic, two-hour repast, we returned to the motel for the New Year's Eve festivities. In total, there were about twelve couples animatedly eager to greet 1998.

Danny and I ordered drinks, danced a couple of slow dances, and then returned to our table, ready to have another round of drinks. I was not a dancer by nature, but fueled by the cool, sweet cocktails I had ingested, I obliged again later on, not only to keep my husband happy but to fit in with the spirited crowd. We danced until the birth of the new year, popping balloons and shouting, "Happy New Year!" and secretly praying it truly would be a good year for us.

Inebriated from overindulgence in libations and still in party mode, we departed and returned to our room, undressed and literally tumbled headfirst into bed. Sleep, I thought, would come willingly after the long, eventful day that had begun predawn.

But, I was in error. Thrashing about, periodically thumping my pillow, rest did not come until five o'clock. Four hours later, I awoke, took a leisurely, steamy bubble bath, and returned between the sheets. Wide awake, Danny eyed me curiously.

"If you don't get dressed, I'm going to tackle you," he whispered raucously.

"Are you threatening me?"

"Yeah. Oh, yeah," he continued, grinning sheepishly. "So, what are you going to do about it?"

"Probably nothing at all," I responded teasingly as he rolled over, immediately making good on his threat.

Nineteen ninety-eight arrived interspersed with feelings of positivism and elation. Focusing on optimistic thoughts, I believed, was a valued tone setter and certainly more exhilarating than digging emotional ditches or centering on all the bad that could possibly occur. I always did my best to be upbeat despite the issues and dilemmas I was struggling to overcome. Somehow, the new year sets the pace for the 365 days.

Several days later, sobered from the celebrations, I returned to work, sewing shoulder guards for horses.

When the phone rang, I debated if I should interrupt my stitching to respond or just let it go to voicemail. A raging curiosity determined the outcome.

"Hello, Bảo, this is Pat. I want to tell you about a dance contest on Tuesday. Do you think you would be interested?"

Surprised to hear from my screen agent, I was momentarily silenced.

"Bảo, the theme is California summer," he continued, not waiting for my response. "You must dress in bright colors and wear a straw hat and dark glasses. It's going to be a lot of fun—I think you'll have a good time."

"I don't think so Pat, that's not for me," I began. "You know, I'm not into dancing. It's just not my thing."

"Oh, come on, Bảo," he insisted, chuckling, "Don't be such a drag. Just come on over—it'll be fun."

"Alright, Pat, I'll come to watch, but not to dance."

"Great! Eleven o'clock on Tuesday at the Safeway store."

"Dancing in a grocery store?" I asked, laughing. "That's a new one."

"Sure, why not? It's a big store with lots of room for dancing."

I had to admit that Pat's sense of humor and proposition to dance in the Safeway intrigued me.

My mind created images of couples dancing in the aisles while shoppers

263

maneuvered their carts around gyrating bodies to avoid running them over.

Never one to shy away from a challenge, I drove to Mervyns early Monday morning and bought a straw hat and matching purse, a pair of white pants, black sandals decorated with white, perpendicular stripes, a white-and-pink-print shirt, a silver chain belt and a pair of sunglasses. If nothing else, I would look the part!

Though my arms were filled with packages as I made my way to the car, my purse was $90 lighter. But, I was certain I was ready just in case I had a change of mind regarding participation in the contest.

From the onset, I had assumed we'd be dancing as a group, and I could conveniently get lost among the others. Maybe it would not be all that bad. However, the scenario filmed in my mind little resembled the actual shoot, in which each person was instructed to dance solo for thirty seconds following the start of the music.

The best dancers would receive a thousand-dollar prize and a commercial contract with Very California Avocado Company. When I understood the concept, I stepped back, edging over to the attendance roster to cancel my name. Anticipating my move, the cameraman blocked me. Plan B called for a trip to the ladies' room and an eventual escape.

"Bảo, take your time," the cameraman reassured me when I announced my intention to head for a restroom break. "We'll call your name later."

Rushing out, I tried to review in my mind the two-step, awkwardly moving my feet to simulate the dance moves. I did not feel good about my challenged status and hoped my brief recess would allow the crew to forget about me.

Luck was not my companion that day. My name was called as soon as I returned. Taking a deep breath, I edged myself into the center and waited for the music before performing my rendition of the two-step, secretly praying I would not make of myself a ridiculous spectacle.

"*Brava,* Bảo," a spectator shouted, slamming his palms together. "Well done!"

Uncertain about my performance despite the gentleman's impulsive gesture of approval, I asked Pat for his evaluation.

"You have potential," he said, smiling. "You know the dance steps, but you must work on quickening the pace."

Since I was not interested in a dance career, I thanked him for his input but worried little about improving my performance.

The prize was won by a gentleman who was immediately awarded the contract.

"I won't survive if you ever ask me to try out again for a dancing job," I told Pat. "You'll kill me!"

Though I was being a bit dramatic, realizing that dancing would never kill me, I would soon discover I was harboring a time bomb that would eventually change my life. Awakening one morning feeling exhausted and queasy, I was so weak I couldn't rise from the bed. When Danny returned from work and found me still in bed, his expression changed from perplexed to concerned.

"You've been in bed all day?" he asked. "What's the matter?"

"I'm tired. I think I need to slow down and perhaps get some more sleep."

"How can I help? What do you want to do?" Danny asked, looking to me for a clue.

"Maybe we could spend the weekend in Cannon Beach," I suggested.

"How about a drive to Lincoln City instead?" he asked. "I'd like to visit the casino."

"OK, that sounds like fun. I'd like to see the casino, too. But could we maybe stop overnight at Cannon Beach before returning home?"

"Sure."

"Thanks, dear, I really need the rest. Besides, I don't want to wait another five years before taking some time off to enjoy ourselves. We have the money—all the bills are paid on time."

"That's thanks to you, Bảo. You're an excellent manager. Did I ever tell you I'm proud of you?"

"Well, actually it's a combined effort. It takes both of us to make it all run smoothly."

"I'm really glad I'm married to you," Danny said, planting a kiss on my cheek.

The following morning, after a light breakfast, we slipped our bags into the car and took off for Lincoln City. However, having failed to call for reservations, we were surprised to find the hotel booked to capacity. A quick visit to the casino soon turned excitement into boredom; therefore, when Danny counted a loss of $20, we departed. This part of the trip was nothing to boast about. I was hopeful that things would improve.

As agreed, we headed for the Surf Sand Resort in Cannon Beach. Although Danny was far from shy in critiquing his entree as not quite up to par, we did enjoy a leisurely dinner. Laughing at his furrowed brow every time his teeth clenched a piece of steak, I accused him of being spoiled by the products of my culinary skills.

After dinner, we took a dip in the pool and a relaxing soak in the hot tub, then headed for our room to end the day with a romantic hour of lovemaking. Exhaustion and happiness merged. Once Danny was on his side, snoring, my mind drifted over the past ten years of our marriage.

Although a very deep love kept us together, I had to admit we did have our issues and conflicts. We fought, sometimes violently, and our marital skirmishes often led us to ponder divorce.

However, peeling back the layers and evaluating my husband for who and what he was, I realized he was a man of substance—more importantly, a keeper.

Although he had a bad temper, which I sometimes had difficulties dealing with, Danny was a good man.

In the new year, I vowed to listen more to my husband's concerns and complaints, and to offer suggestions and advice on how to improve his failings both personal and financial. I expended a lot of time and energy to make our marriage work. I had made a commitment and wanted to honor it in full this time.

Towards this end, I explained the principles of correct budgeting to him. I planned money management strategies that involved collecting a monthly paycheck instead of a weekly or biweekly.

"Why monthly? So we can go broke all at once?" Danny asked.

"No, you missed the point. With a monthly paycheck, we can first satisfy all our bills then budget the remaining funds as we please. But, if we do it your way, with a weekly or biweekly stipend, we spend on incidentals, the bills remain unpaid at month's end, and we are in debt due to lack of funds and faulty management."

Danny gathered the simple threads of my reasoning and listened to my words.

Based on common sense, my idea was practical, sensible and realistic.

Furthermore, it contained little substance to breed serious doubt. Therefore, unable to contradict my theory, he agreed to adopt my money-management plan. Once proven successful, my mentoring became credible, inspiring him to work on the next issue: I brought to his attention: his often-out-of-control temper.

Thankfully, it worked. My husband's unruly outbursts subsided, and responsibility defeated his careless outlook. Although it took much sweat, tears and a battle against quitting, I was victorious not only in helping Danny turn his life around but in becoming a better human being.

Often, I pondered what my life would be like had I had a strong man by my side, a man who would have evaluated my strengths and weaknesses, a man who would have deemed me worthy of retuning the balance of my failings and attributes to tip the scale in a positive direction.

Who would I have been today if I had chosen a life companion willing and able to lead the way, making me a better woman? Though a valid query, I had no answer. On the other hand, I sometimes questioned if I was perhaps more significant and productive in the leadership role, sharing the fruits of my experiences and knowledge. After all, isn't it nobler to extend a helping hand than to receive one?

Late spring was a very busy time for me. I worked on three films in addition to my job at Sleazy Sleepwear. Simultaneously, some memorable moments were happening in the family.

On June 6, Danny and I sat proudly as our son, Thaun Nha, graduated from Mt. Hood Community College with an associate's degree in automotive technology. The ceremony was moving, and my mind kept drifting back to the tiny infant I'd swaddled in white linens and rocked in my arms. Now, in the blink of an eye, he was a young man filled with dreams.

Although we invited Thaun to dinner after the graduation, he expressed a preference to celebrate in the company of his friends.

"Have fun," I told him, willing to let him spend the evening as he wished, "but please do not drink too much. Remember, we are leaving for Key West in the morning and you promised to get up early to drive us to the airport."

"Don't worry, Mom, I won't drink too much," he promised me.

After a light supper, Danny and I retired early. The following morning, our Northwest Airlines flight departed promptly at seven o'clock, as scheduled. At midday, we deplaned in St. Paul, Minnesota, and caught a connecting flight to Miami.

Once in Miami, we picked up our compact car at Alamo, which was part of our vacation package. The car was uncomfortable and for some inexplicable reason, I felt the beginning of a migraine accompanied by unpredictable waves of nausea, which I was unable to shake during most of the vacation.

Too queasy to even ponder dinner, I sipped a glass of water and picked at some boiled rice while Danny satisfied his hearty appetite with a substantial selection of food. Wiping his lips when he was through, he pushed his chair from the table and stood.

"Are you up for a drive?" he asked. "I'd like to head for Florida City."

Nodding my head in agreement, I cringed at the thought of another bumpy ride in that uncomfortable toy car. But how much more awful could I possibly feel?

It took an hour to reach our planned overnight destination, the Roadway Inn Motel in Florida City. I climbed out of the car happy to be on steady ground, immediately drawing a deep breath to fight off another sudden wave of nausea that seemed to be surfacing.

"Be calm, Bảo," Danny said, gazing at my green complexion. "We'll be inside, and

272

you can kick off your shoes and lie down. Perhaps that will make you feel better."

I hoped he was right. The awful feeling in the pit of my stomach was rather disturbing. Why couldn't I shake it?

As Danny slid the key into the partially rusted lock to open the door to our room, a swarm of mosquitoes materialized before our eyes.

"Hurry, Danny—these little monsters will eat us alive if you don't get the door open," I screeched, pulling on his shirtsleeve.

"I'm doing the best I can," he said. "The key is stuck."

Eventually, we made our way into the sparsely decorated room. Much to my chagrin, I noticed it was inhabited by another group of famished mosquitoes eager to jab their stingers into our appetizing flesh.

Exhausted, hot and plagued with the throat-stinging thirst of someone who had spent endless days in the arid desert, I opened the faucet. Cupping my hands, I let the cool, running water collect in the hollow of my palms and drank, quenching my thirst.

Danny, instead, had to run out for a soft drink.

"I'll be right back," he blurted, darting out the door.

"Where are you going?"

"I want to get a soda—and a can of mosquito spray."

"We're invaded here. Maybe you better get two cans," I teased.

During his absence, I did as he suggested. Removing my shoes, I reclined on the bed, closing my eyes for a few minutes.

I dozed off, awakening fifteen minutes later just as Danny crossed the threshold swinging a brown paper bag.

"Did you bring me some beef jerky?" I asked, feeling better after my rest.

"You didn't ask me to. Did you?"

"No. Did I have to? You know I like to eat jerky when I travel!"

"Yes, but you were not feeling well. You didn't eat anything and said you were nauseous. How could I even think you would want a beef jerky? But if you want, I'll go back and get some for you."

"Wait a moment," I said, slipping into my shoes. "Let me comb my hair and I'll come with you. I'd like to take a look at the town. Maybe there's a Chinese restaurant around here."

We climbed back into the car and drove down the street until Danny pulled into the parking area in front of a store.

"I don't want to go in there," I told him.

"I thought you wanted some jerky."

274

"I said that I wanted to go look for a Chinese restaurant."

"You didn't say that!"

"Yes, I did. Perhaps you were not paying attention."

Sliding the transmission into reverse, Danny backed up the car. We drove about a quarter of mile before we spotted a Chinese restaurant.

"There's one," I said, pointing towards an illuminated sign with red-and-green, twinkling lights advertising the Asian eatery. My appetite had returned and I was ready to satiate it. Thankfully, I felt well and fully focused on enjoying my vacation.

Dinner was pleasant but I was wise in choosing a light menu to avoid any calamities during the drive to the Keys.

We arrived in the Florida Keys about nine the following morning. The swamps, tall bushes and fishy, humid air stirred my memories, though the change in the architectural panorama was striking compared to our last visit there. Many new, multi-sized, luxury residences sat stately along the oceanfront, altering the view of the coastline. When we drove over the familiar footbridge leading into Boca Chica Stock Island, I knew we had arrived in Key West.

We headed toward downtown, chatting animatedly about the old places I had frequented years earlier.

"I wonder if Lori's Bikini Shop is still here," I questioned aloud as Danny turned sharply on to Waterfront Street, halting at the entry of the Hilton Hotel. Our check-in went smoothly and fifteen minutes later, we headed upstairs to our oceanfront room on the second floor.

Once again, my shoes were off and I was flat on my back, stretching my muscles and tendons after the cramped car ride.

"What would you like to do now?" Danny asked.

"Do you have any brochures? I'd like to get some ideas."

"Yes, the concierge handed me several. I'm browsing through one."

"Danny, I feel so much better now that we are out of that car. Let's do something fun."

"I see that there are boats available to visit Sunset Island. It says here that boats drop people off on the island, then return every two hours to bring them back. And you can remain on the island all day if you wish."

"That sounds nice to me—what do you think?" I said, feeling rejuvenated.

"I'm still reading, Bảo. In the evening, they have a special party boat that transports people to Christmas Island just in time to catch the beautiful sunset. And you don't pay extra—it's all included in the package deal. I think I'd like to do this. How about you?"

"Sure, but I'd prefer going for a swim today and just relaxing. We can book the boat outing for tomorrow."

"Sounds like a good plan to me."

The next day, we slipped into our swimsuits, packed a light bag and boarded the boat for tiny Sunset Island. After a beautiful, twenty-minute glide at full sail, we arrived, awed by the new construction and rows of colonial homes that comprised the resort, which was, surprisingly, scarcely populated. Perhaps the throngs of people arrived in a different season.

Touring the island, we took some photos for posterity and then returned to the hotel around four.

Strolling around town, I tried to ruffle my memory and return to some of my old haunts.

"Excuse me, ma'am," I said, interrupting the quick stride of a passerby, "have you lived here for a long time?"

"Well, I've been here for three years," she said, grinning.

"Then perhaps you will know where the Key West Hand Print factory is?"

"Yes, sure, I know. Turn right," she directed, pointing to the street perpendicular to where I stood. "Then walk down two blocks and make a left. You will see a seasoned building on the south corner. It's right there."

"Thanks," I said, grabbing Danny under the arm.

Before searching for my old workplace, we paused, savoring the amazing view of the city and beach. The contrast was a subtle juxtaposition of sea, sand, brick and mortar. Memories flashed in my mind of the many long, seaside walks that had served as solace during my troubled times. The Atlantic had an electrifying influence—inspiring, rejuvenating, comforting.

There was something mystical about nature; its healing powers, though perhaps scientifically inexplicable, were phenomenal. It calmed my nerves and lifted my mood quicker and more efficiently than the most potent antidepressant, and all without the ghastly side effects.

Reflective and observant, Danny stood quietly beside me, honoring the scenarios he imagined were unfolding in my mind.

278

"Let's go," I whispered, upsetting the stillness. "I'd like to pass by the factory."

Although I found no traces of the factory, walking past the area brought back memories. Later, I learned it had moved to Miami. During the walk, I also discovered that Lori's Bikini Shop was closed due to the late hour.

"Bảo, where would you like to go next?" Danny asked.

"I'd like to pass my old house on Truman Street. It's just five blocks north."

"OK, lead the way!"

When we reached Truman Street, I was stunned. Most of the old homes had been torn down or renovated beyond recognition. Rows of old-style colonial houses decorated the street. My old apartment building had been replaced with a new, unfinished structure. All that remained of the original structure was the address.

The construction facelift and resulting unfamiliar look encouraged me to reminisce about the area where I had lived in military housing, about a quarter mile away. I was certain the military would have maintained its buildings.

I recalled that the Navy barracks was enclosed behind three gates in the front, back and middle. Military personnel guarded the front and back gates whereas the middle, the officers' territory, was always locked but unguarded. Massive coconut trees surrounding the area blocked any possibility for viewers to get a look.

As we walked through the area, I marveled at the wide-open gates. There, in full view, were the stately colonial houses, once almost sacredly concealed, now oozing luxury. Never would I have imagined back then the size and grandeur of these residences.

Moving along on our memory-lane journey, we visited the U.S. Naval Hospital and President Truman's house before opting to use the car to continue touring Key West.

The following morning, bags packed and my memory dusted of its accumulated debris, we departed for Miami and our eventual return to Oregon.

Although it had always been my wish to plant roots in this tropical town, returning after many years as a vacationer and tourist, I realized the impossibility of my reverie. I felt the passage of time and its irreversible effects. True, I would never forget Key West and the part of my life lived among the swaying palm trees, but that day, I realized I had to bury one of my dreams.

Even though I abandoned the time-worn thoughts of my youth, I was certain I would never forget them. The trip to Key West was more than a quick getaway—it was part of my journey of truth.

Was this the Buddha's Noble Eightfold Path? Did I have the Dharma wheel in my hand? Was this the start of my journey to end the *dukkha*—the suffering?

Chapter 13
Sự trở lại đến Việt Nam: Return to Việt Nam I

One afternoon, while cutting some fabric, I was inundated by a sudden nostalgia for my family in Việt Nam. I had left behind my son, Trung, whom my brother had adopted as well as my sister. *Wouldn't it be exhilarating to visit them?* I thought. The idea was tantalizing.

Over the years, I had kept the lines of communication open, sending my family money and gifts whenever possible. Despite the passage of time, I never stopped pining for Trung. Although I had tried to bring him to America, his adoptive status enabled the government to prohibit his emigrating to the United States.

Indisputably, the chaotic events and often dramatic vicissitudes of my life had not weakened the bond linking me with my overseas loved ones. Even though I worked and tended to the needs of my husband and

283

children, an unvarying ache in my heart kept the faces of my family back home forever present before my eyes.

Now, a seed had been planted in my mind—but would I be able to make it sprout and bloom? Would I have the joy of setting my feet on Vietnamese soil?

Would I once again experience the exotic aromas, colorful sights and familiar sounds of my native land?

My six-hour shift at Sleazy Sleepwear terminated around three o'clock. Afterwards, I completed alterations for my private customers, prepared and served dinner for Danny and the kids, and dashed off to my English class. This was my life.

Returning around nine o'clock, I noticed Danny rather involved in a computer game. However, when I crossed his path on tiptoe so as not to break the momentum of his excitement, he rose, welcoming me back with a kiss and hug.

His mood seemed carefree, playful and agreeable, and I thought it would be an opportune time to discuss my feelings about a trip to Việt Nam.

"It's a great idea, Bảo," Danny said after I shared my travel plans. "I think you should go."

"Would you like to accompany me or would you prefer I go alone?"

"I'd love to go with you, but I don't have any vacation time until July."

"That would be perfect. Don't forget, we need time to renew our passports and book the airline flights. I'll check it out after breakfast tomorrow."

Exhilarated about my planned return to Việt Nam, I had a difficult time falling asleep that night. Images of my childhood and the atrocities of war flashed through my mind, keeping me wide eyed and restless.

At the first inkling of daybreak, as a tiny speck of light invaded the darkness, I was already on my feet. Pacing up and down, careful not to tread heavily for fear of disturbing Danny, I waited for the clock to tick a decent hour, giving me a green light to phone Lu. Unlike my nearly twenty-five-year absence, my friend, Lu, had visited Việt Nam just five months earlier.

Thrilled to hear about my plans, Lu shared her contacts, making available the name and number of her travel agent, Kim Pham. When I phoned Kim, I was greeted by a gracious lady who reassured me she would take care of all the travel arrangements, including the necessary visa applications.

285

Kim suggested we reapply for passports at the post office, since ours had long expired.

"It will take about five or six weeks to get new ones," Kim said, asking us to drop by the agency to finish the arrangements.

The following day, Danny and I went to meet Kim.

Petite in stature, with a perfectly proportioned, slender body and black, glistening hair that brushed against her shoulders whenever she moved her head, Kim greeted us with a radiant smile.

"Please, sit down," she said. "I would like to get some additional information from you."

"Sure. What would you like to know?" I asked, reciprocating her bright smile.

"Bảo, I need your first and last names, date of birth, the year you immigrated to the United States, and how long you have lived here."

"Here is my driver's license," I said, pulling it from my purse. "It has my name and date of birth. This should answer some of your questions."

"Great, but I still need the other two dates."

"I'll phone you with that info later. Will that be alright?"

"Sure, perfect. I also need to know your desired departure date and how long you plan to remain in Việt Nam."

"Well, we'd like to leave on August first and stay until August twenty-fifth," Danny replied.

"Let me check the availabilities," Kim responded, swinging her chair to face the computer.

"You can leave on August fifth with an August twenty-fifth departure. How does that sound?"

"Perfect," Danny said. "Would that work for you, Bảo?"

"Sure!" I agreed, too excited to say anything more.

"You have to pay in advance," Kim said. "It will cost seventeen hundred dollars for two roundtrip tickets."

Danny pulled out his MasterCard and, several minutes later, he was in possession of our airline tickets. It was really happening—I was going back to Việt Nam!

Five weeks thereafter, we had our new passports and visas. All that remained was the compilation of a list of things I intended to take with me. The Vietnamese had explicit limits regarding items that could be imported into the country and precise tax restrictions on others.

Diligently, I lined up the items, recording the toys I bought for the grandchildren, the packages of American candy that were always much desired, as well as imperishable food provisions and medicines. I checked several times to be certain I had not been remiss in including everything.

Afterwards, we drove over to the doctor to satisfy the immunization requirements for travel to Việt Nam. Danny and I were vaccinated against Hepatitis A and polio. Additionally, we were administered an oral anti-typhoid vaccine and given a prescription for Ciprofloxacin, an antibiotic for diarrhea, and Malarone, a daily medication with a start date two days prior to departure, to stave off malaria.

Our preparations executed with precision, we were ready, though somewhat anxious when the departure date arrived. Leaving the house at eight in the evening, we drove to Portland Airport for a 4:00 a.m. flight to Seattle, where we would board the 747 that, in ten hours, would land us in Taipei, China.

The final lap of the journey was an Evan Airlines flight to Việt Nam, which brought us to Sài Gòn City at midday. An hour thereafter, we deplaned. Exhausted but excited, we passed through customs with luggage and passports in hand. Thankfully, I had not indulged in libations, even though the temptation was ever present during the endless hours in flight. Although a couple of drinks sipped amid the clouds would probably have helped me relax, from the start.

I knew I wanted be fully present in this emotional moment, which meant that my sensory system had to be as fine tuned and vigilant as possible. Premise formulated, my indulgences were limited exclusively to soda and water.

Stepping into the airport, I was immediately swathed in the bulging population of men, women and children scurrying about. The echoing intonations of spoken Vietnamese warmed my soul, swishing me back in time to my early years. Like a child set free in a toy store, I had to see it all. I was delirious. I was infatuated. I was famished for this different but familiar land that had a powerful, magnetic hold on me.

A prodigal daughter returning to the fold after a lengthy absence, I behaved like a tourist witnessing the exotic Asian culture for the first time.

I marveled at the dress. A *nouveau* influence had redesigned the scenario, enrobing the protagonists in Western garb. Though many women were dressed in the traditional *áo dài* and conical *nón lá* leaf hat, most of the men were in American-style trousers and shirts. One or two elderly gentlemen, holding firmly secured to the arm of a doting son or daughter, wore the *áo gấm* brocade coat that had been very much in vogue when I was a small child. However, it was more than evident that my recollections of Việt Nam no longer reflected reality. An evolutionary process had rearranged part of the panorama.

I questioned if perhaps my family members were realigned with the change. Would I recognize them? Twenty-five years had passed since my departure in 1973, and I was now certain that the images in my mind would no longer correspond. The warm familiarity that had comforted me throughout the years had dissipated.

"Ma! Ma, I'm over here!" a man shouted, pausing my thoughts.

Turning in the direction of the voice, I was stunned to see my son, Trung, standing beside my brother, Nghe. Though both men were obviously older after my quarter-century absence, I recognized them immediately. One fear had been dispelled.

My heart, cluttered with a mixture of emotions, went into race mode. Would my firstborn welcome or chastise me? Drawing a long, deep breath, I surveyed Trung's face, yearning, yet not daring, to expect his love. My son approached. As he wrapped his arms around me, I feared my thumping heart would burst with anticipation.

Often, throughout the years, I had rehearsed this reunion scene in my mind, never calculating the immensity of emotions that would literally paralyze my breathing. Yet, in his arms, I felt the joy of reuniting with a part of my being that had been severed many years earlier.

Trung's absence in my life was a silent agony unshared with anyone. Not a day passed without thoughts of him. Morning, noon and night, he lived within my spirit.

When I left him, he was just eight years of age, and I feared he may not have been sufficiently mature to understand the reason behind my excruciatingly painful decision to leave him behind when I emigrated, and how my plans for his arrival in the USA were thwarted. Destiny was a wicked demon, prohibiting mother and son from a life together.

Today, my prayer was for Trung's understanding and forgiveness in the event he assumed my actions were an unjust wrongdoing.

Fully aware that my criterion was based on what was best for the young child, I often lay wake many evenings, wondering if my firstborn son would see it through different eyes.

Smiling, Trung proudly introduced his wife, Cuc, and four daughters, Ni, Na, Nu and Thu. Overcome by the moment, I tried my best to choke back the tears. Thankfully, my hand was quick in brushing away a few sliding drops before anyone noticed.

We rode in a minivan to Trung's house in the central highlands of Bảo Lộc. As soon as we arrived, his neighbors and in-laws dropped in, curious to meet his American stepdad, Danny. Word spread like a plague, and people who had never before come into contact with a Westerner crossed his threshold to get an up-close glimpse of my husband. There was no mistaking it: He was being viewed as a celebrity.

After the guests departed, we enjoyed dinner and watched as Trung and his family opened the gifts we had brought.

The children's faces lit up, relaxing, perhaps, my own furrowed brow, which was tightly knit with insecurities. Every toy extracted a giggle and an excited, often-inaudible word of exclamation. Tearing open the cellophane bags of candies, they grabbed the treats with outstretched fingers, stuffing their mouths with the most-coveted sweets.

292

Cuc smiled as she unwrapped the canisters of hand and body lotion, Dove soap and Pert Plus shampoo we had brought for her. American products are considered much-desired and valued treasures in Việt Nam, even worthless effects often classified as junk.

A few days later, Danny and I, together with my son's family, visited my brother, Nghe, and his family in Da Kai, about an hour bus ride from Bảo Lộc.

Returning home, I felt it was appropriate to visit my mother's grave, which was situated just a few hundred feet away from the road. Seeing her name engraved on the tombstone brought back memories of that awful day in 1987, in which I was taken aback by a letter I received from my brother bearing the sad tidings of my mother's sudden and unexpected passing. Exhausted and complaining of a headache, she had retired early, and then passed away in her sleep. It was painless, instantaneous and shocking. Life was held by a breath and released in a sigh.

Adding to the tragedy was my inability, due to family issues, to visit her previously and attend her funeral. Heartbroken and despondent over my grave loss, I now broke into uncontrollable sobs.

Nha, who had never enjoyed the pleasure of meeting his grandmother, joined me in my desperation. Gently taking my hand in his, he poised his head on my shoulder and cried with me.

Standing at her gravesite, I wept, unburdening my soul while silently begging my mom for forgiveness, even if I was faultless in the face of my pressing circumstances. Sometimes, guilt is like the sting of a leather whip on bare skin. This was a moment of truth laid bare. I felt as if justice had been served. I had paid for my failing.

After visiting the gravesite, we consumed a quick lunch. Ngoa, my brother's son-in-law, took us to the Dong Nai River waterfall in his tiny, wood motor boat. Diving off, Danny and I enjoyed a refreshing swim. The cool ripples, like nimble fingers, relaxed the tension in my neck and shoulders. Every knot was unwound and ironed out. That evening, I slept like an infant, undisturbed by consciousness, blissfully unknown to sorrow.

The following day, with the intention of visiting my sister in Huế, I asked Cuc about renting a car. Searching the Yellow Pages, we found an auto-leasing company and rented a vehicle for 750 *đồng* a day.

I was, however, unaware that, willing or otherwise, in Việt Nam, the owner of the leased car or van was automatically the chauffeur.

A new experience was about to occur as we climbed into the minibus and discovered that the back seats were occupied by eight individuals—four children, four adults, all comprising the family of the vehicle's owner.

"Who are these people?" Trung asked, visibly puzzled by the overpopulated van.

"They're my family," the driver responded lackadaisically.

"But *we* rented this vehicle today."

"It's yours, but my wife and kids planned to visit relatives in Huế. They will be making the trip with us."

"Well I don't think that is acceptable," Trung blurted angrily.

"Mom, the owner of the vehicle is taking his family along with us. They have filled up two rows of seats," Cuc shouted, agitated. "Will there be enough room for us?"

"Well, my son told me there are sixteen people in your family," the driver said, "so there's still plenty of room for my family to come along. They haven't visited our relatives in ten years."

"I understand your family's reasoning, but the number of people in my family traveling to Huế is irrelevant," I said, ignited by his arrogant attitude. "In fact, we no longer wish to engage your services or vehicle. I'll find other transportation for my family."

"Ma'am, I'm sorry," the driver stammered. "If I send my family home, would you reconsider renting my van?"

"Well, if you're willing to satisfy my conditions, you may take my family to Huế," I responded after comparing his fee against the other, more-elevated bids. Furthermore, time was an important factor. Either we agreed to travel with this man or we just didn't go at all.

Several men loaded the luggage into the bus while, one by one, all sixteen of us— Danny and I; my brother and sister-in-law with their three children, Gia, Cu and Sa; Trung, his wife and mother-in law, Nguyen; their four daughters, Ni, Na, Nu and Thu; and my niece, who had invited her boyfriend— climbed in.

We covered the 900 miles from Bảo Lộc to Huế in a day and a half. Major detours and numerous lane closures for repairs rendered the journey more complex and time consuming.

The route was scenic and as we drove through Khánh Hòa province on the South Central Coast, I asked the driver if we could possibly stop in Nha Trang City.

"I'd like to take some photos of the breathtaking views," I announced, unable to

296

remove my glance from the glistening, white-sand beaches.

Meandering along the outline of the rolling, verdant hills, the aquamarine sea sent foamy waves to the shore.

In the background, a clear, blue sky embraced deep, sunburned mountains hosting tall, angular, evergreen trees at their summit. Sometimes, it seemed as if their narrow heads would spear the downy, white cloud formations sliding by in silence. In a way, Nha Trang's spectacular coast resembled certain northwestern Oregon and Washington scenes.

We proceeded to Tam Ky, a city from my past. The darkness prohibited any view of my old family residence, rescuing me from reviving some of the despondent memories of that era. Basically an optimist, I tried not to resurrect scenes from my tragic past. Although I had been formed by certain life-altering experiences, I accepted my sad yesterdays as part of the character-strengthening process, recognizing in my pain and sorrow today's ability to live my joys with greater intensity and confront my sorrows, pain and disappointments without ever abandoning hope. The trials and failings made of me not only a survivor but a conqueror.

In Huế, my family was thrilled to see us. Amid tears, hugs, kisses and stammering sentences, we expressed our sentiments and filled in the voids left vacant by decades of silence.

After paying Trung's in-laws a courtesy visit, we drove to Son Tung to see Chau. *En route*, we stopped at An Lo market for groceries since, living in the countryside, on the outskirts of the city, the distance made it inconvenient and time consuming for her to fill her cupboards. Armed with provisions, we headed to my sister's house.

When Chau and her three daughters spotted the bus arriving, they ran outside to greet us. Stepping off the bus, I ran into Chau's arms, tightening my grip around her, never realizing I was probably obstructing her air supply. We sobbed as reciprocal tears ran down our cheeks, drenching our blouses

Although Chau's were tears of joy, mine were bittersweet. Aware that my sister felt

298

trapped in a nasty marriage, I now understood the full intensity of her misery as our eyes met. At fifty-seven, she appeared almost two decades older. Hers was a rushed aging based on an unwholesome cocktail of ill health and desperation. In comparison, my sufferings and trials had taken on a lighter tone, even if my own life showed no resemblance to a fairy tale.

"How long will you stay?" she asked, her eyes begging for a favorable response.

"Four days," I replied, turning away from her sad gaze, regretful to disappoint her. "We're on a tight schedule due to visa restrictions. But, while I'm here, I'd like to visit the gravesite of Dad's family, Linh Mu Temple and Castle, the King's grave and Mom's relatives in Co Top. Would you like to accompany me?"

"Sure, I'd love to."

Together, Chau and I made plans, beginning with a memorial gathering to honor deceased family members that very evening at our cousin Tai's house. We agreed to include both immediate and extended family members—about fifty people, many of whom I had not seen since my early childhood. Of course, there was budding interest among my cousins to meet Danny. As an American, he represented a major curiosity to all my relatives. Nghe was selected to extend the invitations.

My nieces, Minh and Oanh, took turns riding the one bicycle they shared to the market. Upon their return, the provisions were entrusted to Chau and me to be turned into delicious meal selections. We did not disappoint.

Afterwards, we filled several large pots with tantalizingly aromatic delicacies and hand delivered them to Tai and Mon's house, where they were then artistically arranged on oblong platters and set on the altar.

In keeping with Vietnamese traditions, we honored our deceased family members with prayers, perfumed clouds of burning incense, ginseng and tall, white candles, their wicks ablaze.

Following the memorial ritual, and prior to the arrival of the guests, I accompanied Danny on a neighborhood tour. Strolling past the rippling Vinh River, I related events from my early life.

"As a young girl, I carried the family's laundry to the banks of this river," I said, pointing to the exact spot as if it had happened yesterday.

"Then, I scrubbed each piece by hand—clothing, bed linens and towels."

"That's incredible, Bảo," Danny said, though he had heard it before. Perhaps standing at the river bank transposed my words into a stark reality.

"In my house, laundry was washed in a machine," Danny began. "Sure, my mom did some things by hand, but not very much," he continued, encircling his arm around my waist.

As we neared the bridge, children skimming pebbles into the currents lightened the moment, switching my memories to more pleasant activities like swimming and splashing my siblings with sprays of cooling water while our giggles echoed, challenging the muffled whistles of the midday breezes.

Like budding blooms, my memories sprouted. The flashing remembrances were interrupted by the sudden realization that an allegedly thousand-year-old tree had been uprooted to expand an existing house. Upsetting my memories, change was a disturbing inconvenience I didn't appreciate dealing with. The spell had been broken, at least momentarily.

"I think we should go back," I said, glancing at my watch. "Everyone should have arrived and I'm really looking forward to greeting my relatives, especially Uncle Hong's family."

"What's the attraction to Uncle Hong's family?" Danny asked.

"Well, they're kind of interesting in an amusing way. All the girls resemble and behave like his wife, Aunt Yen, whereas the boys are copies of Uncle Hong. Apparently, their parental DNA is exclusive and powerful. It's a fine example of nature's ability to clone!"

The evening proved to be as emotional and exciting as I had anticipated. Through hugs, kisses and nonstop chatter, we greeted each other and did our best to catch on up the missing years. At times ,I felt a little sorry for Danny, the outsider, but he claimed to have enjoyed seeing me so animated in my natural setting.

Though exhausted from the prior day's events and the scorching temperatures melting our energy into beads of perspiration, the next morning, I took Danny to visit Linh Mu Temple. Mesmerized by the tall, octagonal structure, he was eager to get a closer look. I explained that each of the eight tiers was dedicated to a human form Buddha.

We each had a photo taken poised on the shell of a turtle statue adorning the temple. Afterwards, embracing the 200-step climb up a steep hill under the blistering sun, we visited King Khai Dinh's tomb.

"What's his claim to fame?" Danny asked, fascinated by the striking richness of Vietnamese history and traditions.

"He was the rather-docile successor of a king exiled for plotting against the French," I explained.

"Look at the wall," Danny urged, pointing to the structure surrounding the gravesite. It was heavily designed, with colorful formations depicting animals, pieces of furniture, birds and flowers.

"All those interesting designs were hand-glued together," I told him. "Millions of fragments of broken china! Isn't that absolutely amazing?"

"It's totally mind boggling, Bảo. What patience and tenacity that must have required."

"Danny, it's an extraordinary work of art—worth climbing all those steps to see."

Although the return downhill was much less challenging, we reached the bus, recklessly near exhaustion and dehydration. Yet despite it all, to cool off and slow our tourism pace, we opted to head for Thuan An Beach for a reinvigorating swim. Reposing in a tent I rented to shelter us from the blistering

303

sun, we were able to relax, unwind and recuperate our forces before undertaking the next lap of our journey, a trip to Co Top to visit my mother's family. I wondered what surprises, if any, I would encounter while digging into the maternal side of my family.

Chapter 14
Sự trở lại đến Việt Nam: Return to Việt Nam II

First on the itinerary was a trek to the grocer's to purchase some candy and tea. In Việt Nam, gifts of tea and candy are offered to adults and children, respectively, when paying a courtesy call or accepting an invitation. Excited about my adventure to pursue my mom's relatives, I retired early, after separating the hostess gifts into individual packages.

As is customary, the journey began once again with a stopover at the cemetery to pay respects to my deceased ancestors. We offered traditional prayers while burning incense before heading off to Co Top.

It was amazing how suddenly time seemed to have stood still. Within just a few short days, dormant memories and feelings sprang to life as mysteriously as a caterpillar awakens as a beautiful butterfly. I questioned if a quarter century had really passed since I had last walked on Vietnamese soil. Yes, there was concrete evidence of time's flight, but in some instances, change was a nonexistent factor in the cultural preservation of this country.

Despite the historical evolution and lengthy absence, my heart still beat for my native land.

If I was moved to tears, it was because I had returned to my roots. Though dressed and reconfigured like a *nouvelle* American, I was still attached to the apron strings of my birth land.

The initial entry on my list of place to visit was Uncle Xon. I knew this would be an experience. Knocking on his door, I prepared myself and Danny for his seven children, a son-in law and daughter-in-law, and a handful of grandchildren who would jump to their feet to greet us. Believing this welcoming committee to be sufficient, I was unprepared for the extras. As if my Uncle's family were inadequate company, some neighbors dropped in to meet the American delegation of his entourage.

Confused and caught off guard by the numerous components of the welcoming committee, I was unable to draw the line between family and friend. Gazing around the room, I realized that with the scurrying of years, it was not easy to identify some of individuals. Time is sometimes unkind to many fresh faces, leaving deep footprints in its wake.

Reason and courteous manners took the reins of the communications, enabling me to smile, hug, kiss and extend my hand, mimicking the lead of the individual greeting me. *Who are all these people?* I asked myself nervously. Would I remember names even if faces were redesigned by age?

Finally, amid the many strange, semi-familiar and recognizable physical aspects, I spotted my cousin, Tha, who, I marveled, had succeeded in retaining her girlish looks.

Making a mental note to eventually approach her, I ran to Uncle Xon and greeted him with a big bear hug.

"*Cậu* Xon, it's me, Bảo," I blurted, noticing his eyes moistening with tears. "Don't you remember me, *cậu?* I know many years have passed, but it is me, even if older! I don't see *Mợ* Chieu," I barged ahead, neither expecting nor awaiting any response. "Where is she? Where is *mợ?*"

"She's outside in the backyard," *Cậu* Xon said, clearing his throat. I could see he was clearly moved. "My dear Bảo, you have to realize how many years have passed. We are no longer young. Your *mợ* recently turned

307

eighty-eight! Often, she is forgetful. Sometimes, she's confused and doesn't know where she is. These are things that happen to older people." Pausing to catch his breath, I noticed his eyes taking on a pained expression. Taking his hand in mine, I smiled reassuringly.

"Tha, go into the garden and bring your mother here," Uncle Xon said. "Tell her there is someone from far away who would love to see her."

Obediently, my cousin did as she was told. Jumping to her feet, she dashed out the door. When Aunt Chieu stepped in, tiny, bent over and slowed in her stride, I leaped to my feet, eager to give her a hug.

"*Mợ* Chieu, do you remember me? I'm Bảo, Kieu's daughter!" I told her, raising my voice to accommodate any hearing challenges. Grabbing Danny by the arm, I pulled him closer. "And this is my husband, Danny."

"*Thật hả... Really?*" Aunt Chieu sputtered through a less-than-perfect set of teeth, almost disbelieving what her ears were hearing and her eyes seeing. All and any memory issues seemed to vanish.

We chatted, hugged and kissed. As expected, I tried my best to answer the torrent of questions fired at me. Certainly, they were curious to learn about my exciting adventures in a new world, and I did my best to be as responsive as possible. Afterwards, prior to parting, I reunited everyone for a photographic memento.

Once the flashes calmed down and the lineup dismantled, Danny and I distributed monetary gifts to Uncle Xon and his family. Smiling faces and grateful hearts bid us a safe journey and a quick return.

Next on the to-visit list was Aunt Dung, who, like Uncle Xon, was thrilled to greet us with smiles and kisses, catch-up banter and endless questions. More gifts were distributed as exhilarated relatives clutched their newly acquired *đồng*, which amounted to approximately the equivalent of a year's pay. It was as if the skies opened up and let loose a deluge of manna. Of course, our parting was tearful, though buffered with promises to revisit.

Exhausted from the emotional energy expended during our family tour, we eventually arrived at Chau's house eager for the luxury of quiet relaxation. But, it was short lived. A half hour thereafter, we received an unannounced visit from the mayor, Mr. Quyen.

Slender and of average stature, he extended his hand as if setting the tone for a business meeting, then addressed me without blinking an eye.

"I understand you and your husband are visiting from the United States," he began, glancing in my direction. "In case you were not informed, tourists and visitors from foreign countries are required to seek accommodations at a hotel of personal preference. We require this protocol as a security precaution to guarantee your safety. However, if you choose to stay with family or friends, you must register at the courthouse and give notification of all your travels plans while in Việt Nam."

His words and delivery were so smooth and unfaltering, it seemed as if he were reciting in lieu of speaking.

"If visitors and tourists fail to do this," he continued, "the Vietnamese government will be absolved from all responsibility in the event of a mishap."

The mayor's voice was strong, his message emphatic and to the point. There was room for neither doubt nor error.

"Mr. Quyen, it is my understanding that our visit here has been properly documented with the appropriate authorities," I responded, mimicking his militaristic tone and precision.

"Yes, I am aware that your niece notified my office of your arrival. However, she did not approach the proper authority. I went to the courthouse and was informed there was no paper work documenting your arrival and presence here."

Hearing his words, Chau stepped forward. "I'm sorry. It's my fault," she admitted, flustered. "Since my sister and her husband were just paying us a short visit, I thought it was not necessary to give notification."

"Mr. Quyen," I interjected immediately, eager to change the topic to ease worries over Chau's failings, "are you from the north or south?"

Although my question left him momentarily bewildered, his composure remained unruffled.

"I was born in Son Tung and eventually migrated north," he replied without relinquishing his dry tone. Courteous, his words were measured and far from plentiful, perhaps an intentional deterrent for me to proceed further. Inarguably, he cared not to discuss his personal history.

Taking two steps back, he bowed his farewell and took leave from our company. After his departure, Chau confessed the real reason for not reporting our visit.

"I owe you an apology, Aunt Bảo," she whispered contritely. "I was remiss in reporting your visit at the courthouse because I feared they may have denied my request, forcing you to spend money at a hotel."

"Relax," I said, "I don't blame you. I know it was not your fault. You acted in good conscience. However, I do feel a bit nervous about the situation and don't want to place either of us in jeopardy. Since the mayor is aware of our irregular status, I think it is best for all if we return to Bảo Lộc this evening with Cuc and Trung."

Although Chau felt culpable despite my reassurances to the contrary, she did little to conceal her sadness when we announced our decision to leave that evening after supper. Apparently, the mayor's admonition had ignited her. In tears, she helped me pack, realizing that perhaps I was just exercising a bit of caution and was not cross with her. It was clear to me that she need more words of reassurance, which I imparted.

Once outside, she refrained from any conversation. Tense, her jaw trembled. Tears, mine and hers, continued to spill profusely along the contours of our cheeks throughout the farewell. She accompanied us to the bus, dabbing at her eyes with a neatly folded, linen handkerchief.

"*Tiếng chào nhau*—goodbye, *Cô* Bảo," she sobbed. Giving her a quick hug, I slid into the vehicle. Neither of us knew for sure if we would enjoy each other's company again.

The bus driver took off slowly, then increased his pace. I took a deep breath and settled in my seat, convinced I had made the right decision. Sometimes, failing to err on the side of caution can result in serious consequences.

"Hold on," the driver shouted, abruptly suspending my thoughts. I felt myself glide along the vinyl seat as he swerved to avoid colliding with an apparently distracted bicyclist, In so doing, he narrowly missed hitting another pedaling on the opposite side of the road.

What began as a ballerina-like sashay ended with an unexpected brunt. Extending my arms to hold my position steady, I protected myself from slamming into the front seat. Unexpectedly, he turned sharply, then slammed his foot on the brake. Like ingredients in a tossed salad, the sudden impact shuffled us into each other. Arms and legs merged, tangling us in a knotted skein. Thankfully, no one suffered any serious injury.

However, though grateful to have escaped with merely a thumping heart and a few beads of sweat on my brow, I was unaware that our road troubles were not yet over.

The next morning, nearing the Nha Trang border, the bus collided into a mobilette, a small-scale quadricycle very popular in Asia. This time, the impact caused the mobilette driver to lose control. Flying into the air, the young man landed on a patch of unidentifiable debris scattered on the side of the road, skinning his knees and elbows.

Tiny drops of glistening, red blood oozed from his fresh cuts, bringing back to me memories of my childhood scrapes and injuries while escaping bombings in war-torn Việt Nam. Certainly, I understood the physical and emotional sting of bleeding wounds and could not stop the knots from forming in the pit of my stomach.

Scared, the owner of the bus scurried over to the cyclist, offering 200,000^d in

314

reparation for damages inflicted. In shock, and disconcerted by the unforeseen, the wounded man refused the offering.

However, several minutes and many words later, reconsidering and reversing his rather hurried decision, he allowed the bus driver to coerce him into acceptance.

Both parties were far better off settling without police intervention, which would have involved squandering time and energy under the blistering rays of a torrid sun. Appreciative of the quick resolution, I sat back and enjoyed the rest of the trip, absorbing in my mind the sights and sounds of Việt Nam, committing every detail, scent and echo to memory, realizing it would be perhaps a long time before I would return.

When the driver came to a halt at a congested intersection, I dismissed my thoughts.

"Excuse me," I blurted, sliding forward in my seat to get the driver's attention. "May I ask you some questions, Mr. Tanh?"

"Yes, ma'am, how can I be helpful?" he responded, without removing his glance from the windshield.

Inquisitive by nature, I was also impassioned about the modern Việt Nam and the stories of the people who called it their country.

315

"Thank you, Mr. Tanh. I appreciate it. I would like to know a bit about your background."

"Well, I was in the military—spent fifteen years in the infantry, five out in the field and ten in rigorous training. I was discharged on April thirtieth, nineteen seventy-five."

"What was your rank, and where were you stationed?" I asked, eager to get all the pieces of the puzzle.

"Ma'am, I was a first sergeant stationed in Da Lat at the time."

"You've had quite an impressive military career. How do you feel about the political situation of Việt Nam today?"

"What exactly do you mean?"

"I mean, what do you think about the current government and its effect on the people? You are old enough to have lived through the change of power."

Caught off guard, Mr. Tanh shifted his gaze from the road, rotating his focus from Danny to me without uttering a word. More appropriately, I would say, his silence and furrowed brow spoke of indignation and animosity. Since I had been told that the general consensus was anger over the Communist takeover, his reaction did not surprise me. Therefore, I concluded that Mr.

316

Tanh shared the wrath and consternation of the majority of Vietnamese people.

I also realized that the presence of my American husband was not only intimidating but a plausible motive behind his reluctance to verbally express any anti-American sentiment. Furthermore, Mr. Tanh may have feared instigating a confrontational discussion or offending the sensibilities of American guests visiting his country.

Understanding his hesitancy in pursuing any political conversation, I rested my case, turning my attention back to the picturesque scenery through which we were driving. I was certain that a bit of consideration on my part would put him an ease.

"Well, ma'am," Mr. Tanh began, drawing a deep, slow breath, "the South Vietnamese government couldn't do very much for anyone but themselves."

"Are you saying that the people are better off and happier today with the new government?" I snapped, taken aback by his comment.

"Well, haven't you noticed all the new construction throughout country? Cities are being rebuilt as citizens strive to recuperate from the dire affects of the war." Clearing his throat, he lit a cigarette—a tactic, in my mind, to stall for time to reflect. Taking a few puffs gave him a moment to reflect on his answers.

"Everyone is hopeful for a promising future," he said. I wasn't quite sure if I was willing to be satisfied with what he stated. Eyeing me, dismayed at my surprise reaction to his response, he took a drag, exhaling clouds of smoke.

"We're all working to rebuild the country so we can have a better future." Though he was snaking his way through my interrogation, this last thought was unanimously shared.

"Amen," I whispered under breath. If such could be reality in lieu of a visionary dream, I would celebrate with my compatriots.

Yet, in spite of his positive attitude, I was not swayed by the certainty he was trying to project. I questioned if, in effect, he truly attributed any credibility and worth to his conviction. In addition, unsure of whom Danny and I were, he opted, understandably, to keep his personal opinion regarding government preference, shrouded in the unstated unknown. Apparently, he appreciated our company and business and tried his best to preserve our relationship for the duration of our stay in Việt Nam.

The next day, my niece, Nhan, her son and her husband, Ngoa, paid us a farewell visit. Although I detected a clear-cut northern accent at various intervals during the conversation, I remained dubious about my nephew's birthplace.

Secrets and riddles always fascinated me, though they represented a challenge I had to affront. Plus, inquisitive and probing as I was, I had little choice but to unmask the uncertainty.

"Where were you born, Ngoa?" I asked bluntly.

"I was born in the north, but my family immigrated south about ten years ago," he said hesitantly, betraying his disinclination to be put on the witness stand. In all probability, he felt ill at ease and unaware of my bias for either north or south.

To my knowledge, before 1975, most South Vietnamese categorized all North Vietnamese as the Việt Cộng—guerillas, or, in their own words, the army units of the *Mặt trận Dân tộc Giải phóng miền Nam Việt Nam,* the National Liberation Front of South Việt Nam. We, however, never considered them liberators, but invaders. Nevertheless, unknown to Ngoa, I was of the opinion that all Vietnamese were victims of Communism.

I enjoyed interacting with people and digging into their thoughts and feelings, perhaps to gain new perspectives about my birth country. Therefore, later that evening, I settled on the front porch with a woman who worked as a nanny for my son's family. Although I knew she had birthed five boys and had been forsaken by her husband, who, disgruntled over her failure to give him a daughter, ran off with another woman, it was her turn to brace for my line of questioning.

"Did your husband provide financial support after he left?" I asked, flashing a faint smile to soften the mood.

The sadness in her eyes made me regret my question.

"Bảo, he sent me just enough money to cover the house payment. I had to work as a nanny to put food on the table for my sons. Our well-being was never his concern."

"Can you tell me a little bit about yourself?" I asked, moving away from focusing on the scoundrel who had abandoned her and their children.

"I'm a kindergarten teacher, but during the eight years in which I lived here, I was unable to find employment in a school."

"What about your sons? Don't they have jobs?"

"My two older sons married and returned up north. I don't see them very often."

Relentlessly, I pursued the line of questioning. "Do you think the government discriminates between north and south? I mean, are people treated differently? I guess what I'm trying to figure out is if it is better in any one area."

"Today, it really makes no difference where you live. Since the 1954 Communist takeover of the north, life became a hardship," she said, sighing. It appeared as if the silent pauses enabled her to extract buried memories.

"I remember one day, the Communists barged into my house," she continued, visibly agitated, "and made me a prisoner. Together with thousands of others, I was dragged into the woods, where we were forced to dig holes, gutters and canals every day for three months."

"Why?" I questioned, puzzled.

"To prepare for war. It was debilitating work and certainly not for a woman. Most of the time, we were hungry and tried."

"Hungry? Didn't they feed you?"

"Yes and no. They offered us birds' rations. Hardly sufficient to satisfy the appetite of an adult. Plus, we were working hard and consuming energy."

321

"Why did they take a woman to do a man's job?" I asked.

"Since my parents had only girls, they took me. I was the oldest of five daughters."

Listening to her tale of woe brought to mind a similar story related to me in 1973 by Bon, Nha's nanny. Her saga took place in 1954, when the country was divided into North and South Việt Nam.

I could still hear her words as, flushed and nervous, she said:

"Many northern citizens dreaming freedom immigrated south via the waterways. People crowded into boats, paying little heed to capacity regulations and the possibility of sinking. Hundreds of boats teeming with people anxious to escape headed south until a group of armed men appeared, preventing any and all boats from sailing.

"In particular, they were trying to locate and halt the departure of a wealthy man. Threats were shouted, forcing the occupants to disembark or face immediate death.

Fearing for their safety, the people returned the boats to shore, where the wealthy man was taken prisoner and escorted away at gunpoint.

"Though he agreed to go without resistance, he yelled over his shoulder, instructing the boat's captain to await his return. Several minutes thereafter, he re-boarded dressed only in his underwear. Apparently, he had been stripped bare of all his possessions."

Able to visualize the humiliation and fury of being relieved of all possessions at gunpoint, I was overcome with sadness. However, reflecting, I realized it was a small price to pay for freedom—the very same freedom we often take for granted in the USA. Instead, we should treasure and protect our liberties as precious blessings. Such liberty is coveted by many born into political captivity.

I felt extremely fortunate to have departed Việt Nam prior to 1975 and to have avoided any encounters with the Việt Cộng. Luckily, all my awareness and knowledge of their sinister dealings was through the painful narratives of others—no firsthand experiences. Now, as a daughter of Việt Nam, I was merely a tourist with a visa, free to enter and, more importantly, at liberty to leave.

Before bidding farewell to Việt Nam, I had two last items on my itinerary to satisfy. The first was a tour of Sài Gòn, officially renamed Hồ Chí Minh City in 1976, though the former name is still more commonly used.

While visiting there, Danny and I were literally flabbergasted to bear witness to a building boom that had completely redesigned the panorama and demography of the city.

The second thing I had to do was begin the bureaucratic process of revoking Trung's adoption, to permit him and his family to immigrate to the United States. I informed myself of the protocol, obtained the documents and completed the paperwork.

I had revisited the places of my youth, sat and broke bread with my maternal and paternal family members, and listened attentively to the suffering and tribulations of the Vietnamese. Undoubtedly, I gained new insights and perspectives regarding what I had and what I would have had today if I had been faithful to my birthplace. Furthermore, I learned exactly what I relinquished and what I gained when I choose freedom, opportunity and free enterprise in the United States.

Recognizing the gifts I had received from life, I was ready to turn the page on my quest to discover and reunite with my roots. Any doubt I may have had was quashed. Convinced I made a brilliant decision, on August 25, accompanied by Cuc, Trung and Nghe, Danny and I boarded the plane at Hàng không Quốc tế, Sài Gòn's Tân Sơn Nhất International Airport. Though travel weary, I was rejuvenated and happy, fully cognizant of who I was, and, more importantly, where I was.

Chapter 15
The Demon Within

My journey into the past left me with a very diverse perspective of who I was and who I had become throughout the years. I was encouraged to see what could have been had I continued life in the same vein in which it had begun.

Revisiting my birthplace and relatives provided ample substance for serious reflection. I, too, could have been like my cousins and siblings, living under a stifling Communist regime disallowing any and all private enterprise.

However, does the end always justify the means? Perhaps it was still too soon to respond.

Despite it all, I felt heavily indebted for the hand destiny had dealt me. I surely had not led a life of ease, but my fate of suffering and hardship had played a major role in my development as a human being. Furthermore, immigrating to America had left me free to profit from the many opportunities offered as a citizen living in a free land.

Once home from my trip, I walked though a muddled gauntlet of weeks and months. Then, in 1998, I reached the half century mark, having extinguished fifty candles on my birthday cake.

It was a time of introspection during which I evaluated from whence I had come, where I stood today and where I hoped to go. A productive year, it seemed to have literally evaporated into my memory.

Shortly thereafter, at the turn of the millennium, I was back in the maelstrom. My relationship with Danny was sailing through a nasty tempest. Trying to keep afloat challenged my stamina and, often, my willingness to overcome. Sometimes, the convenience of slipping into a defeatist mode seemed like a plausible solution to a difficult dilemma. But, denial is not without consequences, and certainly not imperishable.

Suddenly, serenity and well-being were just illusions. My energy was seeping away. It seemed as if my body was reacting to the emotional mutiny with a slow, steady leak. Listless, I felt miserable, drained of my forces shortly upon awakening in the mornings. I was too young to feel so depleted and frazzled.

In 1999, Danny retired from military duty after almost a quarter century of service. To honor his loyalty and dedication to the Army, a group of friends organized a farewell party, the date of which was kept secret from me until the evening of the event, even though my presence was expected.

Upset with Danny for this puzzling and senseless nondisclosure, I tried my best to regard it as a careless oversight. I dressed hurriedly, and applied some rouge, lipstick and a bit of eye make-up. Smiling reluctantly, I accompanied my husband to the reception. Danny seemed to approve, and grinned as he walked me to the driver's seat.

When we arrived, the guests—twenty men, impeccable in dress uniform, and one tall, slender woman with a thick mane of long, dark hair, tightly gathered in a low ponytail— greeted Danny. No presentations occurred. It was as if I was invisible, a nonentity in a room of animated guests.

Unlike the uniformed gentlemen, the lady's attire was a sexy, floor-length, body-hugging, chocolate sheath decorated with an intricate, red-floral print—not exactly a subdued look. She was definitely looking for attention. As Danny approached, she flashed a coquettish grin, similar to the coy smiles shared between individuals engaged in an intimate relationship.

"You look beautiful this evening," Danny whispered. "I have never seen you in an evening dress before."

Perhaps the timing was poor, or perhaps Danny didn't care if I heard his innocuous compliment—but I did. It wasn't so much his gallantry but the woman's response that sent the alarm buzzing.

"Thank you, Danny, I wore this dress just for you," she cooed, rolling her eyes.

Pretending not to have heard the enticing comment, Danny escorted me to the table and held my seat until I settled in. Just as he sat, the woman slid into the chair on his left. Immediately, we were served dinner while loud, rhythmic beats of music echoed, trumping any attempt to converse. However, I noticed Danny and the woman repeatedly exchanging decisive glances that spoke of a familiarity unquestionably improper between them. The very thought set my heart thumping.

Was I just an apprehensive wife, insecure in the company of my husband and an attractive younger woman? Or did I have a valid reason to suspect he had been unfaithful? Was I justified in mistrusting him?

At the stroke of midnight, like Cinderella fleeing Prince Charming, we departed the party, slipping into the car for the drive home. Neither of us spoke. An eerie silence prevailed, weaving a thick barrier of tension. The quiet begged to be shattered. I knew that if I didn't confront Danny, I would explode.

"Did I understand correctly? She wore a long dress just for you?" I asked him.

Meeting my gaze, Danny remained silent, leaving my question unanswered.

Indomitably, I persisted. "From what she said, I had the impression she never wore a long dress before. So, how did she dress on your dates?"

Shifting his glance, silence was once again the only response I would get.

My blood was boiling, my pressure rising. I entertained thoughts of leaning over, lifting the door lever and pushing him out, though I recognized the implausibility of my sweet reverie.

Powerless in the light of a suspected betrayal, I realized how often Danny and I bickered lately. It didn't take much for our tempers to flare. A word hurriedly said, a word left unsaid, and we were at war. At one point, in a heated argument, he had even spoken of divorce.

Perhaps the alleviating panacea of denial prohibited me from seeing the whole picture. Reflecting, I recalled how, during one of our Christmas shopping trips, Danny had asked for advice in selecting a present for a co-worker. "It's part of a holiday gift-exchange program," he'd said, justifying the request.

Once inside the shop, Danny had dashed over to the women's perfume and cosmetics counter as if there were free handouts for the first person to arrive. Quickening my stride to keep pace, I'd arrived just as he was browsing through the various gift items—aromatic soaps and scented candles.

"I'll take this," he announced, lifting a silver, heart-shaped basket filled with miniature perfumes.

"Do you have a secret lady friend?" I asked, realizing his gift selection was not exactly innocuous.

"No, I don't have anyone," he replied dryly.

"Then why did you buy a heart basket? That makes a statement. It sends a message of love!"

"Really? I had no idea. No reason—I just like the way it looks."

If any husband actually believes a wife would digest a comment of that nature without suffering an attack of acid reflux, physically and emotionally, he's living an illusory moment. Of course, my considerations were not without a basis in

333

truth. Danny was a man with a philandering eye, and it gave me reason to doubt his spousal integrity.

I never forgot his father's and grandmother's funerals. An old flame that had fallen in love with and married his close friend had been in attendance when the remains were laid to rest in Longview, Washington. On both occasions, she had awaited Danny at the church entry, enveloping him in a full-body, condolence-conveying embrace, oblivious to my feelings.

It didn't end there, however. Afterwards, at lunch, overcome with sorrow, she had failed to fill her plate. Coming to her rescue like a knight in shining armor,

Danny had made certain his damsel in distress was nourished, giving from his own rations. So much for diplomacy, discretion and the preservation of a wife's dignity.

Enraged, I had fought the urge to hurl my plate at her. I maintained my composure, at least outwardly, in respect for the somber occasion. Instead, I excused myself and parted company, giving him the opportunity to collect her phone number if he was so inclined, to pursue an adulterous relationship.

That evening, we quarreled like archenemies. Hurt and offended, I sulked in silence for five days thereafter, shutting down the lines of communication. A funeral silence prevailed. Then, one evening, unable to bear my repressed rage, I jumped into the shower fully clothed, turning on the cold water.

Springing to his feet, Danny pulled me from the icy downpour.

"What are you doing, Bảo?" he shouted, wrapping a towel around my trembling shoulder. "What are you, nuts? What's going on? You must be sick. Something is very wrong with you. Sane people do not behave in this manner."

"Of course something is wrong with me," I responded. "You've made me ill—you made me crazy!"

Deeply concerned and scared, he removed my saturated garments and slipped a warm, dry nightgown over my head. Still in silence, I climbed between the sheets. If only I could drift off, all the pain would all go away—at least for a few hours. I could maybe dismiss the betrayal, forget that my husband had cheated on me. However, sleep was not a gallant savior, offering me a release from my torment.

Twisting and turning to the point of sheer annoyance, I rose around four and headed to the kitchen, intent on targeting the refrigerator. Emptying the contents, I switched to the cupboards, pulling out whatever filled the shelves—food, plates, pots, pans, cups and glasses, dropping it all on the floor. Glass and china fractured in hundreds of pieces. Cataclysmic, the noise was painfully ear shattering. But, I heard only my thoughts.

However, the clamor of my predawn tantrum did little to release my anger. Frustrated, I grabbed a long kitchen knife. Running my fingers along the icy, polished ridges, I questioned why it was firmly lodged in my right hand. Was I entertaining thoughts of suicide—or worse? Was I pushed to the limits and capable of committing murder? Did I believe I could eradicate my pain by killing both Danny and myself? Was I really out of it? Had all the tragedies of my life gained the upper hand?

The ruckus awakened Danny, who, terrified the house had been invaded by thieves, followed the light into the war zone. Seeing the knife clasped in my hand, he inched over to where I sat, tiptoeing like a child trying not to bring attention to his presence.

Lost amid the tormenting thoughts of my silent monologue, I was startled when he yanked the weapon from my hand.

"I'm so sorry, Bảo," he whispered, dropping to his knees beside my chair. "It will never happen again, please believe me. If that woman ever crosses my path again, I promise you I will not have anything to do with her."

Through tear-filled eyes, I noticed the remorseful expression on my husband's face—a retiring look of repentance that spoke of earnest contrition. Taking me in his arms, he repeated his promises, holding me close. Desperate to give credence to his apology and pledge of repentance, I choose to accept his words as true. They were what I wanted and needed to hear.

337

Still smarting from the wrongs committed against me, I sat quietly, nursing my bruised feelings as Danny cleaned up the mess I had orchestrated. Trash bagging most of the ruined food, he dragged it outside, returning to mop the floor and reorganize the cupboards.

Perhaps it was a penitential settling of the score, or perhaps just a means of being in my company without any further confrontations. It could also have been a strategy to demonstrate good will. I churned endless uncertainties in my mind, never really expecting or desirous of a response.

Although the nature of the underlying motive may have been disputable, it worked, consoling my restless ire while calming my nerves.

More importantly, a lesson was learned. Throughout the ensuing years, Danny's behavior became a testament to the value of our marriage. He neither strayed nor indulged in any action or deed that would have jeopardized our relationship. At least that part of my life was at peace.

338

However, not a stranger to setbacks, I knew life sometimes has an ironic way of pitching unexpected curve balls. Furthermore, the surprise element often leaves us defenseless. We know not what sinister nemesis lies in ambush around the corner, and not knowing hinders the ability to strategize.

When the agonizing pains started, I realized something was very wrong. Nauseous most of the time, I began suffering from intermittent bouts of diarrhea and uncomfortable bloating.

"Danny," I stammered one morning, barely able to lift myself off the mattress, "I feel terrible. I think I need a doctor. Something is really wrong."

"Get dressed and I'll drive you over before work," he replied. "You look terrible and I think you have lost weight."

I tried my best to shower, dress and climb into the car. Believing I had caught some terrible virus, I was eager for whatever medical remedy my physician would offer. It had to stop. I needed my strength. There was too much to do, and I could not squander any more time being sick.

When Dr. Bernier entered the exam room, I was ready to begin my litany of complaints.

"Bảo, how are you?" he asked, extending his hand. "You look awful. What's wrong?"

"Doctor, I don't know what's happening to me. I feel sick most of the time. I'm exhausted, nauseous and have such terrible cramps, I can't straighten up."

"I think she has lost too much weight," Danny interjected.

"We'll run some tests and try to find out what's going on. I'd like to schedule some blood work and a series of upper and lower gastrointestinal exams."

Several days thereafter, Dr Bernier informed me there were traces of blood in my stool.

"Bảo, I'd like to schedule an appointment for you to see Dr. Colip. He's a specialist in gastroenterology at Adventist Medical Center."

"Just give me a time and date and I'll be there. I want to get to the root of this as soon as possible."

On June 17, I met with Dr. Colip.

"I have been looking at your file," he said, "and I understand you have a problem that has been unresolved for many years."

"Yes, I've been suffering from bloating and intestinal irregularities for fourteen years."

"I'm going to schedule a colonoscopy. We will see what's happening."

The receptionist gave me a June 24 appointment. Handing me a patient information folder, she emphasized that I must read and follow the instructions carefully, especially the part about avoiding ibuprofen and aspirin as well as irritating foods such as popcorn, nuts and seeds.

Though this was not exactly amusement-park fun, I realized that I had little if any choice if I wanted this agonizing nightmare to come to an end. I had never before been subjected to such poor health; therefore, my attitude was one of total submission and optimism.

I presented myself on the twenty-fourth for the colonoscopy. Of course, I was nervous and anxious; fear of the unknown is difficult to deal with primarily because of its unfamiliar nature.

Considerate, compassionate and caring, the nurses and physicians were true professionals committed to the well-being of their patients.

Understanding the intricacy and anxiety involved, they were gentle and patient even with complex individuals.

Ignorant of what was about to ensue, I put myself in their hands. It was an action of blind faith on my part. Minutes later, the process was explained in more detail than I actually needed or cared to have, and I was anesthetized. When I awakened, Danny was standing beside my bed, holding my hand.

"Hi, Bảo. How're you feeling?" he asked, smiling. "It's over. Are you in any pain?"

"No pain… Just sleepy. Did they tell you anything?"

"The doctor said they removed a tiny lump from your colon."

"A lump! What kind of lump?"

"Stay calm. I don't know what kind of lump. They told me they would phone when the biopsy results are in."

Several hours thereafter, I was discharged and informed that as soon as the verdict was in, I would be contacted. Consequently, when the receptionist phoned to schedule an appointment with the physician, I was relieved it would all soon come to a conclusion.

Danny accompanied me the following morning.

"Hello, Mr. and Mrs. Lindner," the receptionist told us, "the doctor will be with you in a few moments."

We grabbed a couple of magazines and selected two seats relatively close to the door, to avoid having to traipse through the entire waiting room when summoned.

"Danny, do you think everything will be OK?" I asked as a sudden fear of the worst settled in my stomach.

"I'm sure everything will be fine," Danny said. "Anyway, we will see the doctor soon, so there is no need to fall into dark scenarios."

"Mrs. Lindner," the tall, moderately overweight nurse said, walking through the door, "please come with me."

Drawing a deep breath, I rose and took several steps towards the door.

"I'm coming with you," Danny blurted, closing the *Sports Illustrated* magazine he had been nervously flipping through.

The doctor greeted us with firm handshakes.

"Bảo, how are you feeling?"

"I'm a bit better today, thank you." I responded.

"Well, I have all your test results," he began, opening what looked like an extensive dossier. "I'm afraid the situation is somewhat serious." Nervously clearing his throat, he paused before continuing.

"The colonoscopy and biopsy revealed a malignant mass in your colon. Thankfully, the bone scan was negative, which means the cancer has not metastasized."

Cancer, I thought. *He said cancer! I have cancer!* My body froze. My breathing became labored. My stomach, invaded by hordes of warriors, somersaulted. Was that a death sentence? Was he telling me I was dying? Grief stricken, I turned to Danny.

"Bảo, we will schedule you for surgery as soon as possible," Dr. Colip said.

"Then what? Am I going to die? How long do I have?"

"Relax—there is no need for pessimistic thoughts. After surgery, we will monitor your health. Luckily, we caught the cancer in the initial stages, therefore it will not be necessary to undergo chemotherapy. The good news is that you will make a full recovery and be able to enjoy a long, fruitful life. Much progress has been made with respect to colon cancer, and survival rates are encouraging when the illness is caught in time. This is why we urge patients to have colonoscopies at regular intervals after the age of fifty. The sooner we discover a malignancy, the better the odds are of defeating it. Patients have higher survival rates and treatment options are often less aggressive and debilitating."

"If I would have done chemotherapy, I would have lost all my hair?"

"Yes, I'm afraid so, but for cancer patients who need it, the chemo is a small price to pay for life. Furthermore, once the treatment is completed, hair regrowth is automatic. Also, the hospital has a great support system of competent professionals who are qualified to answer questions and assist patients psychologically and provide important nutritional information to promote quick healing."

"I am fortunate not to have to go that route. When will I have the surgery?" I asked, feeling decidedly relieved about my post-op course of treatment.

Lifting the telephone, Dr. Colip dialed hurriedly. "I'm going to set a date for your surgery right now," he said, covering the receiver with his hand.

Several minutes later, he informed us that there was an opening on the first of July.

"We'll take it," Danny blurted.

"If you have any questions or concerns regarding the surgery, please free to contact me or Dr. Hayes," Dr. Colip replied.

"Thank you," I said.

"I'll have Bảo at the hospital on June thirtieth, ready for the surgery," Danny reassured the doctor as he rose to his feet.

"Fine. Do you have any additional questions?"

"Dr. Colip, tell me the truth. What are my chances for survival?" I asked him. "What kind of life expectancy can I count on?"

"Well, Bảo, the good news is that your cancer has been diagnosed in the early stages, therefore with surgery and treatment, you have a ninety-percent chance of a full recovery."

Although Dr. Colip's words created a reassuring impression, I was still riddled with doubts and fear. What if I didn't survive? What if my cancer was more sinister than originally thought? What would the surgeon find once he sliced though my abdomen?

I was silent and reflective during the drive home. Sensing my vulnerability, Danny left my thoughts uninterrupted. Prayer, I thought—prayer was a powerful ally, one I needed to win this battle.

When we arrived home, I played my telephone messages to be certain there were no changes regarding my surgery date. Surprised to hear Pat's voice, I listened to his proposal for participation in a television show

347

the following morning, for Channel 2. The short message said, "Be here at eight o'clock if you're interested."

I debated all of five minutes before deciding to accept Pat's offer. Life was far from over and I was not going to curl up and hide in a pity womb.

This illness was certainly an obstacle but I had no intentions of admitting defeat even before the battle began.

I dialed Pat's number.

"Pat, this is Bảo. Count me in for tomorrow."

"Great, be here at eight o'clock."

Re-energized with the verve of survival, I jumped out of bed the following morning, showered, dressed and departed. This would be another adventure, and adventures were the pulse of life.

Awaiting the show's director, I noticed an older woman literally thinking out loud. At first, I chuckled to myself as she mused, "Maybe I should not have worn this dress... After all, I'm sixty-three years old."

Sobering, I thought. I was fifty. Who knew if I would ever reach sixty-three?

Maybe Dr. Colip had made an error, or perhaps the ten-percent fatality possibility would kick in and the cancer would get me.

"Follow me, please," a gentleman carrying a note board, said. His words shattered my less-than-sunny reflection.

Several minutes thereafter, I was oblivious to all negative thoughts as I laughed and applauded with the rest of the audience. Sometimes, prayers are answered when we least expect it, and sometimes, the answer is disguised in laughter.

Chapter 16
Saṃsāra: Endless Suffering

A voice message from the physician's receptionist confirmed my surgery was a reality. Returning the call, Danny spoke with the doctor. Upfront, and irrespective of my presence, he inquired about the prognosis. The concern in his voice was unmistakable. His countenance, viewed in the dimming light of sunset, took on an ashen hue, his eyes darkened in distress. I had cancer and my life was being threatened.

"Thank you, doctor," Danny said, jumping to his feet. "I'll have Bảo at the hospital in the morning."

Much as I would have welcomed the comforting refuge of a blissful slumber, I slept little that evening, plagued by a vibrant imagination working overtime to produce the bleak scenarios and possibilities that could befall me.

The following morning, I dressed quietly, packed a few personal belongings, slid into the car and eventually followed Danny into the reception area of Adventist Hospital as if I were a robot set on automatic pilot. It was July 1, 1999, a date I would never forget, a date I now think of as one of the most significant turning points of my life.

Scared and apprehensive, my thoughts turned morose. Would I be able to face the battle ahead? Would I be triumphant after all the anguish, or would I succumb? Was it really all worthwhile?

Faced with endless uncertainties, the issue of my wavering mortality could no longer be pushed into denial. But, I was suddenly cast in an unfamiliar scenario. Not a stranger to suffering and war, I realized that this was very different from running through the dusty streets of war-torn Việt Nam, fleeing the bombing raids. I was fighting an enemy within. Beleaguered by a heartless traitor, I was taken prisoner by my own body.

"Mrs. Lindner, we have some forms for you to sign."

Hearing my name called lowered the curtain on my drama. I approached the desk, wondering if my trembling knees would collapse.

Once officially admitted, I was escorted to my room, asked to undress and informed I would be completing a series of pre-op exams for my surgery.

"Nothing to concern yourself about," the slender, young nurse chirped, exposing a perfect set of pearly, white teeth. "It's just some routine blood work and a chest X-ray."

Nothing to concern myself about, I thought. *Doesn't she know I have cancer?*

The day unraveled peacefully despite the presence of an almost-irrational anxiety of the unknown, which seemed to surface from time to time. Nevertheless, resigned to my fate, I tried the calming, slow, deep-breathing exercises that various gurus of medicine and psychology promoted in their self-help manuals.

If I could relax, perhaps I would be able to pass a restful evening. In this moment, only the quickness of time's passage would hasten the conclusion of my nightmare.

Finally, dinner was served. Although I was limited to intolerably unappetizing liquids, receiving the evening rations signaled the imminent conclusion of an inauspicious day.

Clutching my pillow, I remained wide-eyed, pondering my future while my heart thumped in synchrony with my breathing— the verification that I was still alive. Thoughts of surgery invaded my final moment of consciousness. However, exhausted, I was encouraged to yield to sleep and leave tomorrow's outcome to my creator.

Awakening suddenly from a substance-induced sleep, I was greeted with the image of a surgeon's scalpel slicing through my stomach. I broke out in a cold sweat as I imagined, step by step, how he would cut into my flesh. Would the anesthetic be sufficient to put me to sleep?

What if I awakened in the middle of the operation? How badly would all this hurt? Tears rolled down my cheeks.

"Am I dying? Am I dying?" I cried.

"Bảo, what's wrong?" Danny whispered, walking over to my bed. "I'm glad I decided to stay the night. Are you in pain?"

"I'm scared, Danny. What if I never awaken from the surgery?"

"There is nothing to worry about. You have an excellent surgeon and these operations are performed quite frequently. Everything will be just fine. Try to get some rest."

Danny used the typical response, custom designed to suit the situation by truncating any remnants of negativity. However, his words did little to reassure or calm me.

Receiving a cancer diagnosis was like

ingesting a torrential downpour of water, one full swallow after another, without pausing to breathe. I was drowning and unable to help myself. Cancer invaded my life, took possession of my thoughts, sequestered my emotions and suffocated my breath, ambushing me from within.

However, empowered to triumph over adversity by the often-overwhelming catastrophic misadventures I had overcome, I knew I was neither willing to allow cancer to dominate my existence nor ready to relinquish my hold on life.

Repudiating the depression demon, I quashed its bittersweet, force-fed despair aimed at tempting me to surrender. Undoubtedly, I was going to arm myself for combat and, more importantly, I was going to win.

Deep down I knew I had not waded through all the calamities, fought all the battles and affronted all the hardships to be vanquished and outwitted by a nasty cancer. I would not let this happen.

As soon as the first ray of sunlight peeked through the blinds, a nurse came in to take my temperature. Placing a thermometer under my tongue, she slipped a cuff around my arm to check my blood pressure. Putting a pulse oximeter on my finger, she monitored my breathing.

"We'll be taking you to the operating room in about an hour," she announced, smiling. "Just try to relax." I heard but didn't hear her words.

Afterwards, I was visited by the anesthesiologist, who verified my weight and asked if I had any questions.

After he left, there was a knock at the door. Danny rose and greeted a middle-aged woman dressed in a dark suit. Her manner was reserved, her wide smile genuine.

"Good morning," she said, "are you up for a brief visit?"

My gaze was as gloomy as a swollen cloud riding into a storm, my response just a faint nod.

She presented herself as a spiritual guide who spoke to and prayed with patients before surgery. An empathetic woman, she seemed to understand my terrified state of mind.

Informed of the gravity of my illness, she listened to my concerns, neither wincing nor batting an eyelash.

"Do you belong to a church or synagogue?"

"No, but I'm a Buddhist."

"Would you like me to pray with you for a successful surgery and full recovery?"

"Yes I would like it—that would be reassuring."

"Let's join hands and ask God to watch over you during the surgery," she whispered, approaching my bed. Danny walked over and took my hand and hers. I looked down and closed my eyes.

Certain that there really was a God, I begged for His intervention and solidarity. Amazingly, such unwavering faith is often confirmed during moments of despair.

"Lord, please protect Bảo during her surgery and restore her to us in good health," the woman prayed.

"Amen "I whispered as Danny squeezed my hand. My fate would now be written according to my creator's will.

Just as we released our hands, the nurse knocked on the door and announced that I was ready for surgery. Directly behind her were two husky men dressed in blue scrubs.

"I guess it's time," I said.

"Yes, we are here to take you up to the operating room," said one of the men.

"OK, let's go," I responded, eager to get it all over and done with.

"I'll walk with you to the elevator," Danny said.

"You will be fine," one of the aids said, pushing my bed out the door. "It will be over soon and you will feel so much better."

I had no choice but to trust his words.

It was freezing cold in the operating room and the bright lights forced me to shut my eyes. I was hooked up to various machines; a blood pressure cuff was placed on my arm and a mask was put over my face.

Post-op, excruciating pain was my first sensation. It radiated across my abdomen and around my back. When I tried to scream, I felt a stinging burn in my throat as if a scalding liquid had been poured down my esophagus. My cries had volume but no coherency.

Hearing the ruckus, the nurse, intent on liberating me from the agonizing pangs, came running to medicate me.

Upset and frustrated by his inability to comfort me, Danny held my hand. Leaning over my bed, he covered my forehead with kisses.

"I'm so sorry, Bảo. Is there anything I can do for you? The nurse has given you more painkilling medicine. Is it getting any better?"

"I'm tired—so tired," I stammered. My eyelids, feeling like steel shades, drooped.

Witnessing my exhaustion and agony was too much for Danny. Anxiety and frustration had entered the room while he spoke. Believing it best for both of us, I dismissed him with a faint smile.

"Go home, Danny," I whispered. "Try to get some rest. Don't worry, the nurses will take good care of me. I'm going to be OK."

During my hospital recovery, Danny visited faithfully every morning before work, and Thaun Nha arrived directly from the office, shortly before sunset. My room resembled a florist's shop as colorful, aromatic bouquets arrived from my coworkers at Sleazy Sleepwear, my neighbor, Debbie, and her family, Tan, my best friend, and other family members. Sometimes, the fragrance was so overpowering, I asked the nurses to open the windows to weaken the scent.

Cards and well wishes also poured in. Valerie, with whom I had a close relationship, visited several times a week.

Despite the mood-elevating attentions and nurturing, I was in agonizing pain and still uncertain about my survival potential. Sure, the tumor had been aspirated, but what about the cancer? Nobody pronounced a reassuring word—at least not yet.

Fearing blood clots, the doctor had me immediately on my feet. At first, I was reluctant to budge; the staff literally hoisted me from my bed and set me down on my feet.

"Come on, Bảo, you have to walk. We must get your blood circulating."

Miffed by their insistence, though recognizing that they made sense, I dragged my feet a few steps. Through half-closed eyes, the hall appeared to be a less-than-shimmering mirage. Every move sent a stabbing pain through my body. The air was full of

361

discomfort. However, one thing was certain: If I failed to cooperate, my convalescence would be delayed.

In my mind, I wandered through the joy of living pain free, enjoying good health. Thankfully, by the third day, I was able to ramble up and down the hallway unaccompanied. While time usually escaped with uncontrollable rapidity, in the hospital, every hour seemed like an eternity, although the doctors and nurses were exceptional and played major roles in my healing.

In particular, I recall Cynthia, the empathetic, warm-hearted nurse who diligently tended to my needs daily. Her beautiful face wore the brightest smile, which illuminated the room whenever she entered.

Meticulous and nurturing, she made certain, to the best of her ability, that I was comfortable and serene. Discreet and considerate, Cynthia easily handled the rather embarrassing and unpleasant chore of inquiring about my bowel movements and checking my stools for blood.

"Have you moved your bowels today?" she would ask me.

"Not yet," I would reply.

"Do you wish to do so?"

"Yes."

"Let me help you," she always said, gently offering her arm as I walked to the bathroom. Like a sentinel guarding a top-echelon politician, she stood guard until I exited.

"Bảo, I'm waiting for you near the door. Let me know when you're ready," she would call to me.

Afterwards, she would do her due diligence, as required by the physician, and accompany be back to my bed. Undoubtedly, she was a guardian angel.

One afternoon, during a visit, Valerie informed me that she would be out of town for a week to attend a trade show.

The room was filled with vivacious chatter, poignantly animated by my irrefutable return among the living.

"How are you today?" Cynthia crooned, waltzing into the room.

"Much better, thank you," I replied.

"I'd like check your blood pressure."

"Sure, go right ahead."

"Bảo, today is my last day at Adventist Hospital," she said, inflating the cuff.

"Your last day? I didn't know you were leaving!" I gasped, surprised.

"Yes, I'm going to spend the rest of the summer in Japan."

"Are you Japanese?"

"My birth father is Caucasian and my birth mother Japanese," she said. "But I was adopted by a Caucasian mother and Japanese father. It's strange, but all my siblings have dark skin. I'm the only light-skinned child in our family."

"How did your mother handle her Japanese husband's culture?" I asked.

"Very well. She soon learned how to be quietly obliging. She bathed his feet, massaged his back and graciously performed every service expected of Japanese women."

"Really? I'm shocked! I would never have thought a Western woman would be so agreeable to the Asian ways."

Smiling coyly, Cynthia just nodded her head.

"Will you return in the fall?" I asked her.

364

"Yes. I'm a med student. I would like to be an obstetrician. I have about two more years of studies remaining."

"That's wonderful, Cynthia You'll be a great obstetrician."

"Thanks, Bảo, I hope so. I wish you all the best. I know you will make a full recovery, and I enjoyed assisting you."

We hugged and said our goodbyes, and Cynthia departed. Grateful, I recognized how blessed I was to have had this dedicated and committed woman attending to my needs in such a delicate time.

After the surgery, I noticed that my life took on a different twist. Debilitated, vulnerable and repeatedly harassed by morose thoughts centered on my mortality, I was unable to re-acclimate to the lifestyle I'd once had.

Incapable of fulfilling my professional obligations, I loitered around the house, sliding into a deep pit of depression. Dressing and caring for my personal needs became a hardship and with my pride and vanity waning, I abandoned my reliance on cosmetics. Nourishing myself was a new challenge, since most of my menu staples were no longer compatible with my fragile digestive system. I felt as though my life was running out of steam.

Noticing my out-of-character lethargy and accompanying psychological weariness, Danny took control of the situation, impressing upon me the importance of positive thinking in the healing process.

"Bảo, everything will be OK, but you have to take action. You cannot just sit around and wait to get better. You must help yourself."

Recognizing the truth in Danny's words, I became a model patient. I listened to my physician's advice, intent on following his instructions regarding the inclusion of dried beans, rice and fiber supplements in my diet. I also paid strict attention to his words regarding proper hydration and the integration of an exercise regime in my daily routine.

Researching my illness, I became knowledgeable concerning the importance of a healthier lifestyle. I avoided the spicy fish sauce that had been a part of my nourishment since childhood as well as fried and greasy foods that were high in trans fats and low-density cholesterol, all of which had been proven to increase the risk of certain cancers in human beings.

Realizing I was overburdened with dangerous stress, I turned to my religion for a means of attaining inner serenity, self-acceptance and some measure of contentment.

Aware that toxic elements in my surroundings were poisoning me, I weeded out the negative people in my life, embracing instead family and true friends. I had to believe in myself. I had to do all that was humanly possible to stay the course. I had to trust that I would not succumb under the weight of this life-threatening illness. By no means was it easy, but if I wanted to believe there was life after cancer, I had to do my part.

Eventually, my doctor decided that I should undergo chemotherapy, and during my frequent hospital stays for that, I took inventory of my life. I switched my focus away from the egotistical spotlight, centering my attention on the inclusion of altruistic endeavors in my life. It was no longer exclusively about satisfying my wishes and wants but about doing for those who had less than I did.

Danny stood by side, offering solidarity and guidance. He knew of my love for nature and the outdoors and often suggested day trips to distract me from the debilitating treatment. Sometimes, he would load the car with some blankets and a picnic lunch and take me for long drives along the coast.

On one of our day trips, we drove to Multnomah Falls, about thirty-five miles from Portland. On our return home, we chose the scenic highway, visiting Vista House to savor the panoramic, breathtaking view of the Columbia River Gorge.

Built in the early twentieth century as a memorial to pioneers, the towering, octagonal Vista House served as an historical feature and rest stop for tourists.

Walking through the area, I noticed a group of volunteer's intent on asking if they could be of assistance. Impressed by the beauty of the surroundings and the graciousness of those who gave of their time, I wondered if perhaps I could participate.

"I think I would like to volunteer here," I said enthusiastically.

"Let's find out what you have to do," Danny said, encouraged by my sudden rebirth of initiative.

We walked over to the information desk, where Danny spoke of my intentions. We were given an application, which I immediately filled in and returned.

"Thank you, Bảo" said the pretty, blonde volunteer, gazing at my name on top of the page. "Someone will call you shortly."

Her word was law—two days thereafter, I received a phone call from the administrative office thanking me for my interest. In the same breath, the caller mentioned that I would be required to attend a class for volunteers.

I quickly agreed, signed up and began working at Vista House in 2001, assisting the hundreds of thousands of visitors hailing from all over the world.

I began doing the things that gave me the most pleasure—walking on the beach at the coast and along the Columbia River, and in the woods. I also became interested again in home gardening, my favorite hobby.

As a volunteer, I worked for the benefit of others. My goal was to remove the focus from myself and shift it onto others. In recompense, my interactions with people distracted my less-than-sunny thoughts, thus lifting my spirits.

The beauty of the landscape and the almost-dizzying aroma of budding flowers reawakened my love of nature. Encouraged to conquer my frailty and get well, I was motivated to continue as an active participant in life, not a morose spectator awaiting the end.

Listening to the stories and experiences of others gave me a new dimension of well-being, but more importantly, I gained a diverse perspective of my own purpose here on earth. I was on a very unusual path. My journey was leading me towards a different destination…but where?

Chapter 17
Pañña: Wisdom and Insight

My time was filled with good days and terrible days in which I was far too incapacitated from the debilitating, post-op effects to do anything but lie prostrate in bed. Though frustrating, the intermission gave me ample opportunity for thoughts and reflections.

Of course, prayer was always part of my life, especially during my surgery and rather trying convalescence. When I prayed to God or Buddha, I was dedicated to maintaining my promises to become a better individual. In my daily dialogues, I pledged repentance for my errors and amended my ways accordingly, to avoid repeating the same aberrations.

I also believed in the cleansing power of atonement for sins committed in my past lives. In retribution for forgiveness received, it was my obligation to perform charitable works, indulge in almsgiving and give of myself to assist the needy.

Sincere in my request for pardon, I felt it was essential to turn my words into actions if I truly desired forgiveness. Convinced that we could all make a difference, even one person at a time, I intended to play a part in changing the world.

However, even if my faith was intact, I had not worshipped in a temple since my childhood, forty years earlier. This was, in a sense, somewhat shameful. It is not gracious to ask for favors without giving in return.

When I recuperated, I found myself meditating on the possibility of attending services at a Buddhist temple. I felt an irresistible pull towards spirituality, urging me to follow that path. I had shed many tears during my implorations for healing. But now, I felt as though I should make a special commitment to worship more devoutly.

"I think it's time I return to the temple," I said one morning after breakfast.

Gazing across the table, Danny nodded his head. Not a confirmed disbeliever nor a dullard, he understood my draw towards spirituality, fully recognizing the benefits I had reaped from my faith and the power it had over my ability to survive.

Decision made, I drove over to the nearest temple in Portland. Somewhat apprehensive after my prolonged absence, I paused for several minutes, drawing a series of long, deep breaths. Feeling empowered, I decided to cross the threshold.

Cautiously stepping inside as if I feared the reception I would receive after my willful disregard, on tiptoe, I made my way to the main shrine. Although a faint aroma of incense burnt earlier created a welcoming familiarity, I wrestled with a bit of guilt for my negligence. Focusing on the intensity of the moment, I repeated, mantra style, "I'm in a sacred house in a divine presence."

Shutting my eyes to escape the banalities of life, I waited, not knowing why or for what. Suddenly, I felt two arms encircle my waist. Ever so gently, they lifted me off the ground. I felt weightless, removed from my trepidation and concerns. Gazing down, I confirmed that my feet were still firmly on the ground. Yet, I felt totally buoyant. Engulfed in a new sensation, I recognized the compelling power of spirituality.

Of course, the lifting feeling was the unburdening of my soul—part of the reward for my faith and the journey I was pursuing. Certainly, I received a message: I should not absent myself ever again from worship. Not connecting to the spirit, not bonding with the inner energy and actually living in that dimension severs much of life's significance, leaving everything flat and without greater insights.

Making a commitment, from that moment on, I attended services every Sunday and on Fridays, I volunteered to help the staff with their errands.

Commitment to worship was insufficient; I had to go further. I had to be actively involved in good deeds.

During the services, I felt a very gripping communion with my creator. Undoubtedly, I belonged there, in this sacred house of worship. A mysterious calm settled over me. Relaxing yet energizing, it empowered my thoughts and recharged my body and mind, replenishing the energy the cancer had drained.

As I prayed, fond memories of my childhood worship with family and friends in the Son Tung Temple sprang to mind. Sadly, many unforeseen circumstances had prevented me from attending temple in Việt Nam during my teens and early adult years. The frequent, unexpected bombings made traveling risky and difficult, and most of the time, my mother felt it wise to avoid worship for the safety of her family.

In good conscience, I cannot exonerate my spiritual negligence, which coincided with my immigrating to the United States. It happened without dwelling on any specific motive, forcing me to admit a falling out of practice though my faith remained intact. On the other hand, Buddhist temples were not found easily in most suburban, American neighborhoods. Truly, I'm not seeking to rectify my delinquency by seeking lame excuses and prefabricated, convenient loopholes. In the end, when it's time for judgment, it will all mean nothing.

However, throughout my forty-year hiatus, I had been plagued with endless challenges, always finding the strength to overcome and survive. Although I suffered, fought and endured without the guidance and empowerment of a compassionate, Buddhist community, I never lost hope, holding firm to my belief in the mercy and goodness of God. I respected His influence and presence in my life and acknowledged that I could not make it without him.

Rekindled and reestablished in my spiritual identity, I undertook a deeper study of Buddhism. Surprisingly, an interest in the Buddhist philosophy and faith began to sprout. My fervor was not only noticeable but contagious. Fascinated by my dedication, Danny expressed a desire to accompany me on this new, life-turning journey.

I know in my heart that the influence of Buddhism reshaped my life. It allowed my cluttered mind to open up with the same wonder and awe as clusters of clouds that slide away to reveal a sunny, unmarred sky. I was liberated from my confusion and chaos within. Defined by my credence, I recognized that who I was the result of my adherence to Buddhism.

Furthermore, it was the motivating force behind my decision to become a better person and help others who were trudging and struggling along obstructed paths by writing this book as a testament to the winning power of faith and the unwavering belief in my own ability to survive. I could not have succeeded any other way.

Learning the Buddhist way of life is different from learning the lessons parents impart to their offspring. Actually, most mothers and fathers inculcate children with the rules of proper behavior and the obligation to respect and obey teachers as well as elders. Children are also taught the importance of studying to earn good grades in order to qualify for professional careers that will elevate their statuses in the community while fattening their bank accounts and financial portfolios.

Buddhism, however, steps further, teaching that every living being has an immortal soul or spirit that can be reborn over and over, within all different forms of living matter. Thus, it follows that all levels of life should be treated with the utmost respect and dignity.

Actually, an animal could more than likely house the reincarnated soul of a human being born centuries or even millennia ago. In fact, a pet welcomed into the home could possibly be a distant relative returned to earthly life. An interesting but mind-jostling theory, it certainly offers much substance for thought.

When men and women perish, their souls are infused into other living forms, be they other humans, animals or plants. The goodness factor—how a person lived while on earth—determines his or her future status among the hierarchy of life. Virtue, generosity and a compassionate openness to the trials of others constitute a worthy existence. Therefore, how a person lives his or her life sets the stage for eventual reincarnations.

Repeating the words of Buddha, "The secret of health for both mind and body is not to mourn for the past, nor to worry about the future, but to live the present moment wisely and earnestly." I strove to adopt his mindset as my own.

Living in the present moment, giving of myself to others, keeping a positive outlook, altering my dietary and lifestyle habits, and eliminating negative influences, together with a staunch refusal to die, led me to victory not only over the malicious cancer but the pestiferous Hepatitis C I contracted midway through the healing process. It seemed as if the cancer plague was insufficient penance. I had to battle still another debilitating illness.

True to my Buddhists beliefs, my faith was, in the end, the lifeline keeping me afloat despite the murky shadows that hovered above me. Believing in a compassionate God, I was confident that He would not let me perish. Prayers are usually answered, even if it's not always in ways that are compatible with our wills and intentions. But, God awards persistence and tenacity.

The proof came soon enough. Happily, in 2005, after a hellish journey back to health, I was pronounced cured of Hepatitis C. Two years thereafter, following my final checkup, the surgeon declared me cancer free. I had overcome all the odds and won my battle.

Much as I was convinced that my religion was a panacea in my struggle against cancer, I later found myself hoping I could depend on Buddha and his wisdom to heal all the other woes pertinent to the human condition.

Though suffering builds strength, we shun all that causes pain and grief, refusing the existence of our own failings while pointing fingers at others or at the creator for misfortunes encountered during the course of life. We are human. Consequently, due to this condition shared by mankind, we are prone to misguided errors and noxious misdeeds, which, more often than not, injure the physical being of others, leaving open wounds on their hearts and minds.

However, regardless of which label I pinned on faith, at the core of all beliefs is forgiveness. I believe it is a necessary good to be able to forgive those who have trampled upon us. After all, who among us is without fault? Who among us is never culpable of committing a wrongdoing? Who among us has never drawn a tear from the eyes of a loved one?

Many had hurt me in the past, just as my words and actions had undoubtedly caused others grief. I knew the right way. But somehow, it is not always easy to put into action what we preach and often, even in pardoning, we are not quite exonerated from the memory and stinging aftershocks of an evil deed that left painful scars. Consequently, the recollection of my husband's heartbreaking indiscretion lingered, haunting my thoughts and feelings long after I had forgiven him.

I also learned, though my Buddhist studies, that due to the transitory nature of souls, animals have feelings just like humans. They feel frightened, suffer pain and form emotional attachments both with other members of their species and with humans. Most people seeking to gratify their appetites for food seek out and brutally kill animals without realizing the agony they inflict. Believing that life does not exist without a hearty slab of meat on their plate, they go after it, paying little heed to the gravity of their behavior.

I'll admit that I'm not perfect yet in this regard, though I do limit myself to the occasional consumption of fish. In principle, I'm an animal-rights activist—no furs, no chops, no drum sticks, no wings, no ribs, no burgers and no steaks.

If people would take the time to know and understand animals, they would perhaps modify certain thoughtless or even cruel behavior patterns. I made it my business to pursue knowledge of my four-pawed friends with whom I share space and time on this planet.

Often, I like to tune in to the animal channel just to get a momentary respite from the global horrors occurring at the hands of *Homo sapiens*. We like to perceive ourselves as the superior species; however, sadly, raw evidence sometimes contradicts this fabled mindset.

Learning about the wonders of the animal kingdom rattles the conscience. Making comparisons to human behavior leaves me shocked. Yet, there are individuals who continue with an impertinent disregard for life, using the killing of animals as a pastime! Calling hunting a sport is absolutely ludicrous. It is, instead, the destruction of life.

Is it a proud achievement to massacre God's creatures for selfish needs? Don't all breathing creatures have the right to live out their designated life expectancies, just as men and women do?

Most of the animals featured on these programs are intelligent, beautiful beings that care for, nurture and protect their innocent offspring with more diligence, love and respect than some humans who abandon, neglect and abuse theirs.

Difficult as it is to believe, some animals even behave better in social settings, tending with loyalty and unflinching integrity to their adopted parents, children and the physically or emotionally challenged they faithfully serve.

On a personal level, my study of Buddhism gave me a different perspective of and feeling for animal life. I learned to appreciate my beautiful, white cat, Luan, who, with his loving, sweet personality, resembles the virtuous side of human nature. Awakening around seven o'clock, just as the first rays of sun penetrate the room. Luan runs through his feline Pilates with grace and ease that leave me envious. Satisfied with his limbering ritual, he jumps onto the bed and blithely inches up to my head, maintaining a low profile. Once in his strategic position, he rubs his face on mine several times in preparation for his *pièce de résistance*—a sloppy, wet kiss on the lips. Afterwards, he curls up in my arms and, like a satisfied lover, purrs in soft, melodious whispers before drifting off to sleep.

When it's time to quench his thirst or appetite, Luan blazes a trail to the kitchen, positioning himself either in front of the refrigerator to communicate his desire for a bowl of milk or near the cupboard to announce his hunger. It's amazing how studied and exact his maneuvers are, leaving little if any room for failure.

However, before obliging his whims, I check his bowls to be certain he had consumed the previous repast before setting down another meal. If he has not cleaned his plate, I admonish him for trying to solicit more food. Of course, my reluctance to please him does not sit well. A spurt of feline vindication compels him to leap up and entwine his lithe body between my legs in an attempt to topple me.

"Luan, it won't work," I shout. "You can knock me to the floor but you're not getting any more food until you finish what's in your bowl."

My furrowed brow confirms that I mean business. Acquiescent, Luan steps back, fixes his glance on mine and meows.

"OK," I tell him, "go finish your lunch and I'll get you some milk."

Slowly strutting to his bowl, he demonstrates his obedience. In less than a minute, the leftovers are history. His FIQ— feline intelligence quotient—is visibly elevated.

The intelligence of animals always catches my interest. Sometimes, I think we take their abilities for granted and fail to respect their thoughts and emotions as living sentient beings with very real feelings.

However, anyone who enjoys the privilege of sharing their lives with a four-pawed creature fully understands the precious nature and value of that special relationship. It's called unconditional love, and it's precious and unique.

Luan is a loyal companion, willing to love unreservedly. Genuinely enjoying my camaraderie, he gets perturbed when I depart his company. Retreating behind the door, he sulks for a while like a frustrated child wanting his way, then darts off to a secret hiding place. When Danny wants to find him, he has to scout around the house to uncover the location of the secret refuge. It's a game of hide and seek every time, with Luan in the role of undefeated champion.

Nevertheless, as soon as I cross the threshold into the foyer, Luan leaps out, meowing a greeting. If I understood the feline language, I would be certain he is saying, "Mom, I'm so happy you're back." Like most cats, Luan has a funny, feisty nature. Once in a while, he'll rise up and arch his back, resembling a shrimp. Then, in the blink of an eye, he jumps sideways, like a Ninja cat.

Sometimes aggressive, he enjoys confrontational interaction, engaging in battles with Danny and me. Preparing an ambush plot, he conceals himself until the appropriate moment. Then, striking like a bolt of lightning, he lunges forward, landing in my arms, amused by my scared, surprised reaction, though often, his antics draw only a hearty laugh.

Although my mother had a cat while I was growing up, the experiences with Luan encompass my maiden involvement with actually getting to know what makes these interesting animals tick. Like a firstborn child, he was fascinating and mysterious until we became better acquainted and I realized how much love and attention a pet requires.

385

Through Luan, I grew to understand the role of animals in Buddhism. Essentially, they are thought to be in possession of the Buddha nature, which allots them a potential for enlightenment similar to humans. Perhaps not intellectually gifted, they live more by instinct than knowledge. Today, the authenticity of Buddha's words—"Animals feel as much as humans"—leaves no doubt in my mind.

Unfortunately, my earliest memories bring to mind the story of a cat my mom had when I was about nine years old. At the time, we lived on a small farm in the country, adjacent to a rice field. Harvesting rice and vegetables crops, we dried and stored them in our home for consumption during the barren, winter season.

One year, the mice, permanent inhabitants of the village, dug tunnels into the surrounding houses, burrowing their way into the storage areas to snatch the provisions. Disturbed by this unpleasant invasion, my mother realized that opening our door to a cat would eventually stave off the mice, since felines have reputations as mouse-haters.

Searching around the village, she located a neighbor who had access to a litter of newborn kittens. However, to retrieve the pet, she faced a sixteen-mile round-trip trek. Since the Vietnamese believe that bad luck befalls

386

anyone who allows a cat to enter their car, my mother completed the journey on foot, unwilling to test the validity of the age-worn, cultural superstition.

Departing at dawn, she returned shortly before sunset cradling a six-week-old, brown-and-white-speckled kitten with glowing, green eyes. Tiny, he slept nestled in the bend of her elbow.

"Mom," I said, glancing at the tiny, frail creature, "he's just a baby. I don't think he'll be able to handle those big mice!"

"It'll be just fine," she replied. "He won't be a kitten forever. For now, all he has to do is make enough noise to scare the mice away."

It all sounded so easy. However, although my mom's idea was clever, the inclusion of the cat in our family turned my relationship with her somewhat aggressive. Angered because the little kitten had decided to use the ashes from the kitchen hearth as a litter box, she repeatedly admonished me.

"Bảo, it's your responsibility to keep the kitten away from the kitchen," she shouted. "I don't want him messing with the ashes. Let him go outside if he has to relieve himself."

Easy to pronounce and difficult to execute, I thought. How would I possibly manage this? Since the doors to the house and kitchen remained open until bedtime, as was

387

customary in Vietnamese homes, I knew it was virtually impossible to keep the kitten from urinating in the ashes

"Mom," I responded franticly, exasperated by the unfair responsibility with which I had been saddled. "There is no way to stop him from coming into the kitchen."

And, unfortunately, I was right! One afternoon, he crept in unwelcomed and unannounced. Minutes later, he relieved himself in the ashes, kicking up a mound of dust afterwards to hide the confirmation of his crime. The evidence left behind proved my culpability, thereby sealing my condemnation. My mom's quick, open-palmed slap across my face stung my cheek. Offended and irate, I could not understand why the kitten's defiance and disobedience were my wicked deed.

Unable to justify my punishment, I realized that if I intended to prevent encore slaps, I would have to guard the kitten like a sentinel. He became my obsession. Following his sprightly jumps and runs, I kept my glance glued on his lithe body, controlling every stretch, trying to anticipate when he would head towards forbidden territory. When he turned in the wrong direction, I was on my feet, shooing him away.

One afternoon, momentarily distracted, I raised my eyes just in time to catch him squatting over the ashes to relieve himself. Enraged and already feeling my mom's calloused-palm swat my cheek, I grabbed him by the neck and slammed him down on the floor.

"How many times have I told you not to go into the kitchen," I screamed as if admonishing a child for a wrongdoing.

The kitten first whimpered then lay motionless. Leaning over, I noticed a few drops of ruby-red blood drizzling from his mouth. Scared I had hurt him, I knelt down to caress his head. A pair of glassy, motionless eyes met mine. It didn't take much to realize he was lifeless. In my rage, I had accidentally killed the little kitten!

A knot formed in my throat. Swallowing hard, I tried to dislodge it. Realizing the severity of my actions, I feared my mother's wrath. Confused and devastated, I broke into fitful sobs. What would I do now?

Though momentarily in shock, I knew I had to take action. Gathering my wits, I entertained a sudden idea. Lifting the stiffened carcass, I carried it outside, making certain to wipe away the blood stains—irrefutable evidence of my misdeed. Even though it was

389

unintentional, the truth was, I had killed the kitten.

Once in the backyard, I dropped the dead animal, fell to my knees and, with my bare hands, dug into the parched soil. The tiny pebbles ingrained in the sod chafed my fingers, eventually drawing blood as I labored hurriedly, trying to avoid any possibility of getting caught red handed.

As soon as my makeshift gravesite was ready, I reached for the kitten, whispered "goodbye" and "I'm so sorry—but it was an accident," and slipped him into the hole. Afterwards, with the back of my hands, I brushed back and forth, returning the mound of dirt I had removed. Removing the evidence, I had cancelled the crime.

Later that evening, upon my mom's return home, she questioned the kitten's absence. Walking to and fro, she searched under chairs and in the closets."Bảo, have you see the kitten?" she asked me.

"No, I haven't," I lied, biting my lip.

"Help me look for him. I don't see him anywhere."

Pretending to collaborate with the search, I walked around the house, feigning ignorance over the whereabouts of the missing kitten.

With her energy and patience depleted, it was obvious that our efforts would bear no fruit. "I think someone has stolen our kitten," she said, upset and exhausted. Lowering my eyes, I escaped into the quietness of presumed reflection. Thankfully, she pursued it no further.

My kitten-killing crime, though unmediated and accidental, left me traumatized and with recurring memories. Still today, my misdeed remains vivid in front of my eyes, an equitable retribution for a reckless sin of my youth. Though I was unaccountable at the time, eventually, I was saddled with the consequences.

Responsibility is attached to every action, to every thought and every feeling. Even if it seems as if we escape certain penalties, eventually they come back to haunt us—and to claim their due.

A lesson was learned, though it took years to sink in. At this point in my life, I had acquired *Pañña*—the infusion of wisdom and insights derived from a serious striving for awakening.

It was a long, tedious journey filled with sometimes seemingly insurmountable obstacles; yet, I was so close to reaching my destination.

Chapter 18
In the Shadow of Serenity

I've never forgotten the awful day I killed my mother's cat. Although some events of my past are shadowy, I remember that incident almost with exaggerated clarity. On the other hand, why should such a traumatic situation easily be obliterated? After all, people should be accountable for their actions and though my deed was far from premeditated, it did demonstrate a reckless carelessness in addition to a lack of respect for a living creature in my charge.

Although many of my memories are draped in dark clouds, some of the vibrant ones persist, passing through my mind, haunting me. A few have been demolished either by the passage of time or my own unconscious quest to seek a reprieve from some of the early horrors. However, during quiet, reflective moments, I often feel as though I've missed a big portion of my life because I was caught up in the turmoil of fighting for survival.

From time to time, I remember being nineteen years old and running from my first husband, Sang, to escape his humiliating bouts of physical and emotional abuse. Vivid in front of me are the disturbing images of his violent acts.

It seems as if one moment, I'm bent over crying in pain, actually feeling the burn from his slaps, and then the scene shifts and I'm nearly sixty years old. Life has gone by so quickly. At times, I feel as though I didn't get to enjoy it as much as I would have liked.

It was counterproductive, if not destructive, to dwell on past gloom and doom scenarios when present worries continued to overwhelm me. My children were and will always be a source of apprehension and frustration, even if they are young adults. Although I have good relationships with my sons, Thaun Nha and Trung, my interactions with the other three children have been distressing and, in some cases, continue to cause anxiety.

Phuong refused to move to Oregon with us, remaining instead in Oklahoma to conclude her studies. While still in school, she worked at Oak Tree, a clothing store. In 1991, she decided to join us in Oregon, transferring to the Oak Tree store in Clackamas Town Center.

While working and attending Mt. Hood Community College part time, she lived at home. A year later, having accumulated a modest savings account, Phuong moved into her own place. Now and then, we exchanged visits, though eventually, she slipped into the role of phantom daughter, distancing herself from us for months at a time.

The absences grew longer and more pronounced until, in December 2001, Phuong and I ran into each other while shopping at Clackamas Town Center. When I asked her why she no longer visited her family, she just smiled. Ignoring her reluctance to respond, I invited her for lunch, an invitation she graciously accepted.

Phuong arrived vivacious and prompt, eager to spend an afternoon with her mom. I prepared a repast based on my daughter's preferences. We had a delightful visit, sharing the most recent events from our lives. She spoke easily and seemed relaxed after the first few uncomfortable moments. Embarrassing pauses were sparse and eventually nonexistent.

Prior to departing, Phuong offered to come over the following week to decorate our Christmas tree. Pleased by her interest, I agreed, welcoming her whenever she was available. Six days later, she knocked on the door. With a smile and a hug, I welcomed her. We chatted briefly. Midway through the conversation, Phuong jumped to her feet and headed over to the unadorned tree.

I seized the opportunity to absent myself and slip into the kitchen to get some lunch on the table.

"Mom, the tree's done," she said about a half hour thereafter, walking over and positioning herself behind me.

"I'm almost finished here," I told her. "I'll come take a look."

Glancing at the Christmas tree, I was filled with amazement. Phuong had demonstrated an artistic side I had never known. The tree was glowing, each ornament in place according to size, and color coordinated. I wondered if such creativity was inborn or governed by a special fervor—the type of energy that elevates mediocrity to excellence.

After offering due praise, I summoned her to the table.

"Let's sit for a bite and catch up on lost time," I said.

Smiling, she joined me in sharing the rations I had spooned onto the serving dish.

"Mom, you were right about so many things," she blurted, raising her eyes from the plate. "I may have not have shown it always, but I remember all your words and the many things you taught us while we were growing

396

up. Though I acted as if I wasn't listening, I heard every word. You always worked hard to provide us with a warm, secure place to live and plenty of good food to eat. A silly girl, I used to think that our family was crazy. However, since moving out on my own, I've learned that the people I thought were my friends, those who seemed to have all the answers, really were the crazy ones, whereas my family, who I thought knew nothing, were actually normal.

"I used to be firmly convinced that you were wrong to bug me about the kind of clothes I wore. That was annoying and angered me. I thought I should have been able to choose my own fashion trends. Part of the fun of growing up is the ability to express one's personality."

Though I didn't recall pestering her about the outfits she'd selected, I had to admit that I never did understand the attraction to some of the awful dress trends that captivated the young people's fancies. Then again, every generation has idiosyncrasies that appear bizarre if not horrendous to a previous one. However, despite all the conflicts and past rebellions, Phuong's words triggered a flow of tears—tears of joy.

"And I recall talking with Thaun. I can still hear him say in his pubescent, crackling voice, 'Mom is a wonderful mother but all of us kids are crazy!'" she continued, giggling. We both laughed.

We concluded the day with a long embrace at the door.

"I'll be back, Mom, to dismantle the tree," she yelled, running out the door. I watched as her long, shiny hair bounced in the late-afternoon breeze. Indisputably, she was a beautiful, young woman.

But Phuong's promise was merely a string of empty words. When I called her, she neither lifted the receiver nor responded to my voice mail messages. She'd always been a difficult child, and I didn't really focus on her misbehavior, though I had hoped maturity would have altered her faults. Often, long periods of silence would follow her visits. This was who she was, and I had to accept it, though it was a painful reality.

About six months thereafter, distraught over the prolonged silence, Danny and I decided to go to Phuong's apartment in Lake Oswego to discover why she failed to return our calls. She was young, vulnerable and alone, and I feared the worst. Something had to justify her disappearance from our lives.

Upon our arrival, the landlord promptly reported in a jabbering tone that Phuong had moved months earlier, leaving no forwarding information. Danny and I exchanged troubled glances. Was he telling us our daughter was lost? I felt my heart pound in double time. I had no idea where my child was. Was she safe? Had she gotten herself into trouble?

These and many others were questions not destined to obtain answers. Sadly, we never received word from Phuong again.

I can only hope and pray that my daughter is well and that one day, she will come to her senses, pick up the phone and call us.

Tram, on the other hand, roomed with a friend in South Carolina until her eighteenth birthday, after which she met and married a soldier in the U.S. Army. Relocating to Orange County, California, they eventually started a family. Years later, one evening, while relaxing in front of the TV, the ring of the phone startled me.

"I'll get it," I shouted, jumping to my feet.

"Hi, Mom," a female voice chirped. "It's Tram!"

"Tram? H-h-how are you?" I stammered, barely able to get the words out.

"Mom, I'd like to come visit. You really should meet Gabby and Zachary! Gabby is nine and Zach is eight. They are your

399

grandchildren! Can we pay you a visit, Mom?"

My heart skipped a beat. Her voice was tinged with excitement.

"That would be nice, Tram, I'll ask Dad to send you the tickets."

"Great. We'll come for a long weekend because I have to get back to work."

Much as I would have preferred a longer visit, I was excited about Tram's arrival. As soon as I told Danny, he ran out to book the flights. I guess we feared a change of mind and heart on her part.

Revved up by the anticipation of seeing Tram after years of silence, I could hardly get to sleep that evening. Destroying my bed, twisting and turning in rhythmic, nerve-wracking gyrations, I realized I was impeding Danny from getting a merited night's rest. Rising, I headed for the living room. Seated in the stillness, I visualized what it would be like to see Tram after so long and meet my grandkids for the first time.

Sometimes, the images and scenes we orchestrate in our minds to suit our wishes bear no resemblance to reality. That night, I created the visit I desired. I wrote the dialogue and choreographed the scenes one after the after. However, I soon realized the disappointment attached to wishful thinking.

My house was sparkling clean, the refrigerator filled to the limits. Everything was perfect. Nervously awaiting Tam's arrival, I jumped to my feet when the door knocker sounded. Running to get the door, the curtain was lowered on my thoughts. This was for real. Tram and her family were here. I drew a long, deep breath to steady my racing heart.

"Hello, Mom," Tram blurted, hurriedly stepping across the threshold. Her exuberance, though endearing, was in net contrast to the children's poignantly apathetic approach. Two sets of eyes glared at me as if I were a piece of sculpture on public view.

"Mom, this is Gabby and Zachary," she said, pointing to each child.

An uncomfortable interval of hesitancy increased my anxiety. The children stood emotionless, frozen, knowing full well that I was their grandmother. No smiles, no giggles, no hugs, no coy glances. Leaning over, I put my arms around Zachary. Stepping back, he freed himself from my embrace, instinctively rejecting my gesture of love.

Gabby's behavior was similar. Never anticipating the children's reaction, I was painfully disturbed by their aloof manner. Certainly, this was not a manifestation of the timid, retreating nature of young children. The children outwardly rejected me. Something was not quite right.

Flipping the pages of my memory, I recalled how Tram had always considered me the enemy. All the intrigues she'd engaged in to dupe me came to the surface. For a few moments, I relived all the challenges and dilemmas I endured while she was growing up. She certainly had consumed much energy plotting to hurt me. Much as I thought it was all over and done with, I had to question if perhaps she was still holding on to her rebellious nature.

Did she sow seeds of defamation in the minds of her children? Had I been the victim of a smear campaign? Was it possible that my daughter would speak ill of me to my grandkids?

Shocked by my own questions, I had to admit the evidence pointed in that direction. But, unwilling to surrender, I attempted to break the wall Tram had constructed around her children. My efforts met with failure. Much as I tried, Gabby and Zachary would not warm up to me. Once poisoned, the mind of a child does not rid itself of the toxins easily or quickly.

Leaving to return home, they stood as two alabaster statues, icy and stiff, while I planted kisses on their cheeks. The parting was beyond the bittersweet flavor of the arrival. Gone were excuses of timid children confronted by a stranger called "Grandma." They knew me now, and they knew who I was.

Several weeks thereafter, the phone rang shortly before dinner.

"Hello, Mom, it's Tram," she said when I picked up the call. "Can you send me two thousand dollars?"

"May I know what for?"

"Can you just send me the money, Mom?"

"I'm sorry, Tram, I cannot send you any money."

When the voice on the other end faded and the receiver went down, rudely, I hung up.

Sadly, the echo of her disgruntled sigh faded, in no way to return.

Tram never phoned or visited again. Repudiation, especially when unwarranted, on the part of children towards their parents is a monumental tragedy. I gave her the gift of life. In return, she cast me away like a pair of scuffed and torn, seasons-old shoes. Discarded, I had no recourse but to surrender to her will. With her absence from my life, I forfeited her love and the love of my grandchildren.

403

It was suddenly clear: Tram had never altered her opinion of me. In my daughter's mind, I was still the enemy. Her estrangement was heartbreaking and no less excruciating than the actual, physical demise of a daughter. Only this time, it was not an act of God, therefore exceedingly more agonizing to endure. Since there has never been closure for this "death," there cannot be healing. Consequently, I walk each day with a thorn in my side, though in my heart I have forgiven her.

While writing this memoir, I often paused to catch my breath and recollect my thoughts and feelings. Though many years have passed, time has not softened the circumstances of my life, even if the dust of decades has covered some of the pinnacles of my pain.

Although I felt the need to share my story with others, many times during the vivid, dramatic flashbacks and emotional outbursts, I questioned my motives for retaking this painful journey. Why would I spend time and energy reopening old wounds? Why would I give new life to injuries already healed?

Perhaps, in the back of my mind was the hope that I could turn this return journey into a cathartic process that would free me from my demons, cleanse my mind and reenergize my spirit. There were things about my life I didn't fully understand until now, and repressed feelings that lingered, creating unresolved dilemmas in need of reparation.

As I wrote, I noticed that new perspectives and insights sprang to mind. There were endless, puzzling aspects still trapped in the darkness even though a new light had broken through some of the murkiness. In those moments, I felt overwhelmed by it all. Then, the storm gradually subsided. When the clouds parted, I drove to the Ross store in Gresham and bought a box of my favorite Belgian chocolates.

Hurrying back to my vehicle, I unwrapped the box, disrespectful of the pretty packaging, and plucked from the box a luscious, nut-topped square. The encounter between the sweet milk chocolate and my tongue was nothing short of scrumptious.

Each tiny morsel brought an incredible sensation of pleasure. It took so little.

Placing the box on the passenger's seat, I ran back into the store to purchase two additional boxes of this divine manna. At this point in my life, I make it almost an obligation to enjoy every moment of every day while recognizing and appreciating all my blessings. I see no reason to deny myself life's little pleasures—a viewpoint I have adopted and molded into a daily philosophy.

Although I retired after my surgery and battle with cancer, I seldom, if ever, have an idle moment. Determined to perfect my English-language skills, I continue to attend classes, trying my best to gain more fluency and perhaps even conquer the frustration of my difficult-to-eliminate, pronounced Vietnamese accent.

During my leisure hours, I try my best to give back in thanksgiving for blessings received. My volunteer work at Vista House continues, and I do enjoy being of service to others, even if in my own puny way. It is an uplifting experience when someone says, "Thanks, Bảo, you're a big help." It makes me feel as if I have a worthwhile purpose in life and a valid reason to get out of bed every morning.

Gardening has gained equal time with volunteering and studying English in my itinerary.

The feral beauty of nature works like an elixir, sending me soaring to extraordinary heights. Each season, thousands of multihued bulbs promising an extravaganza of full-blown tulips create a phantasmagoric aura enhanced by the splendor of oversized, swell-headed petunias. It is almost idyllic. Birds in song fly over the voluptuous roses and seem to laud my creative genius.

Often, I've caught passersby as they've aimed their cameras to immortalize a scene that truly shares a resemblance with an exotic garden in some far-off paradise. And my neighbors are delighted when spring blooms, spraying a mass of color and scents throughout the neighborhood.

"I bet this garden cost you thousands of dollars," my neighbor, Bud, said one day. From his kitchen window, he was able to enjoy a bird's-eye view.

"That's a pretty good guesstimate," I responded. "Between the flowers and the stone for the sidewalk, we're pretty much there. Actually, most of the plants are holiday,

407

special-occasion or birthday gifts from Danny."

"Really? You mean to tell me that Danny knows what plants to get?"

"Well, not exactly," I responded, chuckling. "He gives me the money and I do the shopping. Since I love a beautiful garden, I buy plants and flowers. It's that simple."

"I get it," Bud chuckled. "You're the one doing all the hard work and I'm getting all the enjoyment." He eyed me sweetly, like a father enjoying the antics of his toddler daughter.

I smiled, happy that my elderly neighbor found my garden pleasing. It always made me feel uplifted when others expressed joy or gratitude for a deed I had completed.

Bud was a gracious gentleman. His open, casual manner and congenial personality reflected the demographics of the neighborhood. The area was formerly a wetland bordered by wild-growing blackberry bushes. Thaun and his friends had spent many afternoons picking berries and casting their rods for fish in the rippling waters of Fairview Lake. The area had been redeveloped at the turn of the twenty-first century.

Situated in the Blue Heron II development, less than a mile from the Columbia River, our single-story, 2,300-square-foot house with French architectural design was considered within the boundaries of Fairview City. Boasting a low crime rate, the neighborhood was ideal for rearing a family.

Relatively spacious, our residence was a four-bedroom home complete with three full baths, an office, a formal dining room, a living room, a family room, a contemporary kitchen, a laundry facility and a two-car garage.

Light and cheery, the house was constructed with six skylights and twelve-foot, vaulted ceilings, which grew to fourteen feet in the entrance and living room. To create drama, the builder had decorated the ceilings in the kitchen and dining and family rooms with iridescent, black paint and mounted track lights to create a shimmering, almost twinkling effect.

With a flip of a switch, we played the masters of the universe, enjoying a romantic dinner and relaxation under a ceiling illuminated with a thousand glittery stars— our very own starry sky. The ambience was truly unique, as was the foyer carpeting, which was designed with twelve-inch-square cut outs filled with diagonal tiles, to produce a stepping-stone effect all the way to the kitchen. These features, along with the many other unusual touches, gave our home a truly special quality.

Dan Miu, a Romanian-born architect, was responsible for the unique features that enhanced the ambiance of the house. Believing that he would personally occupy the residence with his family, he'd focused on going the extra mile, adding special effects to suit his distinctive whims.

Eventually, he'd decided to sell, and when we'd bid on the property and questioned his vision for the house, he'd responded with a whimsical smile. "The ceiling depicts our solar system," he'd told us, "but you have to realize that you are viewing it from another planet, not Earth. And the inimitable flooring, mixing carpet and tile, represents the path to the future."

After we closed on the house, I decided to reinvent the garden. Though it was much smaller than my previous backyard, I tried to recapture the lushness by planting fruit trees, lots of multicolored flowers and rows of vegetables. Although far from spectacular, the end result did satisfy my green thumb, encouraging my lips to curl in a smile whenever I strolled through it, centering my gaze on the simple yet exhilarating beauty of nature.

Even though I'd always loved my home, I was not yet ready to script a finale for my imaginings. Believing we never get too old or too busy to indulge in reveries, I often fantasized about a dream house set either on the ocean or high in the mountains. Water and mountains always had held a special fascination for me, captivating and nourishing my craving for the wonders of nature.

To live on the sea and have acres of fertile land to develop into a lush, flourishing garden would be the perfect fantasy turned reality.

Some people search endlessly for simple pleasures, switching their interests and pastimes to dissolve a deep-rooted dissatisfaction with life. Maybe I'm easy to please.

Despite all the conflicts and dilemmas I have had to overcome, nature and the outdoors have always been my sources of joy and refuge. When Danny and I drive for enjoyment, I focus on the mountains and valleys. I breathe deeply, savoring the varied aromas of freshly mowed lawns and budding blooms. The gurgling echoes of meandering waters are like dramatic symphonies, powerful music stirring my soul. Undoubtedly, I'm happiest with nature and

411

the awe-inspiring grandeur of unmarred purity.

Often, I daydream about building a large-scale pond to welcome and accommodate visiting wildlife and any homeless animals that drift along. I'd also like to have a couple of pets—four dogs and four cats would be a nice-sized family.

The unconditional love animals give so freely is priceless. Whenever I would leave my house, I had the certainty that upon my return at day's end, my four-pawed, faithful friends would be there to greet me with tail wags and wet licks regardless of my state of mind.

Instead of arguments, contradictions, rebellious actions or sly intrigues, there would be excited greetings and the expectation of a pat on the head, a walk in the garden and a bowl of nourishment. Animals are not as complicated as human beings—so little gets their tails wagging.

However, much as I recognize and appreciate the extraordinary magnificence of the Earth, I realize I am not a fairy-tale character existing in a fable. In my right mind, I cannot deny the dangers and threats draining the joy out of life. One burning question awaits a peaceful rest: How can anyone ever obliterate the memory of the deleterious attacks of 9/11? Devoid of a response, the question lives and continues to frustrate and disturb.

Before these vicious acts of terrorism poisoned the American dream of guaranteed homeland serenity and an almost-untouchable aura that bred security, my concerns were limited to the threats of foreign wars, domestic violence and the possibility of nuclear conflict, which invades everyone's thoughts from time to time.

Contemplating the probabilities that threaten global peace, I attended class a couple of weeks prior to 9/11, never imagining how perilously close to reality my fears were. It was Friday, August 31, 2001. On that particular day, before concluding the lesson, our teacher, Mary Rose, addressed the class.

413

"Your assignment this week is to write about life in the United States. I want this paper to reflect your own perspectives, thoughts and feelings. Next week, one by one, you will come to the head of the class and read your essay. Does anyone have any questions?"

No one raised their hands, and Mary Rose smiled, wishing us a good week. The following week, on Friday, September 7, I was summoned to present my paper. Drawing a slow, deep breath I stood and steadily walked to the front of the room. Clearing my throat, I grabbed the attention of the students and teacher.

Once I had the interest of my classmates and Mary Rose, I opened my discourse on the merits of the United States as a leader and super world power, always ready to jump in and give political and financial aid when needed by other nations.

I mentioned the generosity and altruism of Americans on an individual and collective level. Undoubtedly, this was a country of givers willing to go the extra mile for the less fortunate.

"I feel safe," I said, gazing up from my paper. "We have a strong defense department, a well-trained and well-funded military, and a political philosophy that favors reaching out

414

to other nations as ambassadors of good will and peace intent on defending and preserving human rights while promising US citizens safety.

"I feel safe when I leave my house to begin the workday, and I feel out of harm's way when I return in the evenings. My fear of warfare and its devastating consequences on my family dissipated when I left Việt Nam. Gone was the terror of death at any moment that tormented me through my childhood and young life.

"I'm also thankful for the ability to better my circumstances. Hard work and diligence have allotted me a decent paycheck, a nice home, full plates on my table and all the comforts of American life.

"I'm grateful for the privilege of being a citizen of this great country. Not only has my dream come true, but I have the possibility and encouragement to keep on dreaming in this land of opportunity."

My presentation was met with a hearty round of applause and a superlative comment form Mary Rose.

Four days thereafter, on September 11, 2001, I awakened, turned on the radio and slowly stepped out one foot and time from between the covers. I had no definite plan but thought I would work a bit in my garden,

415

gathering the first autumn leaves carpeting the lawn.

In a somber voice, the newscaster reported a terrible air crash in downtown New York City—a jet had smashed into one of the towers of the World Trade Center!

"Danny!" I shouted, raising the radio volume. "Something terrible has happened. Come listen to this."

As Danny entered the room, the newscaster announced that a second plane had crashed into the other tower. Chaos and panic had hit New York!

What had happened? Was America attacked? Who was responsible?

Taking my hand, Danny led me into the living room. I stood trembling while he turned on the TV. The images were shocking—fire, clouds of dark smoke, bloodied people running for safety. People screaming, children crying. This was war!

"Danny, we are at war" I shouted. "I have seen this before. I have been there. The US has been attacked."

"Calm down, Bảo. Let's listen. Maybe we'll find out what happened."

The news was devastating, overwhelming. Having experienced the Việt Nam War firsthand, with all the hardships, the bombings, the loss of property and loved

416

ones, and the terrifying escapes in the night to save our lives, I understood the tragic repercussions of violent conflicts.

War was an eternal shadow draped over my native land. But did 9/11 alter my sense of security here in the USA? Did I doubt American supremacy? Was the dream shattered? Or was my perception of American incomparability still intact?

Though my faith in God and in the USA's ability to defend and protect its territories and citizens remains firm, I have not fully recovered from the shock and awe of that deleterious incident, which reshaped the perception of every American.

I face life differently today, with more caution and more appreciation but the same gratitude, always mindful of the vulnerability factor. No one is immune to tragedy, and no one enjoys unconditional security. However, the USA has stalwart resources and the wherewithal to overcome adversity. Reassured, I'm hopeful. This is my new dream.

EPILOGUE
Last Trip to Việt Nam: The Promising Wings of Hope

Once again, I felt a longing to revisit my native land and reunite with my family. My health had improved, my energy was flourishing and I was reinvigorated even if the mounting, autumn winds had saddled me with a busy gardening schedule.

The shedding of a mass of orange, yellow and golden-brown leaves left lanky trees clad only in a few remaining blooms too resistant to surrender without a fight. Having lived out their natural life cycles, it was time to crumble and fall, making way for new blooms in the spring.

Stepping outside, I watched as the last, curled leaves pirouetted like novice ballerinas, dainty yet a bit unsteady, gradually floating to the ground. I shivered, pulling the sweater loosely knotted around my neck over my shoulders. The crisper temperatures confirmed that summer had passed.

When I mentioned to Danny my yearning for another trip back home, he received my suggestion with eagerness.

419

"That sounds wonderful, Bảo. When would you like to go?"

"As soon as possible," I chirped, already drawing up plans in my mind.

"That's just fine with me. Let's do it. I'll book the flights."

The following morning, soon after sunrise, Danny was on the computer, confirming our travel arrangements. Two weeks later, on the evening of October 24, 2007, we closed up the house and left Portland several minutes after ten o'clock. Boarding an Alaskan Airlines jet, we flew to San Francisco, arriving just in time to catch a connecting flight to Taiwan.

Following an endless period of slicing through milky-white clouds, the EVA Air jet made a smooth landing on the runway of Taiwan Taoyuan International Airport, at seven-thirty in the morning on Friday, October 26. Exhausted but not yet at our destination, we flew from Taiwan to Sài Gòn, planting our weary feet on Vietnamese soil at nine forty-five that same morning. Tabulating the hours in flight and awaiting connection at various airports, I calculated twenty-six hours for the trip from Portland to Sài Gòn.

Spotting Trung and Cuc lifted me from the sheer exhaustion that had overtaken my body. I was revitalized with joy and

420

exhilaration. We had not seen each other since my last visit to Việt Nam in August 1998.

After the tears, hugs and kisses, we loaded the rental van and climbed in, chatting without pausing even to breathe.

Driving along the narrow, two-lane Nguyen Trong Tuyen, my eyes focused on the hundreds of cyclists riding their bikes and motorcycles everywhere—in the streets and on the sidewalks, respecting neither pedestrians nor autos. It was such a contrast to the orderly traffic routes in the United States. Some things just never change, despite the passage of years or even millennia.

Often, the cyclists careened dangerously close to the van, actually risking accidents. However, with extended arms, they pushed themselves away from the rapidly moving vans, avoiding calamity. Apparently, years of experience had rendered them secure in their own recklessness, though I would never have advised such perilous tactics.

Horns bleated, augmenting the ear-splitting, roadway chaos. Thankfully, I half expected the ruckus. Still, whenever a cyclist or another motorist cut us off, I flinched and shut my eyes. Had I anticipated any less pandemonium, I would have been surprised. At first, it was uncomfortable but as I acclimated myself to Việt Nam, my stomach

421

settled down, the ringing in my ears subsided and my eyes shut with less frequency.

Two hours thereafter, the driver pulled on to the Quốc lộ 1 highway. Visible in the background were the imposing Banana Mountains, surrounded by acres of wild banana trees.

A blending of the yellow, green and brown of nature created an impressionistic panorama. Enhancing the natural beauty of the landscape were Buddhist temples intermingled with Catholic churches, structures that added the splendor of unique architecture to the rustic countryside.

The four-hour drive brought us through various, bottleneck traffic jams until, shortly after twilight, we exited in Bao Loc and drove the last few miles to Trung's house.

Prior to my departure for Việt Nam, I had written to my sister, Chau, informing her that I would not be able to visit her in Huế since my cancer surgery had left me with depleted energy and, consequently, a propensity to tire easily. Exhaustion was now a very real part of my life, forcing me to manage my activities accordingly.

Compassionate to my plight, Chau, Nghe and his wife, Tru, decided to pay me a visit in Bao Loc, combining the joy of a reunion with the elimination of any hardship on my part.

The date was set and I awaited it, beyond thrilled.

Driving to Da Kai, they had reached Trung's house two days prior to my arrival. Their presence was a true kindness demonstrated in my time of difficulty and a catalyst in reinvigorating my spirit. Seeing my family after many years and ordeals uplifted my spirits. What a panacea!

Feeling regenerated, I accompanied Danny, Trung and the others on a motorcycle adventure. We explored the countryside, visiting the Cac Tien Mountain where, years earlier, a man intent on building a house had uncovered a brick wall while excavating to construct the foundation.

Believing he had disturbed an old war-munitions dump, he'd suspended his work and reported it to the police, who immediately notified the government. A representative was summoned to investigate the findings. Shortly thereafter, further excavations and collapsing walls revealed the presence of twenty-four-carat-gold nuggets, plus an antique sword and crown.

The objects were exhumed from the underground, examined for authenticity and eventually donated to a museum, though the valuable discovery was never publicized.

423

Upon hearing the story, I was both fascinated and curious and could not wait to get there.

Unfortunately, we did not realize there was a guard post.

"May I help you?" the slender, young man in uniform asked as Trung pulled up alongside the booth.

"We would like to drive around the mountain," Trung replied. "My mother is interested in the history of this site."

"I'm sorry, sir," he responded, peering at Danny. "The gentleman with you is not Vietnamese. I cannot let you enter."

"Danny is my husband," I replied. "Why is he being denied entry?"

"My apologies, ma'am" the guard said. "I don't make the rules. The issue is still under investigation and until the government confirms authenticity of the story, no foreigners are permitted to enter."

"Why? I don't understand?" I said, confused.

"Ma'am, the authorities fear that reporters and journalists will write incorrect accounts of the story. We do not wish the international media to build headlines on misinformation or broadcast rumors."

"I understand, sir," I replied. "Thank you for your time."

A bit disappointed, we returned to Trung's house, enjoying the panorama of young schoolchildren and teens, the boys dressed in uniform with long pants and the girls in the traditional *áo dài*, pedaling their bicycles to and from school. My memories came alive. Certainly not filled with beautiful scenes of nature and happy children, giggling and chatting amongst themselves, they were instead full of war, bloodshed and destruction.

After visiting my brother and his family, we rode to Restriction Forest, located in the Cac Tien area—a state-protected park that was very much involved in the preservation of fauna and flora. The landscape surrounding the park was magnificent, a vibrant panorama of the colors and wonders of nature. Happily, I noticed that the local people maintained their native customs and national, cultural identity both in dress and manner of thinking.

At the end of the road leading to the forest, the Dong Nai River greeted us with rippling tides. To cross over, we rode our motorcycles onto a ferry boat. The cost of the trip was 10,000 *đồng* per person. Danny drove and I rode behind him, wrapping my arms around his waist, unwilling to risk a fall.

Once back on land, we boarded a scratched and dented pickup custom fitted with slender, hardwood benches that snugly hugged its perimeters, allowing tourists to sit while they toured the forest. It was a clever idea.

We drove around the monumental Bang Lang Trees, which stood over 200 feet tall with a girth of about forty feet. Long, leggy roots protruded from their massive trunks at a height of approximately six feet. The trees' bright-green leaves were the size of an open adult hand.

We spent a little over two hours admiring the marvels of the forest before initiating our trek back to Trung's house. Though drained from the journey, I was revitalized by the unmarred beauty I had just witnessed.

Our next outing was to Da Lat, a well-frequented, upscale vacation resort patronized by natives seeking rest and relaxation—a refuge from life's stressful professional and personal situations.

When we arrived, I suggested we visit Lam Tu Temple. Located on a hill, it was surrounded by ten acres of meticulously landscaped property adorned with a mass of variegated flowers. Situated between the flowers were miniature trees, in full bloom, spilling out of massive urns. What a breathtaking testament to the existence of a sole divine creator responsible for such awesome beauty.

For lunch, we selected a restaurant in downtown Ngoc Hai, indulging our appetites with a salty fish dish prepared with black pepper, sugar and water; roasted chicken; stuffed vegetables; stewed beef; and a spicy fish soup brewed with pineapple, green onions and bean sprouts.

Undoubtedly due to the variety, there was something to satiate and gratify every taste bud. Best of all, the menu items were served with steamy, hot rice all for a cost of $25!

Afterward, we went on a shopping spree before visiting Ho Than Tho Lake. Named the Lake of Sorrow, it brought to memory the suicide by drowning of a young girl who had sacrificed herself upon learning her betrothed was called to arms during the Việt Nam War.

Later, a torrential downpour forced us to seek refuge in the van. However, despite the unexpected turn of events, I was able to savor the romantic aura of the lake and a beautiful flower garden several miles in the distance. By the time we arrived to preview the blooms, the puddles of water glimmered as the first rays of sun cut through the clouds.

The gardens' unique, thirty-foot gate was built out of tiny flowerpots stacked in a tower motif, forming a gigantic arch. Several meters away, a gift shop provided the opportunity to purchase interesting jewelry and handcrafted items made from cherry wood and mahogany.

Next on our itinerary was a visit to Thien Van Temple. Stepping inside, we noticed two women between fifty and seventy dressed in lay garb in lieu of monks' robes. Graciously, they accompanied us to the rear of the temple. In silence, they unlocked a heavily etched gate, opening the way to a verdant hillside.

Immediately, my gaze rose to a monumental, thousand-foot-tall, glittering icon of Buddha perched on top of a pedestal at the summit of the hill. On the side of the plinth was a staircase leading to the base of the statue.

"How did they get that Buddha up there?" Danny asked, mesmerized by the striking preponderance of the figure.

"Pretty impressive," I said, breathless from the steps.

But our amazement did not end there. Upon stepping off the pedestal, we discovered a hidden patio complete with two long, mahogany conference tables and benches tucked underneath the platform. Gazing upward, we were able to see the entire interior regions of the Buddha seated on a glass surface!

"Bảo," Danny told me, "I could kick myself for forgetting the camera! This is a spectacular scene. Can you imagine what a fantastic video I could have made?"

"That's too bad, Danny, but we had no idea we would chance upon this wonder."

Thankful to have been an eyewitness to this monument was reward in itself, even if we were unable to immortalize it in a video.

On the final leg of our journey, while Danny stayed behind to gather his belongings and prepare for the journey home, I treated the grandchildren to one last shopping spree. We hopped on a bus headed for downtown Bao Loc, where the three girls giggled and chatted as they slipped on jeans, trying to decide which pair caught their fancy.

Na, who adored American music, sheepishly asked if she could add a couple of CDs to her purchases. Agreeing with her wish, I also bought a bicycle for nine-year-old Nu, the youngest, since she did not yet have one. The afternoon culminated with ice cream and the delightful laughter of three very happy girls.

Then, the eve of our departure was upon us. Nghe and Tru arrived for a sleepover, intent on accompanying us to the airport, probably anticipating my sadness in the morning.

It was November 20 and our month-long Vietnamese excursion had come to an end. Reluctant to depart, I nevertheless agreed to it, as Danny's professional commitments warranted his return.

The goodbyes were touching and heartbreaking. The farewell scene was dramatic. Could I ever expect anything different in my life? Teary eyed, we cuddled and kissed, clinging to each other like mothers wishing to protect their newborns.

Unwilling to release us from their hugs, Ni and Nah sobbed. *En route* to school, they were unable to accompany us to the airport.

Loading the van, we prepared for one last drive through the streets and alleys of Việt Nam. The people, the buildings, the hustle and bustle of traffic along the dusty roadways set my memories rolling. Infused in the panorama were vibrant and animated images of my childhood and teen years. But, more important were my thoughts.

I had left Việt Nam, traveling across seas and lands in search of a new and promising life, seeking love, freedom and the opportunity to be who I wanted to be. Along the journey, I met many fascinating, different and interesting people from all corners of the planet, each with a lesson to impart, all with absorbing stories to tell and mesmerizing cultures to present.

The information gathered and experiences lived have served to guide me in my own journey, encouraging me to reap lessons from my mistakes and those of others. Admittedly, I'm guilty of many errors and misjudgments during the course of the years. Perhaps I was too naïve in my expectations and in offering my trust. However, determined to stand tall, I turned each and every failing, every displeasure and tragedy, into a learning event.

Consequently, though repeatedly knocked off my feet by swift curve balls, I refused to relinquish my dream. Instead, fired with the desire to succeed, I battled my demons one at a time. Throughout my early years of enduring the war, my dysfunctional, abusive marriages, my family heartaches and my serious health issues, I kept my core beliefs intact. Faith was my ally and my salvation, making of me a survivor as I sailed though the nasty tides of trials and tribulations. I sought neither to settle the score for the malevolent spins of fate's wheel that caused much agony nor to avenge the devastating misdeeds committed against me.

Mine was a journey of learning, personal betterment and survival, not a crusade triggered by revenge. Mine was a journey of hope and triumph, a dream to build who I have become—the woman, wife, mother and grandmother who, through sharing the vicissitudes of a suffered life in this memoir, has found closure and peace of mind. Perhaps my words will inspire and encourage one other soul to rise from the quagmire of my adversity to embrace a dream. That being the case, I will recognize the merit of my difficult journey.

As our plane left the ground, my mind wandered back to the family I was once again leaving behind in Việt Nam. Could another dream be realized?

Will the government ever allow my loved ones to immigrate to the Unites States? Would my family be united on American soil?

Believing in the power of prayer, and firmly holding on to the promising wings of hope, I await that day.

ABOUT THE AUTHOR

Author Dieu Bao grew up during the Việt Nam war and experienced everything from first love to bombs dropping on her house. She eventually moved to America to escape the madness going on in her country at that time, and has spent the last few decades building a meaningful life devoid of the violence and ambivalence of her youth.

Today, Dieu lives in Oregon She aspires to share her life experience with anyone willing to listen. Her email is DieuBao100@gmail.com

54038685R00253

Made in the USA
San Bernardino, CA
06 October 2017